LINCOLN IN CARICATURE

A Historical Collection
with descriptive and biographical commentaries by
RUFUS ROCKWELL WILSON

Introduction by
R. GERALD McMURTRY

HORIZON PRESS   **NEW YORK**
1953

To my kinsman
IRVIN ELMER ROCKWELL
who shares descent from
John Rockwell of Stamford
one of the builders of New England

COPYRIGHT 1945, 1953 BY HORIZON PRESS INC.

PRINTED IN THE UNITED STATES OF AMERICA

The publishers gratefully acknowledge the
very kind cooperation of Otilie Erickson Wilson
in the publication of this book

Introduction

Political caricature as a medium for the expression of opinion or criticism antedates the modern newspaper which reviews in editorials public men and controversial situations. James Gillray, the English artist, may be credited with the earliest legitimate forms of caricature in his castigation of the social and political evils of the Hanoverian regime. Gillray's great power of scathing, ruthless wit extended from the 1780's through a decade or so into the 19th century.

Next, it was John Doyle, the father of Richard Doyle the artist of Punch, who issued a long series of political caricatures signed "H. B." beginning with the year 1830. Doyle excelled in satirical portraits of contemporary English celebritieswhose administration of the government called for censure. While his work was sensational at the time, his cartoons today are not highly esteemed for their historical or artistic value. Nevertheless, Doyle was the real founder of the modern school of caricature art.

The establishment of this satirical political medium along with the founding in the 1840's of Punch, the English comic weekly, created interest abroad and the art was encouraged and exploited in the United States. It was the presidential campaign of 1832 that first saw the widespread use of the cartoon and it became an effective political weapon almost overnight. Perhaps "Boss" Tweed, that irascible ward heeler of the 1870's, best expressed the effectiveness of the political cartoon by saying that his constituents could not read, but "they can't help seeing them damn pictures."

Politicians have a rough and ready way of expressing their likes and dislikes, particularly in the heat of election campaigns, and the caricaturist with a quick-catching eye and grotesque conceptions was not hesitant to express what he honestly thought. Although many of them may not have been accomplished draughtsmen, there is no mistaking their political preferences, nor is there any doubt as to the identities of the politicians satirized, or the political morals they wished to convey.

Thomas Nast laid the foundations of the modern American political caricature by devising the familiar figures of the Republican elephant, the Democratic donkey and the Tammany tiger. Nast also seems to have contributed most to the development of the national figure known as Uncle Sam with the striped trousers, star-spangled vest, blue coat, and stove-pipe hat—all the more interesting because his general physical appearance was largely copied from Lincoln. With Uncle Sam's accentuated tallness and slimness a very vivid contrast was achieved between the Lincolnesque figure and the stout John Bull. Joseph Keppler, another cartoonist, apparently added the chin whiskers and gave Uncle Sam a more dignified aspect, but Nast had more to do in bringing about the standardized portrait than any other single individual. Perhaps the essentially American type of man, which found its best exponent in Lincoln, is the reason why Uncle Sam has become the best beloved of all our conventional types. Our present conception of Uncle Sam probably owes more to Lincoln than to any other man and the Yankee Doodles and the Brother Jonathans of the earlier English cartoons have completely disappeared from the scene.

Abraham Lincoln's homely features lend themselves to pictorial exaggeration; his long angular figure makes him the delight of the cartoonist. One writer declared that Lincoln was depicted by contemporary caricaturists as "a bearded ruffian, vulgar charlatan and repulsive beast;" continuing the description "his eyes were filled with demonic cunning, his feet stretched to grotesque size, his hair messed till it became a shaggy mane, his face twisted into a sinister look and his back (was) broken until it sagged like a gorilla."

Lincoln over the years has become so legendary that it is hard for many to realize that he was a subject for cartooning which was often neither kind nor just. Ridicule of Lincoln to some bordered on sacrilege. But his was a turbulent period, with the altered state of trade, the embarrassments of a fluctuating currency, and the abominable draft which accompanied the "rich man's war and the poor man's fight." The prospects of the United States government had never hitherto looked so gloomy.

Pens were sharp and the cut was not often gentle in the years of the Civil War. Lincoln, the most universally hated national figure of the period, was fought by the South with cannon and musket, but England fought the sixteenth president with pen and ink—and the London Punch, that popular organ of British laughter, greeted the news of the fall of Fort Sumter with a poem titled, "Ink, Blood and Tears." Between 1861 and 1865 Punch published approximately twenty cartoons which had Lincoln for their central figure. These were largely the work of Sir John Tenniel, the chief artist of the magazine, whose greatest cartoon "Dropping the Pilot," 1890, is a masterpiece of cartoon art.

What interest the London Punch had in the plight of the slave was lost when Lincoln blockaded English commerce with the Confederate States. Certainly Tenniel, Matt Morgan and other English cartoonists were in no danger of incurring reproof in England when they caricatured Lincoln as "a gross and monstrous incubus oppressing Columbia." The earlier presidents of the United States had many points of resemblance to those of the English country gentlemen, but the plain rugged Lincoln was fitted to be the butt of jesters who hung on the skirts of the nobility.

After the terrible years had shown that Abraham Lincoln, though some thought his inherent gifts were not exceptional, might be considered the best man who could have held the helm of the ship of state—he was assassinated by a fanatic. This tragedy tore the veil from all eyes. For once even the caricaturist told the unbiased truth. To be slain in the moment of triumph has ever been regarded as the most apt commentary on the *memento mori*.

Tenniel nearly always followed a satirical trend but his "Britannia Lays a Wreath on Lincoln's Bier," published on May 6, 1865, was an acknowledgment of his error as to Lincoln's place in history and, with the consent of the editors of Punch, although some opposed the move, he made prompt and generous amends. The cartoon was accompanied by appreciative verses from the pen of Tom Taylor, which some students attribute to Shirley Brooks. The poem bore the title, "Abraham Lincoln, Foully Assassinated April 14, 1865." Undoubtedly, Tenniel's picture and Taylor's verses made a profound impression in the United States and went far in easing the diplomatic tension between the two countries. Shirley Brooks' diary gives us an insight behind the Punch curtain, "Dined Punch. All there. Let out my views against some verses on Lincoln in which T. T. had not only made P. eat humble pie, but swallow dish and all."

In the centennial year of 1909, William S. Walsh edited a book "Abraham Lincoln and the London Punch" (Moffatt, Yard and Company), which presented some of the most famous of that magazine's cartoons.

Harper's Weekly and Leslie's Weekly helped to popularize the cartoon during the period of the Civil War, and Vanity Fair with its comic illustrations was the Yankee Journal of wit, which had its existence between 1859 and 1863. Only a few copies of this publication survived the destructive years of the Civil War. Its limited circulation makes it doubtful whether there are many duplicates of the seven volumes issued. The contributors did not affix their real names to their articles, and it is likely that one or two men were responsible for the literary content. Henry Louis Stephens was the chief cartoonist, the originator of nearly every caricature published during the life of Vanity Fair.

Many of the better cartoons appearing in Vanity Fair were published in a magazine called The Lantern in its February 20th issue for the year 1913. Six cartoons and a series of drawings called "The New ABC," drawn for Abraham Lincoln, were used as illustrations. Three years later (February 12, 1916) Bruno's Weekly reprinted the Lantern article, using some of the same illustrations.

Currier and Ives, print makers to the American people, published about twenty-five cartoons in which the sixteenth president appeared. This New York lithograph-ing firm began to issue their sheets in 1848, the year of Taylor's election. These prints are now very difficult to acquire. Other minor lithographing firms also pub-lished caricatures to help sway public opinion one way or another. Many of these cartoons bear no date or imprint or credit line to the artist. However, some are known to have been published by lithographing houses in Boston, Buffalo, Cincin-nati, Chicago, Baltimore and other cities.

A collection of etchings called "Confederate War Etchings," made by Dr. Adalbert J. Volck, a German dentist of Baltimore, and released under the pseudonym, V. Blada, are by far the most important contribution in the South both artistically and historically. While they are anti-Lincoln and wage a vigorous attack on Northern policies and armies, when viewed with an unsentimental eye they are strikingly and masterfully executed. There are twenty-nine plates, three of which lampoon Lin-coln. The Volck etchings were reprinted in book form by William Abbott in 1917.

But Lincoln cartoonists, or any others for that matter, should not be judged by their qualities of craftsmanship alone. Integrity, depth of feeling, humor and power are factors to be taken into consideration. Cartoons are a problem of research. Inter-pretation is important. The attitude of the creator, his motives, knowledge of his subject, judgment and responsibility are the elements which give these early cartoons their importance as history. They express vividly the current trend of events and reflect clearly the main issues of their day. They will always hold interest and value for the historian and student of the political and social development of the United States. Both as true mirrors of history and as intimate diaries of public opinion, their significance increases with the passage of time.

The late Rufus Rockwell Wilson of Elmira, New York, preceded all others in the gathering and compiling of the better known cartoons featuring Abraham Lincoln. The first significant study of the subject was made by Dr. Wilson in the September, 1897, issue of The Book Buyer—A Review and Record of Current Literature. The article bears the title "Abraham Lincoln in Caricature" and is divided into two parts, "Part I—In England" and "Part II—In America." The article is profusely illustrated.

In 1903 Dr. Wilson issued a limited edition of thirty-two full 10″ x 12½″ page cartoons with an eighteen page descriptive pamphlet laid in a stiff board folio con-tainer. The folio bears the title of "Lincoln in Caricature" and the first fifteen numbers of the one hundred sixty-five copies are on japan paper.

Over a period of fifty years Dr. Wilson made a careful study of English and Amer-ican cartoons and from a great mass of material accumulated on the subject he was able to prepare "Lincoln In Caricature" for publication. This is the capstone of his literary achievement, although he made many other contributions in the field of Lincolniana.

Not only was Dr. Wilson discriminating in his selection of the most significant caricatures for publication in this great book, but he was also personally acquainted with some of the caricaturists. As a newspaper correspondent he had occasion to visit frequently with Bellew, Morgan and Nast, men now legendary as recorders of pictorial history.

While other compilers have made contributions to this particular study—notably Albert Shaw who published an impressive collection of thirty-eight prints in the February, 1931, issue of the Review of Reviews and the two volume work entitled "Abraham Lincoln, A Cartoon History," 1929-1930—no one has achieved so close an affinity with the caricatures of the Lincoln period or so deserved the distinction of authority in relation to historical caricature as Rufus Rockwell Wilson.

Certainly no compiler or editor could have been better fitted than Dr. Wilson to interpret the Lincoln cartoons and to write the background descriptions of the 163 drawings which appear in this new Horizon Press edition. Like Bellew, Morgan and Nast, the compiler has made an important contribution to the understanding of United States history. Perhaps no other book in the great field of American history serves so well as a reflector of the events and issues of the Civil War period.

No serious study is necessary to discern, in the work of many caricaturists who made Lincoln their chief theme that, despite false satirical strokes, certain of his important character traits are ever present: namely, an unbounded trust in Providence, a strong reliance upon his fellow-men, an honesty of purpose, a sense of the sanctity of promises, and grave awareness of the tasks that lay ahead.

And what did Lincoln think when he found himself so readily caricatured? The cartoons undoubtedly served for his entertainment and instruction. With his humor, he probably enjoyed as much as anyone else the raillery of the artists at his expense, even when their wit was trenchant and caustic. He could hardly have dreamed, however, that his physical appearance and his qualities of leadership, the stories he told and the renewing timeliness of his insights, would make him the most fertile historical subject for the cartoonist of our present day.

—R. GERALD MCMURTRY

Lincoln Memorial University
1953

Preface

In the years that have elapsed since the close of the Civil War, the fame of Lincoln, the grandest figure in that conflict, has taken on majestic proportions, and, influenced no doubt by the august place he now holds in our history, people no longer recall that he was the most bitterly assailed and most savagely caricatured public man of his time. Such, however, was the fact, and one has but to study the poster cartoons, or to search the newspapers and periodicals of the period to find striking confirmation for it.

The history of political caricature in the United States has passed through four clearly defined phases. Woodcuts and copper engravings, in most cases put out as separate publications, ruled the first phase. The lithograph, perfected in the middle years of the last century, from 1830 to 1865 dominated the second phase. Then, practically coincident with the opening of the Civil War, weekly publications and their artists claimed the field. More recently and long after Mr. Lincoln's time, political caricature has found its fourth, most pervasive and perhaps final medium in the daily newspaper cartoon which now plays a persistent and substantial part in the shaping of public opinion on a great variety of subjects.

The caricatures which had Mr. Lincoln and the unfolding drama of the Civil War as their subjects all fell within the first three phases listed, and the greater number of them were drawn by half a dozen men, now best remembered for their output in this field, but only one of whom, it is worthy of remark, was a native-born American. The group in question included Victor Maurer, Sir John Tenniel, Henry Louis Stephens, Frank Temple Bellew, Matt Morgan, and Thomas Nast, last, youngest, and in many ways greatest of the sextet.

Currier and Ives, the most popular print makers of their period, first began to issue broadsheet lithographic cartoons in a tentative way in the campaign of 1848, continued to do so on a more extensive scale in 1852 and 1856, and in 1860, as will be set forth in the following chronicle, played no inconsiderable part in the election of Mr. Lincoln. The greater number of the Currier and Ives cartoons which had him as their central figure were drawn by Louis Maurer, an artist held in appreciative and affectionate memory by aging men who knew him in the last years of a many-sided career that spanned a full century. The son of a cabinetmaker, Maurer was born at Biebrich on the Rhine in 1832, in childhood and youth mastered drawing, wood carving and lithography, and in 1850 came with his family to America, where in no long time he found employment first with Nathaniel Currier and then with Currier and Ives, when Currier and James Ives formed a noteworthy partnership.

Maurer was in the employ of Currier and Ives for nearly a decade and in close touch with their affairs for half a century. He left the firm in 1860 to secure more profitable employment elsewhere, but continued to work for it on commission. In 1872 he established his own business and met with such success that he was able at the end of a dozen years to retire with a comfortable fortune. When he was fifty he mastered the art of painting which became his major activity during the latter half of his life. Maurer's other activities and interests made his days rich and full ones. He was a sympathetic student of Indian life and on long trips to the West observed it at first hand; he was a lover of the chase and until far past ninety gave proof on the rifle range of his unerring marksmanship, while his success as a collector in widely varied fields made the three floors of his home in West Forty-third Street, New York, a museum of rare and curious things. He died in 1932 in his hundred and first year. Maurer's work as a cartoonist did not have the arresting quality of that of Gillray or of his great contemporaries Daumier and Tenniel, but it was always marked by sincerity and a sureness of detail that never missed its aim.

Until the closing days of the Civil War the attitude of Great Britain toward the Union and its President was one of cynical and scarcely veiled hostility, and nowhere were the sentiments of the English government and of the majority of Englishmen more faithfully reflected than in the cartoons which appeared in London Punch between 1861 and 1865, not less than a score of which had Mr. Lincoln and the contest he was waging for their subjects. With a single exception all of these cartoons were drawn by Sir John Tenniel—he was made a knight in 1893—then and for forty years thereafter the chief artist of Punch. Born in 1820 and living until the great age of ninety-four years, he was already a draughtsman of repute when he joined the staff of that journal in 1851, and for the greater part of half a century he was recognized as incomparably the greatest caricaturist of his time—his pencil a force to be taken into account in every forecast of the drift of public opinion. His range was not a wide one, yet within its clearly defined limits he was nearly always powerful. Although his methods were usually simple, through them he secured signal breadth and strength, while now and then his drawings give an impression of power such as one fancies Angelo might have put forth, had he amused himself by drawings reflecting upon the politics of his time. If there was any doubt in official minds respecting the necessity of sending an army to the rescue of Khartoum, it vanished when Tenniel drew his picture of General Gordon standing behind an earthwork and looking across the desert for a glimpse of the expected redcoats. That touched the heart of England,

and was more potent than the fiercest denunciation from the Opposition bench of the Gladstone ministry's inaction in the Soudan.

Tenniel was first of all a satirist, but he was seldom either unjust or unfair in his work. His longest and most memorable departure from fairness was when, as we have shown, in common with the ruling class of England generally, he misinterpreted our Civil War and caricatured the chief actor therein with astonishing perversity. Still, he was not more frequently or more deeply in the wrong than some of our own politicians, who could not plead his excuse of distance from the scene, and, to his credit be it said, when once convinced of his error he made prompt and generous amends therefor. Nothing could have been more fitting nor finer in its way than Tenniel's design, published on May 6, 1865, which showed Britannia laying a wreath on the bier of the martyred President and which was accompanied by these appreciative lines from the pen of Tom Taylor:

> *You* lay a wreath on murdered Lincoln's bier,
>   *You*, who with mocking pencil wont to trace,
> Broad for the self-complacent British sneer,
>   His length of shambling limb, his furrowed face,
>
> His gaunt, gnarled hands, his unkept, bristling hair,
>   His garb uncouth, his bearing ill at ease,
> His lack of all we prize as debonair,
>   Of power or will to shine, of art to please,
>
> You, whose smart pen backed up the pencil's laugh,
>   Judging each step as though the way were plain;
> Reckless, so it could point its paragraph,
>   Of chief's perplexity, or people's pain.
>
> Beside this corpse, that bears for winding sheet
>   The stars and stripes he lived to rear anew,
> Between the mourners at his head and feet,
>   Say, scurril jester, is there room for *you*?
>
> Yes, he had lived to shame me from my sneer,
>   To lame my pencil, and confute my pen—
> To make me own this hind of princes peer,
>   This rail-splitter a true born king of men.

My shallow judgment I had learned to rue,
  Noting how to occasion's height he rose,
How his quaint wit made home-truth seem more true,
  How, iron-like, his temper grew by blows.

How humble yet how hopeful he could be;
  How in good fortune and in ill the same;
Nor bitter in success, nor boastful he,
  Thirsty for gold, nor feverish for fame.

The words of mercy were upon his lips,
  Forgiveness in his heart and on his pen,
When his vile murderer brought swift eclipse
  To thoughts of peace on earth, good will to men.

The Old World and the New, from sea to sea,
  Utter one voice of sympathy and shame!
Sore heart, so stopped when it at last beat high,
  Sad life, cut short just as its triumph came.

A deed accurst! Strokes have been struck before
  By the assassin's hand, whereof men doubt
If more of honor or disgrace they bore;
  But thy foul crime, like Cain's, stands darkly out.

Vile hand, that brandest murder on a strife,
  Whate'er its grounds, stoutly and nobly striven;
And with the martyr's crown crownest a life,
  With much to praise, little to be forgiven!

The American counterpart of Punch when the Civil War opened was Vanity Fair, which between 1859 and 1863 ran a checkered but lively existence. The designer of a majority of the cartoons which appeared in Vanity Fair during the period mentioned was Henry Louis Stephens, a man of fertile and incisive wit, with much of Tenniel's ability to enforce a pictorial moral by simple yet telling methods. The manner in which these two artists regarded the men and measures of the war period present a striking and instructive contrast. For a brief period Mr. Stephen's attitude toward Mr. Lincoln seems to have been touched by the not always good-natured suspicion with which the public regards a new and comparatively untried man, and to have shared in the very general belief that he would be defeated in his first canvass for Presidency, but when signs multiplied that the shrewd and angular man from the Middle West would triumph at the polls, and Election Day confirmed this promise in a fashion that confounded those of little faith, and when fateful weeks and months sped and the nation took reassuring note that the new President was facing with courage, wisdom and patience a graver and more imperative task than had confronted Washington or Jackson, the Vanity Fair artist was transformed without delay into an acute and discerning but wholly loyal champion of Mr. Lincoln and the cause he was pushing to a triumphant issue. True to this friendly and understanding spirit Stephens cartooned the President in Vanity Fair for the last time on July 4, 1863 in a design which in happy keeping with the day, showed him holding aloft a flag and calling for volunteers, who are flocking to him from every side. A week later the journal ceased to exist.

Frank Henry Bellew was born in Cawnpore, India, in 1825, the son of an Irish captain in the British army and of an English mother. He was educated mainly in France, and at an early age put out his sign as an architect in London, but his labors in this field were broken by a visit to Scotland, which bore fruit in a series of illustrated sketches shortly put into book form under the title A Cockney in the Highlands. This volume brought him growing repute, and helped to shape a decision that his career should be that of an artist and author in preference to his first choice.

Young Bellew came to America in 1853 to join John Brougham, the actor, in the publication of the Lantern, a comic weekly that for a time enjoyed a moderate measure of public favor, and thereafter for more than a generation, except for a brief return to England in 1860, was active as an artist in New York. When the Lantern went out he joined Thomas Strong in founding Yankee Notions, a weekly periodical of the same sort. He also wrote and drew for Harper's Magazine and Harper's Weekly, and as the years went by had a part in the founding of Vanity Fair and Wild Oats. Bellew's caricatures of Mr. Lincoln, which will be dealt with in order, were drawn for Frank Leslie's Illustrated Newspaper, Harper's Weekly and Vanity Fair. He was not a really good draughtsman, but all of his caricatures had wit and point. They were amusing and never vulgar, and the least of them was sure to reflect amenity and good taste. Indeed, it may be said with truth that his humor was a part of himself—kindly, healthful and natural.

In Bellew's latter years his sketches and writings appeared in the Harper periodicals, Scribner's Monthly, St. Nicholas and Texas Siftings. He was ever fertile in ideas, and was especially happy in writing and illustrating stories for children. His deep and tender love for little ones remained with him to the end, and in his last days, attended, it is to be recorded with regret, by poverty, incessant labor and an unhappy home life, he was ever busy devising new tricks and toys for childhood. He died at the Long Island home of a daughter in his sixty-first year.

Matthew Somerville Morgan, best known as Matt Morgan, was born in London in 1839, the son of an actor father and music teacher mother, who made it possible for him to begin the study of art at an early age. An association with the London Illustrated News first brought him into notice as an artist of skill, force, and unusual versatility, and for five years following 1862 he was, despite his youth, perhaps the best known member of the staff of London Fun, which for a time shared favor with Punch. And for Fun he drew a long series of caricatures of Mr. Lincoln, many of which are reproduced in this volume. These caricatures as a whole were animated by bitter hostility to the Northern cause and a strange misunderstanding of Mr. Lincoln's character and purpose. Too late editor and artist awoke to their unfairness and injustice, and following Mr. Lincoln's death these atoning lines, written perhaps by the younger Tom Hood, appeared in Fun:

> The hand of an assassin, glowing red,
> Shot like a firebrand through the western sky;
> And stalwart ABRAHAM LINCOLN now lies dead!
> Oh, felon heart that thus could basely dye
> The name of Southerner with murderous gore!
> Could such a spirit come from mortal womb?
> And what possessed it that not heretofore
> It linked its coward mission with the tomb?
> LINCOLN! Thy fame shall sound through many an age,
> To prove that genius lives in humble birth;
> Thy name shall stand upon historic page,
> For midst thy faults we all esteemed thy worth.
> Gone art thou now! no more midst angry heat
> Shall thy calm spirit rule the surging tide
> Which rolls where two contending nations meet,
> To still the passion and to curb the pride.
> Nations have looked and seen the fate of kings,
> Protectors, emperors, and such-like men;

Behold the man whose dirge all Europe sings,
Now past the eulogy of mortal pen!
He like a lighthouse fell athwart the strand;
Let curses rest upon the assassin's hand!

In 1867 Morgan became chief artist for and one of the owners of the Tomahawk, a fearless and outspoken weekly, written by a group of clever young men and edited by Arthur a' Beckett. Morgan's cartoons in this journal were on new lines, powerfully drawn and fierce in their satire. They made a great sensation, but as many of them had Queen Victoria or the Prince of Wales as a subject, in no long time they brought the artist into disrepute, and in 1870 Frank Leslie, seeking a rival for Thomas Nast, who was then waging in Harper's Weekly his memorable war against the Tweed Ring, induced Morgan to try his fortunes in America. But he failed to score as a caricaturist in his new field his drawings being regarded as not in sympathy with the American scene.

Accordingly Morgan became a showman for a season, and then for seven years following 1880 was a resident of Cincinnati, where he labored with energy as a decorator of art pottery and as a designer of theatrical lithographs, in which latter field he set up a new standard of excellence. After that he lived and labored in New York. He was fond in his last years of doing things on a large scale, and his completed works included a number of vast panoramas of battles of the Civil War, and a canvas of imposing size which depicted Christ entering Jerusalem. His final occupation was scene painting in which he had had early and profitable experience in London, and he was at work on scenes for an opera in process of production at the Casino, New York, when in June, 1890, death suddenly claimed him.

The writer when a very young man had occasional contacts with both Bellew and Morgan, contacts which have now become pleasantly remembered incidents of a long vanished past. Bellew, as the writer recalls him, was an arresting embodiment of Colonel Newcome as Thackeray described and Doyle drew him. He had the same figure, the same face, the same gestures and gentle voice, and in his carriage and the genteel precision of his dress there was a savor of the retired army officer. Nor was he merely an artist. He was as clever with his pen as with his pencil, and he talked better than he wrote. Both in England and in America he had had a wide acquaintance with people of distinction in literature and art—Carlyle, the Rossettis, Wilkie Collins and many another—and his anecdotes and memories of them he related with inimitable skill. He would talk by the hour about them, and so vividly describe them and the incidents in which they had figured, that one could easily imagine that he was about to summon them in very truth into his listeners' presence. Bellew often talked of writing his autobiography, and it is a pity that he did not take time and leisure to do so.

Matt Morgan was another and very different man. He was twice married and the father in all of sixteen children, but the cares of every-day life sat lightly upon him. He had also the courage of his convictions, and was ever ready to defend them, more often than not with words that had a cutting edge to them. This made him a lively if not always comfortable companion, but his sharp sayings were as a rule tempered by a rare and saving gift of humor, and an instinctive loyalty to the major obligations of life made it easy for him to win and hold friends. He never failed them, even if himself sore beset by unexpected misfortune, and they in turn, when the curtain fell, sincerely mourned him, and paid tribute to his sterling qualities as man and artist. There is only one Matt Morgan in a generation.

The writer also recalls delightful and informing hours with Thomas Nast when that artist's great days were already behind him, and he was preparing to set forth on the long journey from which he was not to return. Nast's career affords material for a luminous and stirring chapter in the history of art in America—a chapter charged with a measure of romance and adventure sure to win and hold the interest of men of a later time.

Nast was born in Landau, a garrison town of Bavaria in 1840, and at six years of age was by his parents transplanted to America, passing his boyhood in what is now downtown New York. His father, a political emigrant, found employment as trombone player in the band attached to Burton's Theater, a famous and popular playhouse of the New York of a century ago, and young Nast, now and again carrying his instrument for him in his walks to and from his daily labors, came in contact with and made sketches of the incomparable comedian from whom the theater took its name. These sketches and vivid memories of a striking personality enabled him fifty years later to paint the fine portrait of William E. Burton in character which now hangs in the Players' Club, New York.

From this it will be inferred that young Nast, following a natural bent, had already begun to draw in an untrained way. Soon he found a skilled teacher and secured admission to the classes at the Academy of Design. Then on an eventful morning in his sixteenth year he gathered up a bundle of his drawings and called on Frank Leslie whose Illustrated Newspaper was at that time winning numerous and devoted readers. Leslie was pleased with the sketches shown him, and after one or two trial assignments gave the short, moon-faced lad a place on his staff.

What followed is a familiar story. Young Nast quickly proved his quality, at the same time by unflagging industry improving his craftmanship. He soon found a more generous employer in the New York Illustrated News of which Thomas Bailey Aldrich was the editor and which in February, 1860 sent him to England to picture the Heenan-Sayers fight, an international event holding for the moment first place in the news of the day. Another happy turn of the wheel, and he was commissioned by the Illustrated London News to follow the red shirt of Garibaldi in his redemption of Italy. This task finished, he visited the art galleries of Italy and Germany, passed a joyous Christmastide in Landau, his birthplace, and on the opening day of February, 1861, was back in New York, with a promised wife to welcome him and a dollar and a half in his pocket.

Then came the inauguration of Mr. Lincoln and preparations for a conflict in which Nast, now one-and-twenty, was to play an inspiring and shaping part. "Thomas Nast has been our best recruiting sergeant," said Mr. Lincoln near the successful conclusion of four years of battle. "His emblematic cartoons have never failed to arouse enthusiasm and patriotism, and have always seemed to come just when these articles were getting scarce." The drawings to which Mr. Lincoln referred did not begin until near the end of the second year of conflict between the States when late in 1862 an occasional association with Harper's Weekly dating from 1859 became a regular one.

Nast at first did pictures of camp and battlefields, but soon turned aside from illustrating actual events to arouse the people of the North to the inner and enduring meaning of the conflict in which triumph or failure awaited them. The success of these efforts was immediate and of the first order, and prosecuted with increasing skill and unfaltering faith in ultimate success for a righteous cause, potently upheld the hands of Mr. Lincoln. It is not too much to say that his masterly and moving cartoon, Compromise with the South, dealt with at length in another place, which appeared in the summer of 1864 just after the Democratic National Convention at Chicago had declared the war a failure and demanded a negotiated peace, and which later was circulated by the millions as a campaign document, did as much as any other event to assure the reelection of Mr. Lincoln. And that drawing remains a telling indictment of appeasers in all climes and ages.

Nast was not yet twenty-five years of age when the conflict between the sections became a part of the past. He was still under thirty when he began the savage and deadly war against the Tweed Ring of New York which remains after three-quarters of a century the outstanding incident in the history of American caricature. This war he waged at times almost single-handed, but it developed his highest talent, and ended in the overthrow of an evil force. In 1872 Nast's pencil was directed against the candidacy of Horace Greeley, and in that year he invented the Tammany Tiger which he pictured as being washed by the editor of the Tribune. In sharp contrast to the Tammany Tiger he also created the Democratic donkey and the Republican elephant. Nast severed his connection with Harper's Weekly in 1887, and during his middle and later years his cartoon work, although he contributed to many journals, was of an irregular sort. Success attended his appearances on the lecture platform, but business and other ventures proved losing ones, and in May, 1902, he was glad to accept appointment to the office of consul at Guayaquil, Ecuador, where a seven months' service ended in his death from yellow fever.

The chief criticism of Nast as an artist has been that he was a poor draughtsman; but there is only a measure of truth in this judgment. He did not, it may be admitted, draw with the abandon and easy freedom of the Frenchmen, Daumier and Forain. Instead his was the uncompromising realism of Gillray and Hogarth, a realism that rarely if ever missed its mark. Both a lovable man and a great artist, the memory of Thomas Nast that must endure is that of one who in troubled days wrought valiantly and effectively for his adopted country! And he fairly and honestly earned the tribute Mr. Lincoln paid him when he declared him "our best recruiting sergeant."

PLATES AND COMMENTARIES

PLATE NO. 1 (Frontispiece)

The Comic Spirit had a part in shaping every chapter of the strange and moving career of Abraham Lincoln, and it is therefore fitting that the present collection should have for its frontispiece a reproduction of the appealing and whimsical drawing by Harold Tucker Webster, A New Baby Down at Tom Lincoln's, which first appeared in the New York World on February 12, 1925, and on the instant won a secure place in the heart of every Lincoln lover. Dennis Hanks, who from youth to old age had a habit of recalling things that had never happened, did retain memories of the birth of Abraham Lincoln the accuracy of which can be trusted. Indeed, the description of the home of Thomas Lincoln, the one-roomed cabin on Nolin Creek in what is now La Rue County, Kentucky—where a man child to be called Abraham after his grandfather was born on February 12, 1809—which Hanks delighted to recount in old age deserves a place in every Lincoln biography. But it is well to remember that other descriptions of the Lincoln home which stress its squalor and absolute lack of comfort do violence to the facts. Dr. Christopher Columbus Graham, a truthful soul who knew Thomas Lincoln well, used, with energy, to stamp them as lies. "It is all stuff," he would declare, "about Tom Lincoln keeping his wife in an open shed in a winter. The Lincolns had a cow and calf, milk and butter, a good featherbed—for I have slept on it. They had home-woven 'kiverlids,' big and little pots, a loom and wheel. Tom Lincoln was a man and took care of his wife."

PLATE No. 1 A New Baby Down at Tom Lincoln's, H. T. Webster, New York World,
February 12, 1925

This was Vanity Fair's first cartoon of Mr. Lincoln drawn by Stephens and published on June 9, 1860, with the apt caption Shaky—Daring Transit on the Perilous Rail: Mr. Abraham Blondin De Lave Lincoln. The artist pictures the Republican nominee as an acrobat, with a negro baby suspended from his balancing pole, trying to cross a chasm, on a rotten and broken log, on the far side of which looms the White House, while from the bank, Horace Greeley whose petulant impatience in the days ahead was to give Mr. Lincoln many an uneasy hour, now worried lest the Negro's interests should be neglected in the pending Republican canvass, calls out: "Don't drop the carpet-bag." In the present instance Stephens had not far to seek for a timely and arresting theme, sure to impress the man in the street. Charles Blondin, noted French tight-rope walker and acrobat of the period, had on August 9, 1859, crossed Niagara Falls on a tight-rope, 1100 feet long, stretched 160 feet above the water, and in the summer months of 1860 was performing similar feats in other parts of the country.

Mr. Lincoln manifested a keen interest in Blondin's exploits, and on at least one occasion made telling use of them to confound his critics. To a group who during his first months as President called on him to remonstrate against his methods of conducting the conflict with the South he returned this tart answer: "Suppose all you are worth was in gold and you had put it in the hands of Blondin to carry across Niagara—would you shake the cable, or keep shouting to him, 'Blondin, stand up a little straighter! Blondin, stoop a little more! Go a little faster! Lean a little more to the north. Lean a little more to the south.' No, you would hold your breath as well as your tongue, and keep your hands off until he was safe over." The faultfinders took their leave convinced against their will that the President did not need advice of a conflicting sort.

PLATE No. 2   Shaky—Daring Transit on the Perilous Rail, Vanity Fair, June 9, 1860

PLATE NO. 3

A Currier & Ives print captioned, Taking the Stump or Stephen in Search of His Mother, was issued in early July of 1860 when Douglas had become the regular Democratic candidate for President, Breckinridge the nominee of the Southern wing of that party, Bell the head of the Constitutional Union ticket and Lincoln the standard bearer of the Republicans. Douglas in the center, one leg in a stay, remarks: "Gentlemen, I am going to see my mother and solicit a little help. In running after a nomination I fell over a big lump of Breckinridge and have been very lame ever since."

Bell at the extreme left comments: "I think I will give him a trifle in New York currency," and Wise of Virginia, studying the crippled Douglas, adds: "He looks like a smart little fellow, and if I were not Wise, I would go my pile on him."

President Buchanan, at the rear and right of Douglas, advises Breckinridge: "Here Breck, as Doug has taken the stump you must stump too," and Breckinridge responds: "Well, old Buck, if you say so I suppose I must, but I know it will be of no use, for I feel that I haven't a leg to stand on."

While Lincoln leaning on a rail fence at the extreme right with confident good humor hails the group: "Go it, ye cripples! Wooden legs are cheap, but stumping won't save you."

After Maine's state election in September, 1860, which resulted in a Republican triumph, as a sequel to the foregoing, Currier and Ives put forth another print, which showed Columbia in the role of the mother of Douglas, grasping a switch titled News from Maine and administering a sound spanking to her wayward son with the injunction: "You have been a bad boy, Steve, ever since you had anything to do with that Nebraska Bill and have made a great deal of trouble in the family, and now I'll pay you for it."

"TAKING THE STUMP" OR STEPHEN IN SEARCH OF HIS MOTHER.

PLATE No. 3   "Taking the Stump" or Stephen in Search of His Mother, Currier and Ives, June, 1860

PLATE NO. 4

The cartoon, Uncle Sam Making New Arrangements, drawn by Maurer and issued by Currier & Ives in the last days of July, 1860, reflects the growing confidence of victory with which the Republican leaders neared election day. It shows Douglas, Breckinridge and Bell approaching the entrance to the White House in varying states of mind, while Uncle Sam in revolutionary garb, with Mr. Lincoln, axe in hand, at his left, takes down a help wanted sign, and remarks to the trio:

"You are too late, gentlemen. I have concluded to take down the Notice and let Abraham Lincoln have the Place. I find his record all right, and can safely trust him with the management of my affairs."

To complete the picture from a White House window President Buchanan, while hastily packing a bag with soiled linen, mournfully remarks, more to himself than to others: "It's too bad. Here he has given me Notice to pack up and quit without a character, and I will never be able to get another place"—a regretful forecast of the speaker's lonely last years at Wheatland.

PLATE No. 4   Uncle Sam Making New Arrangements, Currier and Ives, July, 1860

PLATE NO. 5

Storming the Castle: "Old Abe" on Guard, another popular Currier and Ives print by Maurer put forth in August or September of 1860 when Wide Awake marching clubs had become a distinctive feature of Republican rallies, and there were multiplying signs of the election of Mr. Lincoln in November. President Buchanan leaning from a White House window clutches Breckinridge, the nominee of the Southern Democracy with the plaintive remark: "I will do all I can to help you, Breck, but my strength is failing, and I am afraid you will pull me out before I can pull you in."

"Ah, Mr. Buck!" Breckinridge replies, "I'm too weak to get up, and we shall be compelled to dissolve the Union."

Meanwhile Douglas strives in vain to fit a key to the White House door, impatiently exclaiming: "Confound it! None of these keys will unlock this door; so I'd better be off, for old Abe is after me with a sharp stick." This to the acute discomfort of Bell, who prods him with: "Hurry up, Douglas, and get the door open so that I can get in for the watchman is coming."

The watchman is Lincoln, who, wearing a Wide Awake cap, and carrying in one hand a lantern and in the other a spike made from a rail, advances from the left with the sharp warning: "Ah! ha! Gentlemen! you need not think to catch me napping, for I am a regular Wide Awake."

PLATE No. 5   Storming the Castle: "Old Abe" on Guard, Currier and Ives, August or September, 1860

PLATE NO. 6

The cartoon When Washington was the Sole Standard, drawn by Stephens, appeared in Vanity Fair on July 7, 1860. The Goddess of Liberty grasping in her left hand a Fourth of July banner, and flanked on her right by a bust of Washington and a querulous American eagle, studies with disapproving gaze the gladitorial combat in progress at her feet. At one side Breckinridge and Bell, the Southern candidates for the Presidency, are engaged in a hand-to-hand conflict with no holds barred, while on the other Lincoln with one knee on the ground repels an assault by Douglas, sword in hand and guarded by a Squatter Sovereignty shield. This cartoon accurately reflects the sentiments on July 4, 1860, of a considerable body of voters both North and South. The first thought and chief desire of these voters was the preservation of the Union, in the founding of which Washington and his great compeers had led the way, and to secure this they were prepared for any reasonable compromise, but swift-moving events were to prove that only through bloodshed and conflict could a way be found to a restored and reunited country.

PLATE No. 6   When Washington was the Sole Standard, Vanity Fair, July 7, 1860

The cartoon, A "Rail" Old Western Gentleman, put out by a New York publisher in July, 1860, had a wide circulation during the latter weeks of the campaign which resulted in the election of Mr. Lincoln. It also borrows interest from the fact that it was drawn by and bears the signature of Frank Bellew, who had come back to America to write the later chapters in his many-sided career as an artist. The fence rails Lincoln had split in his youth had an appeal for the voter which reached far beyond the frontier States, and contributed in generous measure to his success as a candidate. When in the spring of 1830 Thomas Lincoln, his son Abraham being then twenty-one years of age, moved from Indiana to Illinois, the family settled some ten miles west of Decatur, in Macon County where the first Mrs. Lincoln's kinsman, John Hanks, had already cut logs for their new home. Mr. Lincoln says in the short biography he wrote for John Locke Scripps in June, 1860: "Here they built a log cabin, into which they removed, and made sufficient of rails to fence ten acres of ground, fenced and broke the ground, and raised a crop of sown corn upon it the same year. These are, or are supposed to be, the rails about which so much is being said just now, though these are far from being the first or only rails ever made by Abraham."

Whatever their order they were the most widely known rails ever split by an American. Moreover, splitting them was the last work young Lincoln did for his father. In the summer of 1830 he exercised the right of majority, and left home to follow the road that was to lead to New Salem, Springfield and a great career. And it is in order to recall that the first work he did for himself, lacking a decent suit of clothes, was "to split four hundred rails for every yard of brown jeans dyed with white-walnut bark that would be necessary to make him a pair of trousers."

PLATE No. 7   A "Rail" Old Western Gentleman, drawing by Frank Bellew, July, 1860

[15]

PLATE NO. 8

The cartoon, Lincoln Shows Douglas the Right Road to the White House, appeared in one of the July, 1860, issues of Phunny Phellow, a humorous sheet published for a brief period in New York, which supplied its share of mirth and laughter to a lively campaign. It also adds an illuminating footnote to the story of Mr. Lincoln's relations with his militant rival. When in 1854 Douglas championed the repeal of the Missouri Compromise, and there loomed the prospect of slavery in Kansas, sharp dissensions rent the Democratic party in the free State of Illinois and early in the following year Mr. Lincoln, having led the opposition in that State to the policies of Douglas, narrowly missed election to a seat in the United States Senate.

Instead, at the eleventh hour he threw his support to an anti-Douglas Democrat, Lyman Trumbull, to whom the way was thus opened for eighteen years of weighty service in the Senate. Nevertheless Mr. Lincoln remained the leader in Illinois of the anti-slavery forces now coalescing into the Republican Party, and in 1856, declined its nomination for governor, but secured the choice and election of William H. Bissell to that office. The same year he was second choice for Vice President at the first Republican National Convention held in Philadelphia. In 1858 Douglas again had to fight for his seat in the Senate, and Mr. Lincoln, growing steadily in prestige and political stature, was the "first and only choice" of the Republicans of Illinois, to oppose him. There followed at the instance of Mr. Lincoln a memorable series of debates, which had issue in the reelection of Douglas by the narrowest of margins, but made his opponent a national figure.

Then came the break of Douglas with Buchanan over the latter's doubtful and hesitant handling of the Kansas question, and a sharp and widening division in the Democratic Party which in 1860 made Douglas the presidential nominee of its northern and Breckinridge of its southern wing in a campaign which ended in the election of Lincoln, the Republican candidate. In the cartoon here reproduced Douglas, with a Kansas feather in his cap, is consoled by Lincoln, who good-naturedly suggests that splitting rails is a more effective road to the White House.

PLATE No. 8 Lincoln Shows Douglas the Right Road to the White House, Phunny Phellow, July, 1860

PLATE NO. 9

The Political Quadrille: Music by Dred Scott, one of the poster cartoons put out in New York during the summer of 1860, recalls a Supreme Court decision which made the Presidency of James Buchanan an uneasy and troubled one. Dred Scott, the negro slave of an army officer, contended that he had become a free man when his master had taken him to live for a time in a free State, later returning with him to Missouri. Aided it is believed by well-to-do opponents of slavery, Scott prosecuted several suits in support of his contention. One of the suits finally reached the Supreme Court, and in the first week of Buchanan's Presidency prompted delivery of an opinion written by Chief Justice Taney which declared that Scott was not a citizen, but only a piece of property, and so without standing in the federal courts. Moreover, the Chief Justice declared unconstitutional the Missouri Compromise of 1820, for the reason, he alleged: "that neither Congress nor the territorial governments could prohibit slavery in the Territories."

The Dred Scott decision gave comfort to the defenders of slavery, but provoked anger and contempt in the North. It added bitterness to the fight to plant slavery in Kansas; in 1858 was one of the chief bones of contention in the debates between Lincoln and Douglas, and two years later figured as a major issue in the presidential campaign. The political quadrille in the cartoon here reproduced is made up of the four candidates for the Presidency. Lincoln with a colored maid as a partner is shown in the upper right hand corner with Bell below him and Breckinridge and Douglas at his left hand. It is to be noted in passing that shortly after the Taney decision Dred Scott was emancipated by his then owner, and passed his last days in Missouri.

Roger B. Taney, an able and honest man, and a devoted son of the republic from youth to age, was also a slave to the narrow letter of the law as he interpreted it, and Northern resentment of his Dred Scott decision shadowed his last years and followed him to the grave. Between the election and inauguration of Mr. Lincoln the venerable Chief Justice was seized with what threatened to be a fatal illness, and it was feared by Republican leaders that it would fall to President Buchanan to nominate his successor. Instead he made a slow but complete recovery, and continued to preside over the Supreme Court. Galusha A. Grow in after years was wont to recall with a smile how on a spring morning in 1864 he and Senator Ben Wade of Ohio walking near the Capitol met Taney, who greeted them with ample evidence of mental and physical vigor. "Grow," said Wade, "in the last days of the Buchanan administration I prayed every night that that old cuss would live at least until Lincoln's inauguration. Perhaps I prayed too infernally hard."

As a matter of fact the Chief Justice died in October, 1864. Mr. Lincoln in due course nominated Salmon P. Chase as his successor.

PLATE No. 9   The Political Quadrille: Music by Dred Scott, Poster Cartoon, July, 1860

PLATE NO. 10

This poster, Lincoln, Douglas and the Rail-Fence Handicap, published at Buffalo in July, 1860, represents Douglas, short of stature and with concern as to the outcome, asking: "How can I get over this rail fence?" Lincoln, with the assurance bred by his six feet four, makes confident answer: "It can't stop me, for I built it," while from a black figure between the rails comes this warning to the Little Giant: "You find me in dis yer fence, Massa Duglis." All of which recalls the account by Dr. Allen Johnson in his admirable biography of Douglas of the odd picture the rivals presented when they first met in debate at Ottawa, Illinois, on August 21, 1860. "The crowd," writes Dr. Johnson, "instinctively took its measure of the two men. They presented a striking contrast. Lincoln, tall, angular and long of limb; Douglas, short, almost dwarfed by comparison, broad-shouldered and thick-chested. Lincoln was clad in a frock coat of rusty black, which was evidently not made for his lank, ungainly body. His sleeves did not reach his wrists by several inches, and his trousers failed to conceal his huge feet. His long, sinewy neck emerged from a white collar, drawn over a black tie. Altogether, his appearance bordered upon the grotesque, and would have provoked mirth in any other than an Illinois audience, which knew and respected the man too well to mark his costume. Douglas, on the contrary, presented a well-groomed figure. He wore a well-fitting suit of broadcloth; his linen was immaculate; and altogether he had the appearance of a man of the world whom fortune had favored."

But the fact persisted that the Little Giant's lack of stature was a handicap rather than an asset. "Judge Douglas can never be President," was the grim yet appraising verdict of Senator Thomas H. Benton. "his coat-tails are too near the ground."

PLATE No. 10 Lincoln, Douglas and the Rail-Fence Handicap, Poster Cartoon published in Buffalo, July, 1860

PLATE NO. 11

The poster cartoon Candidates and Platforms was issued at Cincinnati in July, 1860, and makes reasonably clear how a major portion of the people of the Middle West came in no long time to regard a developing campaign and its candidates. Mr. Lincoln is depicted as firmly planted, rail in hand, on a platform declaring for No Extension of Slavery, while Douglas has one foot on the now outdated Democratic platform of 1856, on which Buchanan had triumphed over Fremont, and with the other straddles Mason and Dixon's Line, in one hand waving a Dred Scott Decision flag to win Southern support, and in the other, to win the favor of the North, a second banner inscribed Unfriendly Legislation. A bell hides the face of the candidate of the Constitutional Union party, who is represented as having no platform on which to stand. Nor could the veteran Tennessee leader claim real support for his candidacy. When election day came Bell secured only thirty-nine electoral votes, given him by the States of Kentucky, Tennessee and Virginia.

Plate No. 11   Candidates and Platforms, Poster Caricature Issued in Cincinnati, July, 1860

PLATE NO. 12

The cartoon Progressive Democracy—Prospect of a Smash Up is another of the famous series of posters which during the campaign of 1860 Louis Maurer drew for Currier and Ives. The two pairs of nominees which had resulted from the several Democratic national conventions of a fateful year furnish the artist with a timely and congenial theme. A cart labeled Democratic Platform has a team hitched to each end of it. Douglas and Johnson compose one team driven by an Indian brave who, confirming a current report that Tammany and Douglas had joined forces, shouts: "Now then little Dug! put in and pull while I cry: 'Tammany to the rescue' for I hear a rushing sound that bodes us no good."

The team at the other end of the cart and pulling in the opposite direction is made up of Breckinridge and Lane. It is driven by President Buchanan, who, flourishing a whip, shouts: "Come Jack and Joe, pull up. And don't let the other team stir the wagon. I'd rather the Machine would be smashed than have them run away with it."

That a smash, sure to make an end of a President and two of the aspirants for his place, is a matter of seconds, is made evident by a fast approaching Republican locomotive manned by Lincoln and Hamlin. "Clear the track," shouts Lincoln, and Hamlin adds the warning: "Look out for the engine when the bell rings." The summer days of 1860 were troubled ones for James Buchanan as well as for the candidates of a divided party.

PROGRESSIVE DEMOCRACY—PROSPECT OF A 'SMASH UP.

PLATE No. 12 Progressive Democracy—Prospect of a Smashup, Currier and Ives, July, 1860

PLATE NO. 13

This cartoon drawn by Maurer for Currier and Ives and captioned The National Game, Three "Outs" and One "Run"; Abraham Winning the Ball, had wide distribution in the mid-summer of 1860; and it must have interested Mr. Lincoln, who in his Springfield days always found keen delight in a lively game of handball, never refusing to try conclusions with all sorts and conditions of men. Founded on the old English game of rounders, baseball in the middle years of the last century swiftly and surely claimed its place as first among American sports. The National Association of Baseball Players was set up in 1858; with few exceptions in 1860 every town and city had its team, trials of skill with visiting competitors being sure to draw large and enthusiastic crowds.

Three of the players in the game depicted by Maurer claim, as already noted, a word. John Bell of Tennessee, long a Whig leader in the South, as the presidential candidate of the Constitutional Union Party in 1860, won the electoral votes of only his own and two other Border States. At first opposed to secession, when Fort Sumter was fired upon he espoused the Southern cause, but, heart-broken and in ill-health, took no active part in the war. Breckinridge, candidate of the Southern Democracy, retained his seat in the Senate until mid-summer of 1861, but then entered the Confederate army, and was expelled by his fellow senators as a traitor. Far different was the course of Douglas, candidate of the Northern Democracy. When war came he instantly became Mr. Lincoln's right hand, declaring in speeches that stirred the North: "There are now only patriots and traitors." His untimely and deeply regretted death on June 3, 1861, was a heavy blow to the Union.

PLATE No. 13   The National Game, Three "Outs" and One "Run": Abraham Winning the Ball,
Currier and Ives, July, 1860

The cartoon The Split-Tail Democracy appeared on July 21, 1860, in the Rail Splitter, a Republican campaign sheet established four weeks earlier in Chicago, and which ended a lively existence a few days before Mr. Lincoln's election in November. It was accompanied by this bit of dialogue:

Old Abe—"Here is a rail specimen of the Split-tail Democracy."
Douglas—"We are all Democrats."
Breckinridge—"So we are."

And to the foregoing the editor appended these lines:

> The deed is done, their day is o'er,
> Two possums fought at Baltimore;
> Now let them scratch, now let them wail,
>   Old Abr'm has them "in a rail."
> Well let them fight, and let them bite
>   And quarrel for the bone;
> The maxim says, at such a time—
>   "The honest get their own."

It is interesting to note that in the same July 21 issue of the Rail Splitter appeared these stirring lines, Up for the Conflict by John Greenleaf Whittier to be sung to the familiar tune of Gaily the Troubador:

> Up to our altars, then haste we and summon
>   Courage and loveliness, manhood and woman;
> Deep let our pledges be, freedom for ever;
>   Truce with oppression, never! oh, never!

> By our own birthright, granted of Heaven,
>   Freedom on sea and earth, be the pledge given,
> If we have whispered truth, whisper no longer;
>   Speak as the tempest does, sterner and stronger.

> Still be the tones of truth louder and firmer,
>   Startling the haughty South with the deep murmur.
> God and our Charter's right! Freedom for ever.
>   Truce with oppression, Never! oh, never!

PLATE No. 14   The Split-Tail Democracy, The Rail Splitter, July 21, 1860

PLATE NO. 15

The cartoon The Rail Candidate, drawn by Louis Maurer and issued by Currier and Ives in September, 1860, shows Mr. Lincoln astride a rail labeled Republican Platform and borne on the shoulders of a sturdy Negro and of Horace Greeley from whose coat pocket protrudes a copy of his journal, the New York Tribune. Says Greeley to Mr. Lincoln: "We can prove that you have split rails, and that will insure your election." To which Mr. Lincoln makes mournful reply: "It is true I have split rails, but I begin to feel as if this rail would split me; it's the hardest stick I ever straddled." And the colored bearer of the forward half of the rail proclaims in protesting tones: "Dis Nigger strong and willin', but it's awful hard work to carry Old Massa Abe on nothing but dis ere rail."

All of which again recalls how the rails Mr. Lincoln had split thirty years before played a picturesque and appealing part in the convention which nominated him for and in the campaign which resulted in his election to the Presidency. "Among the common people," writes Ida Tarbell, "the jeer that Lincoln was but a rail splitter was a spur to enthusiasm. Too many of the solid men of the North had swung an axe, too many of them had passed from log hut to mansion, not to blaze with sympathetic indignation when the party was taunted with nominating a backwoodsman. The rail became their emblem and their rallying cry, and the story of the rail fence Lincoln had built became a feature of every campaign speech and every country store discussion. In a week after his nomination, two rails declared to have been split by Lincoln were on exhibition in New York, and certain zealous Pennsylvanians had sent to Macon, Illinois, asking to buy the whole fence and have it shipped East. It was the rail which decorated campaign medals, inspired campaign songs, appeared in campaign cartoons. There was something more than a desire to stand by the candidate in the enthusiasm. At bottom it was a vindication of the American way of making a man."

THE RAIL CANDIDATE.

PLATE No. 15   The Rail Candidate, Currier and Ives, August, 1860

PLATE NO. 16

The title of the cartoon, The Nigger in the Woodpile, drawn by Maurer, and put out by Currier and Ives in August, 1860, supplied a phrase quickly and widely made use of on the platform and in the press. Mr. Lincoln, seated atop a woodpile, labeled Republican Platform and affording a refuge for an anxious Negro, remarks: "Little did I think when I split these rails that they would be the means of elevating me to my present position."

And Horace Greeley, standing at the right of the woodpile with a copy of the Tribune in his hand, advises Young America, uncertain as how he shall cast his vote: "I assure you, my friend, that you can safely vote our ticket for we have no connection with the Abolition Party, but our Platform is composed entirely of rails split by our candidate."

This assurance falls on stubborn soil, for young America replies: "It's no use, old fellow! You can't pull that wool over my eyes, for I can see the Nigger peeping through the rails."

But it was the young voters of the North who, swelling the Republican ranks, a few weeks later effected the election of Mr. Lincoln.

"THE NIGGER" IN THE WOODPILE.

PLATE No. 16 "The Nigger" in the Woodpile, Currier and Ives, August, 1860

The Political Gymnasium, a poster cartoon drawn by Louis Maurer and put out by Currier and Ives in August, 1860, affords an amusing review of the presidential contestants then striving for mastery. At the extreme left Edward Everett holds aloft a dumbbell on which is seated John Bell, his running-mate on the Constitutional Union ticket. "There is nothing," he remarks, "like having the Constitution to give us strength to put up this Bell successfully," and Bell adds: "I have perfect confidence in Mr. Everett's ability to uphold me."

At Bell's left, Horace Greeley, on a horizontal bar, is shown trying to gain the nomination for governor of New York, but, doubtful of the outcome, he mournfully observes: "I have been practicing at it a long time, but can never get up muscle enough to get astride of this bar." In the foreground Greeley's long time rival James Watson Webb, editor of the New York Courier and Inquirer, not to be denied a place in the new lineup of parties, boasts that he can beat any man in his group at "turning political somersets." In the present instance General Webb's change of party had an agreeable outcome for him as in due course President Lincoln appointed him minister to Brazil. To the rear of Mr. Lincoln, Douglas and Breckinridge, the rival candidates of the Democracy, are engaged in a lively setto with gloves. "If I do nothing else," says Breckinridge, "I can at least prevent you from pulling Lincoln down," and Douglas retorts: "Come at me, Breck, and after you cry enough I will take a round with the rest of them."

But in retrospect, aside from Mr. Lincoln, the most noteworthy figure in the Maurer drawing is Senator Seward, who crippled by an untimely fall from the nomination bar, borrows a crutch and cane for support and cautions his successful opponent: "You'd better be careful, my friend, that you don't tumble off as I did before I was fairly on, for if you do you'll be as badly crippled as I am."

For a brief period after the Chicago convention Senator Seward was inclined to sulk in his tent, but did not long delay his public support of Mr. Lincoln's candidacy, and taking the stump at the end of August, 1860, he delivered most effective speeches in Michigan, Wisconsin, Minnesota, Iowa, Kansas, Illinois and other States of the Middle West. On the morrow of the election in November it became known that Senator Seward would have an important place in the new administration, and when in March, 1861, his appointment as secretary of state was announced there opened before him what is now regarded as the most fruitful and weighty period of his public career. When a visitor called on him at Auburn in his last days he pointed to the library shelf on which reposed the bound volumes of his papers as secretary of state, and remarked with quiet pride: "There is my best claim to remembrance."

THE POLITICAL GYMNASIUM.

PLATE No. 17   The Political Gymnasium, Currier and Ives, August, 1860

The cartoon, Political "Blondin's" Crossing Salt River, issued by Currier and Ives in August, 1860, had for its motive a then favorite subject with caricaturists, the exploits of Blondin, who in 1859, thrilled Americans by crossing Niagara on a tight rope. The stream now depicted is Salt River, made to do duty as a chasm separating North and South. A jutting boulder styled Abolition Rock supports a rail which has Horace Greeley crouching at one and Mr. Lincoln from the other end due for an unwelcome plunge into the water. "Hallo!" moans Greeley, "Here I go as usual into Salt River. I have been dipped in it so often that I don't mind the ducking, if the fall don't kill me, for a bag of wool won't sink," while Mr. Lincoln angrily exclaims: "Confound Greeley! He told me that it was not necessary for this end of my rail to rest on anything so long as he sat on the other end, and I believed him and am lost."

Two more of the presidential candidates of 1860 are shown trying to cross the chasm between North and South; but Douglas, hampered by the weight of the Squatter Sovereignty end of his balance pole, is about to fall on the rope. "Help! help," he cries. "I'm falling. That dead weight on my balance pole has ruined me!" Behind him Breckinridge, on the shoulders of his running-mate Lane, feels the Slavery Extension rope parting beneath them and exclaims: "Hurry up, old man! for it makes my blood curdle to think where we'll be if the rope breaks," and Lane assures him: "Hold on tight, Johnny! and trust 'an old public functionary' to carry you safely over."

John Bell, fourth among the candidates of 1860, refuses to attempt to cross the chasm that is threatening disaster to his rivals. Instead, with his running-mate Edward Everett beside him, he stands on a firmly planted Constitutional Bridge and warns Mr. Lincoln and the rest: "It's no use, gentlemen; you'll all go overboard, because you were not satisfied to stand upon this bridge but must needs try some other way to get across." And Everett enforces Bell with this assurance: "Built by Washington, Jefferson and the Patriots of '76 this bridge is the only structure that connects these two shores in an indissoluble bond of union, and woe be to the man who attempts to undermine it."

In the hours of trial the speaker kept the faith. When war came, as history records, John Bell went with his State and died a broken man, but Edward Everett with voice and pen, and with firmness and fervor, supported the Union. His last years were his noblest and most useful ones.

POLITICAL "BLONDINS" CROSSING SALT RIVER.

PLATE No. 18 Political "Blondins" Crossing Salt River, Currier and Ives, August, 1860

PLATE NO. 19

The cartoon, The Coming Man's Presidential Career a la Blondin, which appeared in Harper's Weekly, August 25, again employing the rope-walking exploits of the man from France as a motive, seemed to predict that Mr. Lincoln's advocacy of freedom for the Negro might end in disaster. The outcome, however, gave the lie to the artist's fears. Charles Blondin survived for eight-and-thirty years his crossing of Niagara Falls on a tight rope and died peacefully in bed at the ripe age of seventy-three, while Mr. Lincoln triumphed at the election of 1860 and a little more than four years later, by the exercise of statesmanship of the first order, effected the abolition of slavery. "My paramount object in this struggle," he wrote Horace Greeley, a captious critic of his policies, in August, 1862, "is to save the Union. If I could save the Union without freeing any slave I would do it; and if I could save it by freeing some and leaving others alone I would also do that. What I do about slavery and the colored race, I do because I believe it helps to save the Union, and what I forbear, I forbear because I do not believe it would help to save the Union. I have here stated my purpose according to my view of official duty; and I intend no modification of my oft-expressed personal wish that all men everywhere could be free."

When Mr. Lincoln wrote this letter he had already made up his mind to emancipate the slaves as a military measure, and only waited the opportune moment for so doing. In the end his patience and wisdom, rightly shaping great events, saved the Union and abolished slavery.

PLATE No. 19   The Coming Man's Presidential Career, a la Blondin, Harper's Weekly, August 25, 1860

[39]

PLATE NO. 20

The poster cartoon, Honest Old Abe on the Stump, put out in August, 1860, carried this bit of explanatory text:

At Springfield in 1858:
"Nobody ever expected me to be President. In my poor, lean, lank face nobody has ever seen that any cabbages were sprouting."

At Springfield in 1860:
"I appear here at this time only for the purpose of affording myself the best opportunity of seeing you and enabling you to see me."

Cartoon and text recall an important phase of the campaign of 1860—the silence of the Republican candidate. From May to November Mr. Lincoln remained at his home, and made no speeches except a very brief address at a great mass meeting in Springfield. And to those who sought a fresh expression of his views he replied that already he had expressed himself fully and referred them to printed copies of the speeches he had made before his nomination. Mr. Lincoln's activities during the summer and fall of 1860 have been summed up in admirable fashion by John G. Nicolay, who early had begun to serve as his private secretary. "He employed no literary bureau," writes Mr. Nicolay, "wrote no public letters, made no set or impromptu speeches. All these devices of propagandism he left to the leaders and committees of his adherents in their several States. Even the strictly confidential letters in which he indicated his advice on points in the progress of the campaign did not exceed a dozen in number; and when politicians came to interview him at Springfield he received them in the privacy of his own home, and generally their presence created little or no public notice."

Nor did Mr. Lincoln hasten to break silence and make statements of policy after his election and before he began his journey to Washington to assume the Presidency. When in November Truman Smith of Connecticut, an old-time Whig who had served with him in Congress, urged him to make a statement that would quiet the fears of Northern businessmen and allay Southern threats of secession, he promptly replied: "I feel constrained, for the present at least, to make no declaration for the public. I could say nothing which I have not already said, and which is in print, and open for the inspection of all. To press a repetition of this on those who have listened, is useless; to press it upon those who have refused to listen, and still refuse, would be wanting in self-respect. I am not insensible to any commercial or financial depression that may exist, but nothing is to be gained by fawning around the 'respectable scoundrels' who got it up. Let them . . . repair the mischief of their own making, and then perhaps they will be less greedy to do the like again."

The sequel proved the wisdom of Mr. Lincoln's resolution to speak only at the right time and in the right way.

Plate No. 20   Honest Old Abe on the Stump, Poster Cartoon, August, 1860

The cartoon Dividing the National Map was one of a series of poster caricatures issued by a Cincinnati printer during the summer and fall of 1860. It shows Mr. Lincoln contesting with Douglas possession of the western and northern portions of the Union, while Breckinridge claims the entire South for his own, and Bell from a high chair seeks with a pot of glue to repair the damage that is being done. It is interesting to recall that when election day came Mr. Lincoln carried all of the Free States of the East, Middle West, and Pacific Coast, and Breckinridge all of the States of the Cotton Belt, along with Delaware and Maryland. The States of Virginia, Kentucky and Tennessee gave their electoral votes to Bell and Everett, the Constitutional Union candidates, but Douglas, despite a popular vote rivalling that of Mr. Lincoln, received only the vote of Missouri and part of the electoral vote of New Jersey.

But the Little Giant, after June, 1860, must have been aware that he could not count on effective support from the South. Jefferson Davis, who soon was to lead his section to disaster and defeat, both hated and feared Douglas and could see no good in any of his ways. "If our little, grog-drinking, electioneering demagogue," he wrote former President Pierce in June, 1860, "can destroy our hopes, it must be that we have been doomed to destruction." A true prophecy, although there was to be nearly four years of strife and bloodshed before Davis, a beaten man, was finally compelled to recognize the force of it.

Douglas was in Mobile when news of his defeat reached him. First of all a patriot and lover of his country, in speeches at New Orleans and Vicksburg he urged the South and its leaders to accept accomplished facts, and then returned to the North and to his seat in the Senate to make a stout but unavailing effort to avert an appeal to arms. Then came Sumter, and his quick and heartfelt acceptance of the role of friend and adviser to his old-time rival now a beset and troubled President.

PLATE No. 21   Dividing the National Map, Poster Cartoon Issued in Cincinnati, August, 1860

PLATE NO. 22

The Political Rail Splitter was the title given by the artist to a lithograph put
out by J. Leach of New York in August, 1860, originals of which are now much
prized by collectors. Little is known about Leach as man or artist, but most of his
drawings have strength and directness, and the one here reproduced is no exception
to this rule. It shows Mr. Lincoln having discarded his axe for a Negro-headed
mallet, resolutely splitting the Union in two, this to the confusion and dismay of
Senator Seward and Horace Greeley, who watch him at work. "I will," Greeley is
saying, "give Bill Seward a taste of his higher Law," and the New York senator
mournfully protests: "Call you this *backing* your friend?" In the summer days of
1860 it was the chief contention of the Democrats both North and South and of the
Constitutional Unionists, who had nominated Bell and Everett, that the election
of Mr. Lincoln would split the Union, and for a time the Republican candidate's
self-imposed silence as to his purposes if elected added point to this contention.
But Mr. Lincoln won and it was the men of the South who sought to carry out the
aims they had assigned to him.

PLATE No. 22   The Political Rail Splitter, Lithograph by J. Leach, New York, August, 1860

PLATE NO. 23

The Irrepressible Conflict was the title given two out-of-the-ordinary cartoons which amused and influenced people in the campaign that resulted in the election of Mr. Lincoln. The first, a lithograph which sold for ten cents, was put out at Cincinnati in August or early September, 1860. Because of its packing industry Cincinnati in those days was nicknamed Porkopolis, and this fact supplied an apt and congenial motive for the drawing under consideration. A huge hog flanked by its lively offspring and labeled Raised in Porkolis occupies the foreground. Its head is a portrait of James Buchanan, who on a platform adopted by the Democratic National Convention at Cincinnati in 1856, and which at least by implication had reluctantly endorsed the repeal of the Missouri Compromise, had been nominated and elected President. "I am not (a hog) any more," he declares. "I am the Cincinnati Platform."

Douglas, who had been Buchanan's chief contestant for the Democratic nomination in 1856 and who had soon come to the parting of the ways with him, grasps the tail of the hog, and explains to Lincoln, who confronts the animal, knife in hand and with a map of the territories behind him: "Don't you see Abe that I want to keep her out of the territories?" But Mr. Lincoln makes pertinent reply: "I am sorry for you, Steph; you did not manage her right; she has gone too far already: but I am bound not to let her come in, and send her where she belongs."

This cartoon was the first to use the term "irrepressible conflict" employed with memorable results by Senator Seward in a speech in the Senate on October 25, 1858, in which, to the confusion of the timid, he summed up the growing tension between freedom and slavery as "an irrepressible conflict between opposing and enduring forces." It is fitting to recall, as a part of the history of a mighty agitation, that a little more than four months earlier, at Springfield on June 16, 1858 in opening his senatorial campaign with Douglas, Mr. Lincoln had delivered his equally noteworthy "house divided" speech.

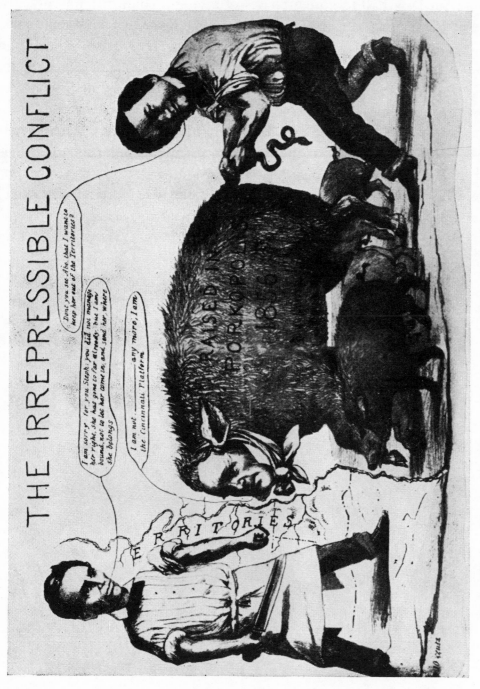

PLATE No. 23   The Irrepressible Conflict, Poster Cartoon published in Cincinnati, August, 1860

PLATE NO. 24

The Political Eclipse of 1860 as It Appears North is another of the poster cartoons put out at Cincinnati during the summer months of 1860, and has to do with one of the tense but now half-forgotten phases of a fateful contest. John Bell, uneasy candidate of the Constitutional Unionists, looking through a telescope notes to his dismay the shadow of Mr. Lincoln eclipsing the New England and Middle States and calls out to Douglas: "Steph, the entire northern limb seems to (have) eclipsed." Whereupon Douglas, ready as usual to meet an emergency, makes reply: "If that is the case John, we better fuse."

As a matter of fact it was too late for heroic measures of any sort to save the Little Giant and his fortunes. In the efforts to defeat Mr. Lincoln, the elements opposing him effected at the eleventh hour a fusion of electoral tickets in Rhode Island, New York, New Jersey and Pennsylvania, but when election day came the Republican nominee carried these and all of the other Northern States.

PLATE No. 24   The Political Eclipse of 1860, Poster Cartoon published in Cincinnati, August 1860

The cartoon, The Great Exhibition of 1860, drawn by Maurer, and issued by Currier and Ives in the late summer, possibly September, of 1860 reflects a belief then held in certain quarters that the trend and character of Mr. Lincoln's campaign was being mainly shaped by Senator Seward and a group of New York editors. Events were to prove this belief in the main a mistaken one, for Mr. Lincoln did his own thinking at every stage, but for the moment it served to lend color and piquancy to the campaign. Horace Greeley, grinding a hand organ labeled New York Tribune, acts as a master of ceremonies, and gives this order to the Republican nominee: "Now caper about on your rail Abraham while I play the Slieve Gammon Polka, All the Way from Oregon, Mrs. Gurney's Love Song and other choice airs from my private collection."

At Greeley's left, Mr. Lincoln, in his shirt sleeves strides a rail doing duty as the Republican Platform, while padlocked lips that of a sudden have come silent infer that Mum is the command of his advisers. In the rear, Senator Seward, clad as a nurse and holding a Negro child, protests to the editor who had helped to bring about his defeat at Chicago: "It's no use trying to keep me and the 'Irrepressible' infant in the background, for we are really the head and front of this party." And a little way removed from the senator and former governor who in hours of need had done him more than one good turn, James Watson Webb, of the Courier and Enquirer, passes the tambourine, and puts forth this plea for dole: Please Gentlemen! help a family in reduced circumstances. We are very hard up, and will even take three cents if we can't get more, just to keep the little Nigger alive."

Perhaps the most amusing figure in the present group is Henry Jarvis Raymond, who in his 'prentice days had served Webb and Greeley in turn as right hand, and then had become one of the founders and the editor of the New York Times. Now with an axe in one hand and with the other clinging to the sturdy arm of General Webb he assures his old employer: "I'll stick fast to you, General, for the present, because I have my own little axe to grind." There is no doubt that Raymond had always an alert eye for the main chance, but first and last he gave Mr. Lincoln loyal support and, unlike Greeley, he was ready when there was need for it to admit the superior wisdom of his chief.

THE GREAT EXHIBITION OF 1860.

PLATE No. 25   The Great Exhibition of 1860, Currier and Ives, September, 1860

PLATE NO. 26

The poster cartoon A Political Race issued by a New York printer in September, 1860, found many purchasers at ten cents a copy. It calls to mind the letter Mr. Lincoln on December 22, 1859, wrote to his friend and champion, Jesse W. Fell, and which, furnishing data for a newspaper sketch of his career, may be said to have marked the beginning of his avowed candidacy for the Republican nomination for President. "If any personal description of me is thought desirable," he informed Fell, "it may be said I am, in height, six feet four inches, nearly; lean in flesh, weighing on an average one hundred and eighty pounds; dark complexion, with coarse black hair and gray eyes." And he whimsically added, in the familiar phrasing of the advertisements for lost and stolen animals, of his period and section: "No other marks or brands recollected."

And while Mr. Lincoln was tall and thin, Douglas was short and stocky, a bigger man above his short legs than he was below them. Volk, the sculptor, measuring both of them for statues in 1860, informed Mr. Lincoln that he was just a foot taller than Douglas. This difference, in the present instance, furnished welcome material for an artist friendly to Mr. Lincoln and a bit critical of Douglas. He depicts them leading in the race for the White House which looms up in the background, with Breckinridge trailing them, and Bell, old and short of breath, bringing up the rear. "I never ran so in my life," says Douglas, and Breckinridge, doubtful of the issue, replies: "That long legged Abolitionist is getting ahead of us all," and Bell adds: "Bless my soul—I give up."

Bell, however, made a respectable showing on election day for he received after Mr. Lincoln and Breckinridge the largest number of electoral votes. Douglas, except in the popular vote, was hopelessly distanced by all of his rivals.

PLATE No. 26   A Political Race, Poster Cartoon, New York, September, 1860

PLATE NO. 27

Louis Maurer was at his best in this cartoon, Honest Abe Taking Them on the Half Shell, put out by Currier and Ives in September, 1860. The people of the North in 1860 classified the Democratic leaders as "soft-shells" and "hard-shells" according to the stand they took on the slavery question. Thus Douglas and Breckinridge were classified, the one as a "soft-shell" and the other as a "hard-shell." Thus Mr. Lincoln, clearly well satisfied with current conditions, is portrayed as surveying his rivals for the Presidency with the smiling remark: "These fellows have been planted so long in Washington that they are as fat as butter. I hardly know which to swallow first." It may be noted in passing that in 1860, as a sharp contrast to Mr. Lincoln's single, ill-starred term in Congress, Douglas had served seventeen years in the House and Senate, while Breckinridge had been twice elected to the House and was then in his fourth year as Vice President. On March 4, 1861, Breckinridge succeeded John J. Crittenden in the Senate, but before the year's end was expelled from that body for treason.

PLATE No. 27   Honest Abe Taking Them on the Half Shell, Currier and Ives,
September, 1860

PLATE NO. 28

The cartoon, Three to One You Don't Get It, first appeared in Vanity Fair on September 1, 1860. It reflects a somewhat cynical interpretation of the popular meaning of the pawnbroker's "three balls." President Buchanan as the Democratic watchdog stands guard at the entrance to the White House, above which hangs three balls inscribed with the names of the candidates, Douglas, Breckinridge and Bell, who, with the several national conventions now a part of history, were opposing Mr. Lincoln, while the Rail Splitter is shown staggering forward, axe in hand and over his shoulder a bundle of rails on which, it is the manifest belief of the artist, it will be difficult for him to secure an advance of any sort. But the sequel was to prove that the Republican candidate's prospects were of another and more compelling kind.

PLATE No. 28   "Three to One You Don't Get It," Vanity Fair, September 1, 1860

[57]

PLATE NO. 29

The unpopularity of President Buchanan during the last months of his administration was a timely subject for comment and caricature of which the supporters of Mr. Lincoln made frequent and telling use. Thus on September 3, 1860, the cartoon here reproduced, The Power of the Rail, appeared in the Rail Splitter, a campaign sheet maintained as previously noted, by the Republican managers in Chicago. It was accompanied by this bit of doggerel:

> Old Buck sat in his chair of state;
>   His face was pale and wan;
> The darkest passions of rage and hate
>   In his sunken eyeballs shone.
>
> Oh! Very uneasy, the Old Man said,
>   Is the head that wears a crown—
> The man who serves the slave-power now,
>   Must certainly go down.
>
> The Covode dogs are on my track,
>   I hear their loud-mouthed wail;
> The treacherous chair begins to crack,
>   Upheaved by Lincoln's rail.
>
> A smile played on old Abram's lips,
>   He sprang the rail upon
> And backward went poor old J.B.,
>   Down to Oblivion.

The reference to "the Covode dogs" in the third stanza recalls an investigation of the Buchanan administration conducted in the summer of 1860 by a committee of Congress headed by John Covode, a stalwart and intensely partisan figure who between 1857 and 1869 was for ten years a member of the House from Pennsylvania. The House in 1860 was controlled by the Republicans, a condition which determined the make-up of the Covode committee, and made its inquiry a savage and unsparing one. The Democrats, in the press and from the platform, denounced the inquiry as unfair and unconstitutional, but it made votes for Mr. Lincoln.

PLATE No. 29   The Power of the Rail, The Rail Splitter, September 3, 1860

PLATE NO. 30

The cartoon, Coming 'Round drawn by Stephens appeared in Vanity Fair on September 15, 1860, when there were steadily growing signs that Mr. Lincoln would triumph at the polls in November. In front of the White House stables stands Jockey Yancey leading a spirited mare on which he has placed a blanket labeled Fugitive Slave Law. Liveryman Lincoln confronts him with the plea: "I say, Yancey. if you'll let me have these stables in peace for the next four years, I'll give you some of the best stalls and see that your nag is well taken care of."

All of which is in keeping with the motives which governed Yancey and Mr. Lincoln. The former, a man of eloquence and unbending will whose career had a turbulent meridian and a tragic close, was through stormy years an outstanding and unswerving advocate of secession. He opposed with voice and pen every plan put forward by Northern moderates for the peaceful adjustment of the slavery question; in the Democratic National Convention at Charleston in 1860 he led the movement which put a period to the presidential ambitions of Stephen A. Douglas, and in January of the following year as a member of the Alabama Legislature he introduced and forced the passage of an ordnance of secession by that body. But when the clash of arms came Yancey was pushed aside by ill-wishers in his own household, and after ineffective service in Europe as a diplomatic agent of the Confederacy passed into an unwelcome retirement which ended with his death in 1863 at the early age of forty-nine years.

On the other hand, Mr. Lincoln, prior to his assumption of the Presidency, never went farther in his avowed opposition to slavery than to protest against its extension to the territories, an extension implied by the repeal of the Missouri Compromise. It was his deep-seated conviction that, confined within its existing limits, slavery, without a resort to violent and, perhaps, unjust measures, would be on the way slow yet sure to ultimate extinction. And he held firmly to this conviction during uncertain weeks and months as President-elect. Witness his letter to Lyman Trumbull on December 13, 1860, when some of the Republican leaders in Congress were seeking in short-sighted and unwise ways to conciliate the champions of slavery and secession.

"Let there be no compromise," he wrote the Illinois senator "on the question of extending slavery. If there be, all our labor is lost and, ere long, must be done again. The dangerous ground—that into which some of our friends have a hankering to run—is Pop(ular) Sov(ereignty). Have none of it. Stand firm. The tug has to come, and better now than any time hereafter."

Time quickly justified the wisdom of this injunction.

PLATE No. 30   Coming 'Round, Vanity Fair, September 15, 1860

PLATE NO. 31

The poster cartoon, The Republican Party Going to the Right House, drawn by Maurer and issued by Currier and Ives in late September or early October of 1860, echoes some of the social movements which claimed attention and provoked sharp debate in the uneasy years immediately preceding Mr. Lincoln's election to the Presidency. At the entrance to a lunatic asylum, Horace Greeley, carrying on his shoulder a rail with Mr. Lincoln astride of it, heads a long and motley procession of would-be social reformers. "Hold on to me, Abe," says Greeley, "and we will go in here by the unanimous consent of the people," while Mr. Lincoln turns to assure those who are following him: "Now, my friends, I am almost in and the millenium is going to begin; so speak what you will and it will be granted."

An arm-in-arm trio heading the group behind Mr. Lincoln consists of an outspoken damsel not easy to describe, an advocate of free love and a Mormon elder. "Oh! what a beautiful man he is," says the woman gazing fondly at Mr. Lincoln. "I feel a 'passional attraction' every time I see his lovely face." The full-bearded man beside her proclaims: "I represent the free love element, and expect to have free license to carry out my principles," and her second companion in the foremost file declares: "I want religion abolished, and the Book of Mormon made the standard of morality."

Behind this trio marches a gallus Negro in the flamboyant garb of a minstrel of the period and a strong-minded female of uncertain age. "De white man," declares the former, "has no rights dat cullud pussons are bound to 'spect. I want that understood," and the champion of equal rights asserts: "I want woman's rights enforced and man reduced in subjection to her authority." Next in the march to a destined haven are two worse-for-wear paraders who also have definite ends in mind. "I want everybody," says one, "to have a share of everybody else's property," and the other also with an eye to the main chance in a doubting and doubtful world, echoes the demands of his mate: "I want a hotel established by the government where people that ain't inclined to work can board free of expense, and be found in rum and tobacco."

All of which bears witness to the fact that the middle decades of the last century were uneasy and, now and again, lawless ones. But when the hour of trial came many of the men and women who had championed the radical movements of those contentious decades were quick to prove their caliber. Neal Dow, father of the Maine law, became a general in the Union Army; Charles A. Dana, who had helped to write Brook Farm history, Stanton's right hand in the War Department, and William Lloyd Garrison and other abolition leaders unswerving champions of Mr. Lincoln and his policies.

THE REPUBLICAN PARTY GOING TO THE RIGHT HOUSE.

PLATE No. 31   The Republican Party Going to the Right House, Currier and Ives, October, 1860

PLATE NO. 32

An Heir to the Throne, or the Next Republican Candidate, a poster cartoon drawn by Maurer and distributed by Currier and Ives in October, 1860, makes amusing use of a minor sensation of the period to point a political moral. When in 1860 that resourceful showman, P. T. Barnum reopened the New York museum bearing his name which had been closed for a time, he announced as its chief attraction a strange creature of manifest Negro ancestry to whom he gave the name, What is It. Maurer makes light of Mr. Lincoln's candidacy by implying that four years hence Barnum's freak, whom he places between Horace Greeley and Mr. Lincoln, will be the Republican nominee for President. Greeley, always equal to an emergency, announces: "Gentlemen, allow me to introduce to you this illustrious individual in whom you will find combined all the graces and virtues of Black Republicanism, and whom we propose to make our next candidate for the Presidency." Mr. Lincoln, with a troubled look on his face, which causes one to question his real sentiments, comments: "How fortunate! that this intellectual and noble creature should have been discovered just at this time, to prove to the world the superiority of the colored to the Anglo-Saxon race; he will be a worthy successor to carry out the policy which I shall inaugurate." And "What can dey be?" is the plaintive question of What is It, which long survived our first Republican President, and in this writer's youth still supplied to the wondering boys of town and country a subject for lengthy and excited discussion.

AN HEIR TO THE THRONE,
OR THE NEXT REPUBLICAN CANDIDATE

PLATE No. 32   An Heir to the Throne, or the Next Republican Candidate, Currier and Ives,
October, 1860

The cartoon, Letting the Cat Out of the Bag! drawn by Maurer, was distributed by Currier and Ives in the closing weeks of the campaign of 1860. Its central figure, Senator Sumner of Massachusetts had made a slow and only partial recovery from the effects of the assault made on him in the Capitol at Washington four years before by Brooks of South Carolina. Hence he was absent from the convention at Chicago, but his radical views on the slavery question played a disturbing part in the ensuing campaign and threatened to alienate a substantial block of votes regarded by some of the Republican leaders as necessary to the election of Mr. Lincoln.

True to his uncompromising nature Sumner refused to abate or forego his demands, and Maurer pictures him letting the Spirit of Discord out of the Republican bag with the scornful comment: "It's no use talking, Gentlemen. I wasn't mentioned at Chicago, and now I am going to do something desperate. I can't afford to have my head broken and kept corked up four years for nothing." Whereupon Mr. Lincoln, clutching a rail, protests: "Oh, Sumner, this is too bad. I thought we had her safely bagged at Chicago; now there will be old scratch to pay, unless I can drive her back again with my rail." At Mr. Lincoln's right Horace Greeley, a copy of the Tribine protruding from his coat pocket, remonstrates: "What are you doing, Sumner; spoil it all? She ain't to be let out until after Lincoln is elected." And at the candidate's left Raymond of the Times barks: "Scat! scat! back with her or our fat will all be in the fire." And from his place at the extreme right of the uneasy group Senator Seward adds this bit of sage advice: "Gentlemen, be cautious. You don't know how to manage that animal as well as I do, and I am afraid that some of you will get scratched."

Mr. Lincoln was elected in November, but Senator Sumner, a stubborn and unyielding theorist, always in love with the sound of his own voice, remained until death claimed the greater man a continuing thorn in the flesh of the first Republican President.

LETTING THE CAT OUT OF THE BAG!!

PLATE No. 33   Letting the Cat Out of the Bag! Currier and Ives, October, 1860

PLATE NO. 34

"The Irrepressible Conflict" or the Republican Party in Danger, a cartoon drawn by Maurer and distributed by Currier and Ives in October, 1860, deals in an arresting way with the unusual role Senator Seward, much against his will, was compelled to play in the campaign of that year. It depicts him being thrown overboard from the Republican barge by other leaders of the party which a few months earlier he had confidently expected would make him its candidate for President. "Don't throw me overboard," he now cries out in angry dismay. "I built this boat and I alone can save it," while on the bank Uncle Sam, a younger and nattier figure than the one with which a later generation is familiar, gazes disapprovingly on the seemingly happy Negro, who, wearing a Discord's Patent Life Preserver, occupies a seat in the center of the boat, and voices this warning: "You won't save your crazy old craft by throwing your pilot overboard. Better heave that tarnal Nigger out."

Mr. Lincoln at the rudder in no way dismayed by this warning, declares: "I'll take the helm. I've steered a *flat* boat before." At his left Horace Greeley, who, at the Chicago convention a few months before had been one of the leaders of the opposition to the nomination of Senator Seward, now shouts: "Over you go, Billy. Between you and I there is an 'Irrepressible Conflict'." And Edward Bates, sitting next to Greeley, who at the Chicago convention had supported his own presidential ambitions, adds: "Over with him, Horace; never mind his kicking." Other occupants of the barge are Francis Preston Blair, longtime editor of the Washington Globe, and James Watson Webb, editor of the New York Courier and Enquirer. Blair, grasping Seward's foot, boasts: "He can't withstand my muscle for I once moved the Globe," and from the bow Webb calls out: "Breakers ahead!" Finally, most hopeful of the barge's crew, its Negro member chuckles: "If de boat and all hands sink dis Nigger sure to swim. Yah, yah."

It is true that Senator Seward's earlier radicalism had bred prejudices that proved disastrous to his later ambitions, but quickly conquering his disappointments he emerged from the shadows to lend Mr. Lincoln effective support in the campaign, and later as secretary of state to give his great chief disinterested and most effective aid.

PLATE No. 34   "The Irrepressible Conflict," or the Republican Barge in Danger, Currier and Ives, October, 1860

PLATE NO. 35

The cartoon by Stephens, Sich a Gettin' Upstairs (Quarrel in the Household), appeared in Vanity Fair on October 27, 1860, where it was accompanied by this bit of doggerel:

> Miss Douglas beller out. Den she jump between us;
> But I guess she no forgot de day when Abra'm show his genus!
>   Sich a gittin' upstairs I neber did see,
>   Sich a gittin' upstairs I neber did see!

Stephens in his drawing depicts Douglas as essaying the role of peacemaker between Breckinridge and Lincoln, but with melancholy results. A week later came the election which was to put an end to the political career of Breckinridge, cause Douglas ere long to write the noblest chapter in an unusual career, and start their successful rival on his way to a place among the immortals.

PLATE No. 35   "Sich A Gittin' Upstairs" (A Quarrel in the Household), Vanity Fair, October 27, 1860

PLATE NO. 36

The cartoon by Stephens, Wonderful Surgical Operation Performed by Doctor Lincoln on the Political Chang and Eng, appeared in Vanity Fair on November 3, 1860, the Siamese twins then on exhibition at Barnum's Museum in New York furnishing a timely and congenial theme. The political twins depicted by the artist were President Buchanan and James Gordon Bennett, the truculent head of the New York Herald, whose close but unexplained community of interest was one of the subjects hotly discussed and argued about during the campaign months of 1860.

Now Mr. Lincoln, about to triumph at the polls, displaying a sword labeled Vox Populi and with a possibly needed saw beside him, announces his willingness to sever the Secret Service Fund bond between two of his political opponents, remarking suavely: "Don't be scared, my boys. 'Tis as easy as lying." On the wall behind the trio hangs a portrait of Roger A. Pryor as Brutus and a huge bowie knife inscribed Potter—eloquent reminders of one of the familiar incidents of a turbulent period.

A ripe and diverting subject fot the explorer of the by-paths of Civil War history would be an account of Mr. Lincoln's relations with some of the leading editors of his period. Early in 1864, Horace Greeley, long hostile to the President, opposed his reelection; but an indirect way was found to inform the editor of the Tribune, ever eager for recognition, that he might be the next postmaster general. Greeley took the bait and in September, 1864, in a ringing announcement proclaimed his unreserved and uncompromising support of the President. No less adroit was the manner in which James Gordon Bennett was changed from a captious critic to a cordial supporter. Always a stout hater whose moods often were unpredictable ones, the editor of the Herald long violently opposed the first Republican President and all his ways, but underwent a change in the fall of 1864 when the suggestion was made to him that the mission to France might become his in season. "The intimation," writes Don Carlos Seitz, "was probably carried by the Chevalier Henry Wikoff, a Philadelphia adventurer who did Bennett's errands in Washington and was much in evidence at the White House." Like Greeley, Bennett took the bait; the Herald championed the President's cause during the remainder of the campaign, and on February 20, 1865, Mr. Lincoln made its editor a tentative proffer of the French mission. Bennett declined with thanks the honor he had already paid for in support. And this, it may be added, was what Mr. Lincoln all along had expected of him.

PLATE No. 36   Wonderful Surgical Operation, Vanity Fair, November 3, 1860

The caricature, Lincoln Thanks Carl Schurz for Help, appeared in one of the December issues of Budget of Fun, a short-lived comic weekly published in New York.

The German of this cartoon, drawn with stein dangling from his neck and pipe in hand, is Carl Schurz—an amusing reminder of the checkered and now and then troubled friendship which had lately sprung up between Mr. Lincoln and the brilliant and erratic spirit who in 1852 had found in America a congenial refuge from the revolutionary storms of his native Germany.

In the Reminiscences which Ida Tarbell helped him write in his old age Carl Schurz gives an extended and delightful account of this friendship. In the summer of 1858 the Republican State committee of Illinois asked Schurz, then a resident of Wisconsin and striving for a foothold in law and politics, to make some speeches in the senatorial campaign in that State. Obeying the call he found that one of his appointments would carry him to Quincy, where on October 13 was to take place the fifth of the memorable debates between Lincoln and Douglas. "On the evening before the day of the debate," Schurz relates "I was on a railroad train bound for Quincy. The car in which I traveled was filled with men who discussed with great animation the absorbing question (of the hour). All at once, after the train had left a way station, I observed a great commotion among my fellow-passengers, many of whom jumped from their seats and pressed eagerly around a tall man who had just entered the car. They addressed him in the most familiar style: 'Hello, Abe! How are you?' and so on. And he responded in the same manner: 'Good-evening, Ben! How are you, Joe? Glad to see you, Dick!' and there was much laughter at some things he said, which, in the confusion of voices, I could not understand. 'Why,' exclaimed the member of the State committee who accompanied me, 'there's Lincoln himself.' He pressed through the crowd and introduced me to Abraham Lincoln, whom I then saw for the first time."

That evening on the train and the following day in Quincy, Schurz had revealing talks with Mr. Lincoln, and thus was laid the foundations of a friendship that in the years ahead was to make the younger man first an outstanding figure in the contest for Mr. Lincoln's election, and later minister to Spain and a general in the Union Army. But it was also to prove a friendship charged with disturbing hours for Mr. Lincoln, for Schurz, ever intent on the making of a new order, was quick to advise and criticize, and his often mistaken zeal more than once sorely tried the patience of the long suffering man in the White House, a condition of things generously admitted by the survivor when his great friend had passed to his long account.

PLATE No. 37   Lincoln Thanks Carl Schurz for Help, Budget of Fun, New York, December, 1860

PLATE NO. 38

The cartoon, Artemus Ward on His Visit to Abe Lincoln drawn by Stephens appeared in Vanity Fair on December 8, 1860. Mr. Lincoln's visitor is Artemus Ward, and the sketch accompanies a letter to the editor giving an account of their meeting by that humorist who was about to become for a brief period the editor of Vanity Fair. Ward, the vagrom owner of an imaginary menagerie keeps a close grip on realities in his text a part of which rightfully claims a place in the present chronicle. Springfield was the mecca for an army of persistent office-seekers in the last days of 1860. Artemus Ward tells how he found Mr. Lincoln sore beset by them, and then continues:

"Two fat office-seekers from Wisconsin, in endevoren to crawl between Old Abe's legs for the purpuss of applyin for the tollgateship at Milwawky, upsot the President-eleck & he would have gone sprawlin into the fire-place if I hadn't caught him in these arms. But I hadn't more than stood him up strate, before anuther man cum crashin down the chimney, his head strickin me vilently agin the inards and prostratin my voloptoous form onto the floor. 'Mr. Linkin', shouted the infatooated being, 'my papers is signed by every clergyman in our town, and likewise the schoolmaster. I workt hard for the ticket; I toiled night and day! The patrit should be rewarded.'

" 'Virtoo,' said I, gittin up, brushin the dust from my eyes, and holdin the infatooated man by the coat collar, 'virtoo, sir, is its own reward. Look at me!' He did look at me, and qualed be4 my gase. 'The fact is,' I continued, lookin round upon the hungry crowd, 'there is scarcely a offiss for every ile lamp carrid round during' this campane. What air you here for? Can't you give Abe a minit's peace? Go home. Stand not upon the order of your goin, but go to onct. Ef in five minits from this time,' sez I, pullin out my new sisxteen dollar huntin casedwatch, and brandishin! it before their eyes, 'ef in five minits from this time a single sole of you remains on these here premises, I will go out to may cage near by, and let my Boy Constructor loose! & if he gits amung you, you'll think Old solferino has cum again and no mistake!' You ought to have seen them scamper, Mr. Fair. They run orf as tho Satun hisself was arter them with a red hot ten pronged pitchfork. In five minits the premises was clear."

What Artemus Ward wrote no doubt was read with relish by Mr. Lincoln, who later in troubled hours as President counted a turning of the pages of the humorist, soon to come to an untimely end in England, among his favorite and welcome diversions.

PLATE No. 38   A Visit to Abe Lincoln, Vanity Fair, December 8, 1860

The cartoon Dogberry's Last Charge, drawn by Stephens, appeared in Vanity Fair on December 15, 1860. It was inspired by President Buchanan's last annual message to Congress, a most disappointing document sent to that body on December 3. One historian terms it "an essay on constitutional law" written in an hour when the supreme call on the head of the nation was for prompt and resolute action. Buchanan, however, had been so long under Southern domination that he was now unable to master it. So floundering in a sea of perplexity, he took counsel of his fears. Although while writing his message word came to the War Department from Major Robert Anderson in command of the Federal forts in Charleston harbor that they must be reinforced without delay, Buchanan consulting with Jefferson Davis, soon to become the head of the Confederacy, modified his views in deference to that insurgent leader's suggestions.

The result was a paltering and feeble document which aroused only anger and dismay in the North, a state of mind clearly reflected in the cartoon under consideration. The artist found a theme admirably adapted to his purpose in one of Shakespeare's comedies. He represents Buchanan and his stout supporter, James Gordon Bennett of the New York Herald, as the two ignorant constables in Much Ado About Nothing—Dogberry and Verges, the latter "a good old man who will be talking." Mr. Lincoln as Seacoal, receives this injunction: "Come hither, neighbor Seacoal. Well for your favor, sir, why give God thanks, and make no boast of it; and for your writing and reading, let that appear when there is need of such vanity. You are thought here to be the most senseless and fit man for constable of the watch; therefore bear you the lantern. This is your charge: You shall comprehend all vagrom men! You are to bid any man stand in the prince's name."

And when Mr. Lincoln as Seacoal demands: "How if he will not stand?" Buchanan as Dogberry makes answer: "Why then, take no note of him, but let him go." A bit of advice as futile and despairing as General Scott's well-known: "Let our wayward sisters depart in peace."

PLATE No. 39   Dogberry's Last Charge, Vanity Fair, December 15, 1860

PLATE NO. 40

In the cartoon, Badgering Him, which appeared in Vanity Fair on December 29, 1860, the artist again pays his respects to President Buchanan's champion, James Gordon Bennett. In the guise of an impatient terrier, the editor of the Herald greets the President-elect in partial concealment with: "Bow, Wow! Come out, Mr. Lincoln." At the moment, following his practice in the campaign just closed, Mr. Lincoln was making no speeches and giving no statements to the press, and so there were in the editorial columns of the Herald repeated demands that he should break silence on the all-absorbing questions of the time. Could Bennett have been privileged to read a letter Mr. Lincoln wrote on December 10, 1860, to William Kellogg he would have had a convincing solver of all his doubts as to what could be expected from the incoming President.

Kellogg, a Republican of the timid sort, then serving in Congress from Illinois, had been a member of the Committee of Thirty-three soon to become a futile memory —appointed by the House to devise some means of conciliating the South. He sought guidance from the silent man in Springfield, and promptly received a reply which was also as wise and prescient an utterance as stands to the credit of any of our Presidents. "Entertain no proposition," Mr. Lincoln wrote Kellogg, "for a compromise in regard to the extension of slavery. The instant that you do they have us under again; all our labor is lost, and sooner or later must be done over. Douglas is sure to be again trying to bring in his Popular Sovereignty. Have none of it. The tug has to come, and better now than later. You know I think the fugitive slave clause of the Constitution ought to be enforced—to put it in its mildest form, ought not to be resisted."

Two days later Mr. Lincoln wrote as follows to Elihu B. Washburne, another Illinois congressman, endowed when the test came with more backbone than Kellogg, who failed to follow the course mapped out for him: "Prevent as far as possible any of our friends demoralizing themselves and their cause by entertaining propositions for compromise of any sort on slavery extension. There is no possible compromise but what puts us under again, and all our work to do over again. Whether it be a Missouri line or Eli Thayer's popular sovereignty, it is all the same. Let either be done, and immediately filibustering and extending slavery recommences. On that point hold firm as a chain of steel."

In the President-elect, as the sequel proved, Wisdom was justified of her children. There could be no compromise with the defenders of slavery.

PLATE No. 40   Badgering Him, Vanity Fair, December 29, 1860

The cartoon An Anxious Mamma and a Fractious Child appeared in a late February, 1861, issue of Phunny Phellow, and reflects the progress of events in the uncertain days preceding March 4, 1861. It was on Monday, February 11 that Mr. Lincoln left Springfield for Washington, carrying with him in a hand-bag the draft of his inaugural address which was to be read by many of his advisers but to suffer few changes or additions during the next three weeks. Seven of the Southern States had seceded from the Union; Jefferson Davis had been elected President of the "Confederate States of America," and his government was already seizing Federal military posts and making preparations for war when on February 23, Mr. Lincoln arrived in Washington. South Carolina through its fire-eating governor was demanding the surrender of the forts at Charleston, and what disposition was to be made of this demand was one of the vexatious problems President Buchanan was about to pass on to his successor. The Phunny Phellow's artist depicts Mr. Lincoln striding into a room at the White House, club in hand and in grim readiness to assume authority, while President Buchanan as an axious mother seeks to still the clamor of a crying youngster, the infant Southern republic, who, wearing a cap made from an issue of the Herald and holding in its arms a warship and fort seized by the Confederacy, cries for possession of Fort Sumter. The moral of the cartoon under review is pointed by this bit of text:

The Infant Southern Republic: "Boo hoo-hoo! I want Fort Sumter."

Mrs. Buchanan: "Now, Baby, you can't have it. You've got two or three forts and a number of ships and arsenals already; and you won't be allowed to keep even them, for here comes Honest Old Abe to take them all away from you!"

The prophecy of the editor, alas, was not to be confirmed by events. Less than eight weeks later Confederate guns were to compel the surrender of Fort Sumter— the prelude to four years of costly and, for those who began it, ill-starred conflict. In truth never did an enemy better serve an intended victim than did the Confederate commander who ordered the firing on Fort Sumter serve Mr. Lincoln and his cause. "At the fall of Sumter, as if by magic," writes James W. Bollinger, in one of the most informing appraisals of Mr. Lincoln that has appeared in recent years, "slavery ceased to be uppermost in the mind of the Northerner. It seemed forgotten. The North quickly rallied and fought not to free slaves, but to save the Union. The North might never have given and expended its countless lives and treasure to set Negroes free, but it would and did to save our country; and its phenomenal struggle to do that never waned. It won—won with the logic that the Union is indestructible, indissoluble."

Plate No. 41 An Anxious Mamma and a Fractious Child, Phunny Phellow, New York, February, 1861

PLATE NO. 42

This drawing by Stephens captioned Alarming Appéarance of the Winnebago Chief had first place in the February 2, 1861, issue of Vanity Fair. It recalls the doubt and incertitude which following Mr. Lincoln's election in November, 1860, attended the make-up of his Cabinet and his first weeks in office. Not the least of the problems of the President-elect was how, without serious sacrifice of self-respect, he could redeem the backstage pledges of high place in exchange for votes his managers had given at the Chicago convention. Thus rumor had it at the time that he was most reluctant to give a cabinet portfolio to Simon Cameron of Pennsylvania, and the drawing by Stephens shows him suddenly confronted in his Springfield home by "the Winnebago chief," a nickname sometimes given to Cameron on account of a not wholly creditable incident of his early career, who says: "You have sent for me and I have come. If you don't want me, I'll go back to my wigwam." A sign on the wall reads: "Offices to Let Here," but it is evident that, in the opinion of the artist, Cameron is not regarded as a desirable tenant.

As a matter of fact Mr. Lincoln, when Cameron visited Springfield at the invitation of the President-elect, proffered him a place in his Cabinet, but later in the face of bitter opposition to the Pennsylvania leader, mainly in his own state, recalled his offer. Not until some days after Mr. Lincoln reached Washington to take office and at the end of tactful handling of a delicate situation was it finally made known to Cameron that he was to have a place in the Cabinet. One of those who stoutly opposed his selection was Alexander K. McClure, long a Republican leader in Pennsylvania. A generation later, when time had softened ancient rancors, Colonel McClure viewed in mellower vein the chain of events which had given Cameron a place in Mr. Lincoln's Cabinet. "Looking back upon that contest," he wrote, "with the clearer insight the lapse of thirty years must give, I do not see how Lincoln could have done otherwise than appoint Cameron as a member of his Cabinet. He felt he was not free from the obligation made in his name by (David) Davis at Chicago. . . . that pledge probably resolved Lincoln's doubts in Cameron's favor, and he was accepted as Secretary of War." But only, be it added, to face a forced retirement within a year.

PLATE No. 42   Alarming Appearance of the Winnebago Chief, Vanity Fair, February 2, 1861

PLATE NO. 43

The cartoon, A Job for the New Cabinet Maker appeared in Frank Leslie's Illustrated Weekly on February 2, 1861, when that journal caricatured the President-elect for the first time. It shows Mr. Lincoln as cabinet-maker, glue pot in hand, seeking to repair the break between North and South. When it was published the President-elect at his home in Springfield was receiving an army of place hunters, and giving the finishing touches to the inaugural address which a little more than a month later was to furnish fresh proof of his mental and moral caliber; at Montgomery the Southern leaders were preparing to set up the Confederacy, and at Washington, the representatives of twenty Free and Border States were assembling for a futile Peace Conference called at the request of the Virginia Legislature.

All of which pointed for many the bold and familiar expression used by Mr. Lincoln in accepting the nomination for the Illinois senatorship in June, 1858, this in the face of the contrary advice of friends whom he trusted: "A house divided against itself cannot stand. I do not expect this house to fall, but I do expect it will cease to be divided." There was both truth and prophecy in this pronouncement so often quoted in the fateful years that immediately followed its delivery. Events confirmed Mr. Lincoln's logic and his intuitive measuring of things to come. A long war, costly in life and treasure was to follow, but in the end the house was to cease to be divided.

PLATE No. 43   A Job for the New Cabinet Maker, Frank Leslie's Illustrated Newspaper,
February 2, 1861

PLATE NO. 44

The illustration Mr. Lincoln Makes a Speech is reproduced from a book entitled The Letters of Major Jack Downing, an ironical treatment of Mr. Lincoln by Charles A. Davis, which followed at a distance an earlier satire on Andrew Jackson which bore the same title. Describing Mr. Lincoln's departure from Springfield in the early morning of February 11, 1861 the author records with small regard for the truth: "He said he jest cum out to see and be seen, and didn't intend to blab anything about public affairs." As a matter of fact the brief speech in which Mr. Lincoln took leave of his Springfield friends was admirable in form and spirit, and by reason of its intimate and moving eloquence holds a place apart among his public addresses.

One of those who heard it and made possible its preservation was Henry Villard, then a correspondent of the New York Herald, who kept Mr. Lincoln company in his journey from Springfield to Washington. "It was a clear, crisp winter day," writes Mr. Villard in his Memoirs. "Only about one hundred people, mostly personal friends, were assembled at the station to shake hands for the last time with their distinguished townsman. It was not strange that he yielded to the sad feelings which must have moved him at the thought of what lay behind him and what was before him, and gave them utterance in a pathetic formal farewell to the gathering crowd. But for me it would not have been preserved in the exact form in which it was delivered. It was entirely extemporised and, knowing this, I prevailed on Mr. Lincoln, immediately after starting to write it out for me on a 'pad.' I sent it over the wires from the first telegraph station. I kept the pencil manuscript for some time, but, unfortunately, lost it in my wanderings in the course of the Civil War."

PLATE No. 44   Mr. Lincoln Makes a Speech, Illustration from "The Letters of Major Jack Downing," February, 1861

PLATE NO. 45

The cartoon The Sudden Appearance of Mr. Lincoln (And the Awful Consternation of the Old Party at the White House) appeared in Frank Leslie's Illustrated Newspaper on March 2, 1861. It depicts in an amusing way one of the incidents of a fateful week—Mr. Lincoln's courtesy call on President Buchanan following his arrival in Washington on February 23. Mr. Seward in the role of Chief Magician produces Mr. Lincoln out of a cloud of smoke.

It is a familiar story of how, to avoid possible assassination in Baltimore, the President-elect, guarded by a single companion, with manifest reluctance made a secret night journey from Harrisburg by way of Philadelphia, reaching at six o'clock in the morning the railway station at the capital, where he was met by his Illinois friend, Elihu B. Washburne, who alone, except for Senator Seward, had been advised of his coming, and by him conducted to breakfast and spacious quarters at Willard's Hotel.

There followed the customary call of the incoming on the outgoing President, Mr. Buchanan and the members of his Cabinet extending a cordial welcome to the man from Springfield; visits to the two Houses of Congress, where the greetings given ranged from the warmth of friends to the half veiled hostility of opponents, and to the Supreme Court, whose aging chief affably received the new ruler to whom he was soon to administer the oath. And in his parlors at Willard's the President-elect was waited upon by President Buchanan and Cabinet returning the call of his late rival for the Presidency, calls by Douglas and Breckinridge, and by the delegates to the Peace Conference of somber memory with its chairman, former President Tyler, at their head.

And to the President-elect's quarters at Willard's there was at all hours of the day and far into the night a constant procession of hungry office-seekers, and of Republican leaders eager to give advice on the make-up of his Cabinet and the policy of his Administration. It has been aptly said that Mr. Lincoln "received worse advice, and more of it than any statesman that ever lived," and the last days of February, 1861, proved no exception to this rule. As was his custom he gave patient audience to all who came, but made few promises, and when his Cabinet was announced on March 4 it departed only in minor details from the list he had prepared in the telegraph office at Springfield on the night of his election.

PLATE No. 45   The Sudden Appearance of Mr. Lincoln, Frank Leslie's Illustrated Newspaper, March 2, 1861

PLATE NO. 46

The cartoon Our Presidential Merryman appeared on March 2, 1861 in Harper's Weekly, accompanied by this extract, real or imaginary, from a daily paper of the period: "The Presidential party was engaged in a lively exchange of wit and humor. The President-elect was the merriest among the merry, and kept those around him in a continual roar." By many, when his first term began, Mr. Lincoln was regarded as a frontier buffoon, and this view of him appears, for a time at least to have been shared by the artist who drew the caricature under consideration where he is pictured cracking jokes with a group of rough companions. It is true that Mr. Lincoln delighted in a good story whether told by himself or by another, but a native dignity which repelled undue familiarity of every sort invariably marked his bearing toward high and low, and never was this trait more constantly in evidence than in the last days of February, 1861. And he had matters of weight and moment to occupy his speech and thought in a troubled hour. Witness his passage-at-arms with William E. Dodge, New York merchant and capitalist, when the group of aging and anxious men who made up the Peace Conference called on him at Willard's Hotel. Dodge, last of the delegates to address the President-elect, made an earnest plea for concessions that would assure peace with the South, and then added: "It is for you, sir, to say whether the whole nation shall be plunged into bankruptcy, whether the grass shall grow in the streets of our commercial cities."

"Then I say it shall not," was the reply of Mr. Lincoln. "If it depends upon me;" this with a twinkle of the eye, "the grass shall not grow anywhere except in the fields and the meadows."

"Then you will yield to the just demands of the South? You will not go to war on account of slavery?"

"I do not know that I understand your meaning, Mr. Dodge," said Mr. Lincoln, a glint of steel replacing the twinkle in his eye. "Nor do I know what my acts and opinions may be in the future, beyond this: If I shall ever come to the great office of President of the United States I shall take an oath; I shall swear that I will faithfully execute the office of President of the United States, of all the United States, and that I will to the best of my ability, preserve, protect and defend the Constitution of the United States. This is a great and solemn duty. The Constitution will not be preserved and defended until it is enforced and obeyed in every part of every one of the United States. It must be so respected, obeyed, enforced and defended, let the grass grow where it may."

Mr. Dodge made no reply, and with this grim declaration of purpose the interview came to an end.

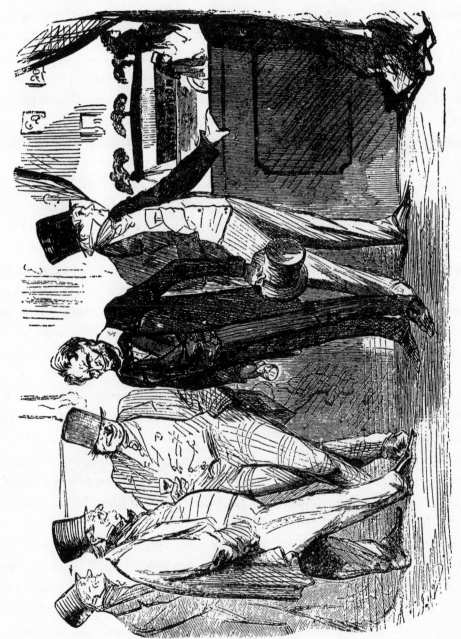

PLATE No. 46 Our Presidential Merryman, Harper's Weekly, March 2, 1861

The cartoon by Stephens The Inside Track appeared in Vanity Fair on March 2, 1861, and recalls in an amusing way Mr. Lincoln's relations with Senator Seward and his friend Thurlow Weed during the last weeks of 1860 and the first weeks of 1861. Horace Greeley, who after long and disappointing association had come to have no use for Weed and his ways, listens behind the door while that master of all wire-pullers in his day and generation, seizing Mr. Lincoln's right arm, with Senator Seward standing in an ingratiating attitude at his listener's left, thus addresses the President-elect: "Trust to my friend Seward—trust to *us*. We'll compromise this little difficulty for you. But trust to *us*. Gentlemen from the country are often egregiously swindled by unprincipled sharpers. (Impressively) Trust to *us*."

It was on December 8, 1860, a month after his election, that Mr. Lincoln wrote Senator Seward: "With your permission I shall at the proper time nominate you to the Senate for confirmation as Secretary of State for the United States."

Senator Seward did not reply to this invitation until December 16. He then wrote from his home in Auburn that his friend and adviser, Weed, had found it "not inconvenient to go West." He added: "I have had some conversation with him concerning the condition and prospect of public affairs, and he will be able to inform you of my present unsettled view of the subject upon which you kindly wrote me a few days ago. I shall remain at home until his return and shall then in further conference with him have the advantage of a knowledge of the effects of public events certain to occur this week."

Weed in due course journeyed to Springfield, and the nature of the talks he had with Mr. Lincoln during a three days' stay is still a matter of varied conjecture with students of an interesting period. This much is history: Senator Seward desired to head Mr. Lincoln's Cabinet but opposed the inclusion in that body of Salmon P. Chase whom he felt had contributed in a major way to his own defeat at the Chicago convention. No doubt Weed made this fact clear to Mr. Lincoln. It is also safe to assume that his visitor found the President-elect a slow promiser and a politic trader. Senator Seward on December 28, following Weed's return from Springfield, accepted the offer of the position of secretary of state, and when on March 5 the names of the new cabinet were sent to the Senate for confirmation those of Seward and Chase headed the list! Mr. Lincoln made good use of the services of Weed whenever there was promise that they would further the general purpose, but in their talks at Springfield, he had taken the Albany man's measure, that of a strong and shrewd personality, and was never misled by his adroit yet rarely unselfish councils.

PLATE NO. 47   The Inside Track, Vanity Fair, March 2, 1861

PLATE NO. 48

The cartoon A President-elect's Uncomfortable Seat, set off with this protest from Old Abe: "Oh, it's all well enough to say, that I must support the dignity of my high office by Force, but it's darned uncomfortable I can tell you," appeared in Frank Leslie's Illustrated Newspaper on March 2, 1861, two days before the inauguration of Mr. Lincoln, which many in the North feared and a few in the South hoped would have a tragic issue. It became clear on the morrow that, much against his will, Mr. Lincoln's policy was to be based on force; that in General Scott, the hero of two wars, but now weighed down by the years, and reluctant to compel the Southern States to return to the Union, he had an uncertain support on which to lean, and that his major problem over a long period would be to seek and find the right man or men to lead the Union armies.

Colonel Alexander K. McClure has put on paper a moving picture of General Scott in futile and pathetic age. "I saw him for the first time," he records in his Recollections, "the morning after the surrender of Sumter, when as chairman of the military committee of the (Pennsylvania) Senate I went with Governor Curtin to Washington to consult with the President, General Scott and Secretary Cameron. The conference was brief, as all agreed as to the duty to be performed by Pennsylvania, but I was anxious to see more of the great hero who had been one of my idols from boyhood. He stood at a window (of the White House) overlooking the Potomac to the Virginia hills, and I saw his eyes moisten with scalding tears as he pointed to Virginia, his home, and in a tremulous voice expressed his fear that she would now join the secession movement. He remained with Governor Curtin and myself a considerable time, and it soon became painfully evident that he was utterly unequal to the task he had accepted. When we descended the stairs after leaving the President's room Governor Curtin threw up his hands and exclaimed 'My God, the country is at the mercy of a dotard' "

General Scott passed into retirement before the first year of war had run its course, but one quality he retained until the end, that of a grim and unrelenting hater. One of the men whom he thoroughly detested was Jefferson Davis, and when in February, 1861, word came to Washington that the man from Mississippi had been elected President of the Confederacy General Scott could with difficulty find words in which to adequately express his wrath. "He is not a cheap Judas," he growled to a group of friends. "He might not have sold the Saviour for thirty shillings, but for the successorship of Pontius Pilate he would have betrayed Christ and the apostles and the whole Christian Church."

PLATE No. 48   A President-elect's Uncomfortable Seat, Frank Leslie's Illustrated Newspaper,
March 2, 1861

The cartoon President Lincoln's Inaugural appeared in Frank Leslie's Illustrated Newspaper on March 9, 1861. It was drawn by Thomas Nast, then twenty-one years old and a recent comer to the staff of that journal. Conflicting views are reflected in Nast's cartoon. At the left the artist wrote: "As the South received it," and at the right, "As the North received it."

The correspondent of the London Times reported to his journal that the composition of the President's message was "generally attributed to Mr. Seward," who was believed in some quarters to favor concessions to the South, while the Richmond Enquirer hailed it as "the cool, unimpassioned, deliberate language of the fanatic," and the Charleston Mercury, to which by the way Mr. Lincoln for long had been a subscriber, announced: "It is our wisest policy to accept it as a declaration of war." Last but not least the Public Man noted in his now famous and mysterious diary that "the great crowd in the grounds behaved very well, but manifested little enthusiasm." Very different was the state of mind and will of the masses of the North as reflected in the warning of an Iowa farmer who a few weeks before had written Mr. Lincoln: "Give the little finger and shortly the whole hand is required."

It is a familiar story to latter day students of how Mr. Lincoln near the close of January, 1861, beside him a few documents for reference, among them copies of the Constitution, Jackson's proclamation against Nullification and Webster's reply to Hayne—locked himself in an upstairs room across the street from the State House in Springfield and sat down to write his inaugural address. A local printer when it was finished put the document in type. Not so widely known is the fact that a gripsack kept close to Mr. Lincoln on his journey to Washington held a copy of it. At Harrisburg the gripsack was given for the moment into the keeping of Robert Lincoln who, when it was shortly demanded of him, could not tell what had become of it. "I guess," said Mr. Lincoln in confidence to Ward Lamon, "I have lost my certificate of moral character, written by myself. Bob has lost the gripsack containing my inaugural address, and I want you to help me find it. I feel a good deal as did the Methodist brother who, having lost his wife at a camp meeting, sought out an elder of the church, and asked if he could tell him whereabouts in the devil his wife was."

An anxious overhauling of the contents of the hotel baggage room brought the missing gripsack to light, whereupon Mr. Lincoln promptly took from it the inaugural address, and thrusting it into one of his capacious pockets declared that it should not again leave his hands, a resolve which, it need not be added, was kept to the letter.

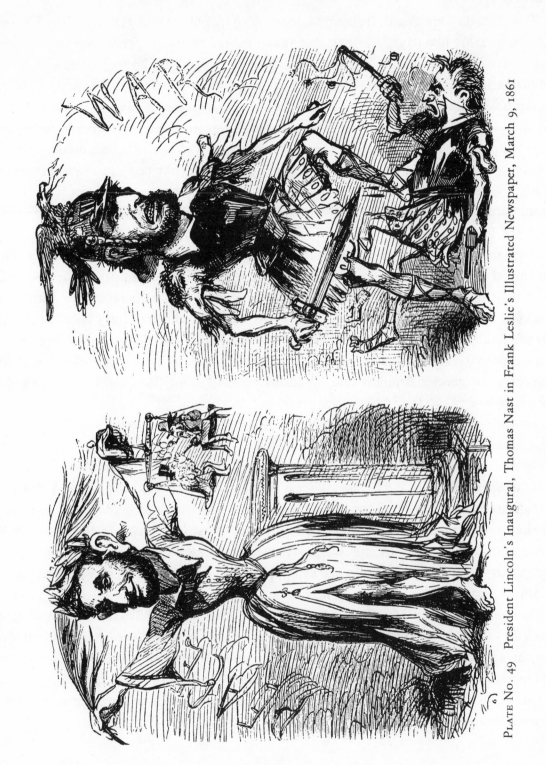

PLATE No. 49 President Lincoln's Inaugural, Thomas Nast in Frank Leslie's Illustrated Newspaper, March 9, 1861

The cartoon Our Great Iceberg Melting Away appeared in Harper's Weekly on March 9, 1861, five days after Mr. Buchanan retired from the Presidency to pass his last years at the home in Lancaster, Pennsylvnaia, to which he had given the name of Wheatlands. Not prone to the ways that win a man popularity, his public career, nevertheless, had been a long and in the main, a useful one. A lawyer by profession, he had served four terms in the House at Washington. After that he had filled for two years the post of minister to Russia, and then had been for the better part of twelve years a member of the Senate. He resigned from that body in 1845 to become Polk's Secretary of State during the Mexican War, and then, after a brief retirement from public office, he had become for three year's Pierce's minister to Great Britain, and had had a hand in the settlement of several diplomatic problems of a major sort.

Buchanan's nomination and election to the Presidency in 1856 were mainly due to the fact that he had been out of the country during a troubled period, and so had had no part in the discussions which then vexed the Democratic party and its leaders. But he came to the Presidency known as one who had long been favorable to the Southern point of view on the slavery question, and the inevitable results of this proclivity were demands from the South that would have sorely tested a chief executive of greater firmness and breadth of vision. Thus he quickly lost favor in the North, and ere long became involved in a bitter quarrel with Douglas which in 1860 split the Democratic party into Northern and Southern wings and led to the election of Mr. Lincoln.

It is a part of the record that during Mr. Lincoln's days in Washington prior to his inauguration Mr. Buchanan did not proffer advice to his successor nor did the latter invite it. Their contacts indeed, were purely formal ones, and when on March 4 they rode together to the Capitol few words passed between them. When they rode from the Capitoi to the White House the former President spoke these last words to Mr. Lincoln: "If you are as happy, my dear sir, on entering this house as I am on leaving it and returning home, you are the happiest man in this country."

The morrow found Mr. Buchanan back at Wheatlands and Washington was soon to know him no more. When Sumter fell he promptly announced his firm support of the Union. After that he gave much time and thought to making up the record by which he hoped posterity would judge him. He died at Wheatlands on June 1, 1868, in his seventy-eighth year, and was duly laid to rest in Woodward Hill cemetery near Lancaster.

PLATE No. 50   Our Great Iceberg Melting Away, Harper's Weekly, March 9, 1861

The caricature The Mac Lincoln Harrisburg Highland Fling which appeared in Vanity Fair on March 9, 1861, holds up to ridicule the unusual and unexpected close of Mr. Lincoln's trip to Washington the preceding month. That journey extending over an eleven-day period, and attended by cordial greetings from the people of half a dozen States brought the President-elect and his party in the mid-hours of February 22 to Harrisburg, capital of Pennsylvania, where there was a noisy reception from another great throng.

It had been planned that from Harrisburg the presidential party should continue through Baltimore to Washington, but in Philadelphia on February 21, warnings had come from Senator Seward and others that a plot was afoot to assassinate Mr. Lincoln during his passage through the Maryland city. However in Harrisburg, the Seward warning was emphasized by reports from other sources, and the members of the presidential party with men of power in Pennsylvania, were called upon for advice as to a prudent change in plans. Mr. Lincoln is reported as asking in the course of this conference: "What would the nation think of its President stealing into its capital like a thief in the night?" But Governor Curtin declared that the question was one to be answered not by Mr. Lincoln but by his friends.

And so after long and conflicting discussion it was arranged that the President-elect, attended only by Ward H. Lamon, and leaving behind the other members of his party to follow him next day by the route originally planned, should return to Philadelphia and there take the night train to Washington. This decision was promptly carried into execution. At six o'clock in the evening Mr. Lincoln and Lamon boarded a special train provided by the Pennsylvania Railroad, and consisting of a single car and a locomotive; shortly after ten o'clock were met in Philadelphia by Allen Pinkerton, the Chicago detective, who had provided a carriage, in which the trio drove across the city to another station. There they found berths awaiting them in the last car of a New York-Washington train. Eight hours later Mr. Lincoln descended to the station platform in Washington to be greeted by Elihu B. Washburne who was there to give him welcome.

Those who were keen to find fault with Mr. Lincoln, and there was a great army of them in February, 1861, promptly denounced the President-elect's secret night journey as the act of an imbecile and a coward, but the long view of it is a very different one, and agrees with Mr. Lincoln's later remark to his Chicago friend, Isaac N. Arnold. "I did not then," said he, "nor do I now believe that I should have been assassinated had I gone through Baltimore as first contemplated, but I thought it wise to run no risk, where no risk was necessary."

The drawing includes the text "HARRISBURG STATION"

PLATE No. 51   The Mac Lincoln Harrisburg Highland Fling, Vanity Fair, March 9, 1861

PLATE NO. 52

The drawing The New President of the United States: From a Fugitive Sketch
was the second of the two cartoons in which in its issue of March 9, 1861, Vanity
Fair spoke its mind in carping fashion on Mr. Lincoln's night journey from Harrisburg to Washington. The figure drawn by the artist, clothed as it is in an atmosphere
of mystery, is not, it must be recorded, in keeping with the facts. Mr. Lincoln was
not clad in a long robe the evening he left Harrisburg, but wore instead as he afterward informed Benson J. Lossing, the historian, an overcoat he had brought with
him from Springfield; and that garment was topped not by a Scotch cap but by a
soft wool hat which he had found in the box holding the new beaver hat given
him a few days before by a New York friend.

Long and oft debated were the pros and cons of the night ride from Harrisburg
through Philadelphia to Washington. As the years sped it became a favorite topic
with Ward H. Lamon, who was, as we know, Mr. Lincoln's companion in that
journey. "Mr. Lincoln," writes Lamon in his Recollections, "soon learned to regret
the midnight ride to which he had yielded under protest. He was convinced that he
had committed a grave mistake in listening to the solicitations of a professional spy
and of friends too easily alarmed, and frequently upbraided me for having aided him
to degrade himself at the very moment in all his life when his behavior should have
exhibited the utmost dignity and composure. Neither he nor the country generally
then understood the true facts concerning the dangers to his life. It is now an ack-
nowledged fact that there was never a moment from the day he crossed the Maryland
line, up to the time of his assassination, that he was not in danger of death by
violence, and that his life was spared until the night of the fourteenth of April, 1865
only through the ceaseless and watchful care of the guards thrown around him."

The "professional spy" referred to by Lamon was Allen Pinkerton whom he,
either fairly or unfairly held in hearty contempt; but the lines here quoted may be
safely accepted as a mellow and reasoned summing-up of a much debated incident
in a great man's life.

PLATE No. 52   The New President of the United States,
Vanity Fair, March 9, 1861

PLATE NO. 53

The cartoon The Flight of Abraham is one of four cartoons in which in its issue of March 9, 1861, Harper's Weekly handled in rough-and-ready fashion Mr. Lincoln's secret journey from Harrisburg to Washington. The first depicts the President-elect aroused from sleep in his room at a Harrisburg hotel with the warning that he is in grave danger and must flee for his life. The second shows him yielding with reluctance to the advice of weeping friends that he seek safety in flight. The third, here reproduced, has him wearing "a Scotch cap and a very long military cloak so that he was entirely unrecognizable," intent, with long strides and outstretched arms, on reaching a waiting train—and safety. The fourth portrays him, shaking and much the worse for wear, calling with Senator Seward on President Buchanan.

The report that Mr. Lincoln had resorted to a Scotch cap and a military cloak as a means of disguise was quickly given prominence in the public prints, and accepted as true by many thousands. As a matter of fact, however, Mr. Lincoln never at any time or under any circumstances wore a Scotch cap and a long military coat. The report that he had done so originated with Joseph Howard, a New York reporter. It was on February 23, 1861, that Howard, then in the service of the New York Times, telegraphed that journal of Mr. Lincoln's arrival in Washington, adding, without warrant for so doing, that the President-elect to prevent recognition had worn "a Scotch plaid cap and a very long military cloak." The Times, although friendly to Mr. Lincoln, printed its correspondent's report; and so a picturesque lie destined to long life took wings.

A little more than three years later Howard again proved a source of acute if passing embarrassment to Mr. Lincoln, for he wrote and in the early morning of May 18, 1864, secured the publication by several New York journals of a proclamation purporting to come from the President, which, implying that Grant's Virginia campaign was a failure, fixed May 26 as a day of fasting, humiliation and prayer, and called for the conscription of 400,000 men for the Union Army. The forgery was intended to further the stockjobbing activities of its author and his associates, but happily failed of its purpose. Publication of the journals which had printed it with no thought of giving offense was summarily suspended, but in a few days their suppression and the arrest of their editors were rescinded by the President. Howard was sent to a cell at Fort Lafayette and there remained for several weeks, but in the end Mr. Lincoln released him at the request of Henry Ward Beecher, whom the erring and now repentant reporter had formerly served as secretary.

PLATE No. 53   The Flight of Abraham, Harper's Weekly, March 9, 1861

PLATE NO. 54

The drawing, The Passage Through Baltimore privately distributed in March 1861, was one of a series of Lincoln caricatures, engraved on copper by Adalbert John Volck of Baltimore and put out by him under memorable and unusual conditions. Volck published a portfolio containing twenty-nine of these remarkable engravings in 1864, under the signature of "V. Blada", his own name reversed; and he gave it a false London imprint—this to avoid detection and confiscation of the plates by the Federal authorities. Volck was endowed with a gift for biting satire allied to rare gifts as an artist, and the portifolio of his caricatures brought into being in such singular fashion has long been one of the items most eagerly sought for by Lincoln collectors. It will be noted that in the plate under consideration he accepts without question Howard's story of the Scotch cap and military cloak, and adds for full measure the disguise of a freight car.

PLATE No. 54   The Passage Through Baltimore, Drawing by Adalbert Volck, March, 1861

The cartoon The Daring Leap Made by the Celebrated Acrobat, Little Giant, appeared in Vanity Fair on March 16, 1861. While it has Douglas for its subject there is excellent reason for including it in a collection of Lincoln caricatures, for no man gave more loyal or more effective support to Mr. Lincoln and the Union cause than did he during what was to prove the last weeks and months of a dynamic career. During the shifting and uncertain deliberations of the session of Congress which ended on March 4, 1861, Douglas, pondering the alternatives of compromise, peaceable separation and war, like many another public man of the period, had little to to say in debate or in the press; but on the evening of the day that Mr. Lincoln reached Washington, he called on his successful rival, and at the end of a sober and earnest talk, in parting gave him this assurance: "You and I have been for many years politically opposed to each other, but in our devotion to the Constitution and the Union we have never differed. In this we are one. Partisan feeling must yield to patriotism. I am with you, Mr. President, and God bless you."

Came April 14 and the firing on Sumter, when John W. Forney, a Douglas lieutenant, asked his leader what course to follow in his newspaper. "There can be" was the prompt reply, "but two parties, the party of patriots and the party of traitors. We belong to the first." There followed before the month ran its course a trip to the Middle West and a series of great speeches which helped to make and keep Illinois firm for the Union, and at the same time, past question, put half a million men into the Union Army. Then came a sudden and unexpected illness that laid the Little Giant in bed at Chicago, and on June 3 resulted in his death at the early age of forty-eight.

A marble shaft now marks his resting place at the spot where he had planned to make a home for his declining years. Atop is a heroic figure of Douglas done in bronze by Leonard Volk, and across its base is graven his parting injunction to his sons: "Tell them to obey the laws and support the Constitution of the United States." Who can deny that the last days of Stephen A. Douglas were his noblest ones?

PLATE No. 55   The Daring Leap, Made by the Celebrated Acrobat Little Giant, Vanity Fair,
March 16, 1861

The cartoon Mr. Lincoln Sets a Style appeared in Vanity Fair on March 16, 1861. A druggist who holds the agency for the Lincoln whiskeropherous advises a visitor: "Try one of these pots, sir, and in three weeks you will be as hairy and handsome as he is." All of which recalls a delightful incident of Mr. Lincoln's campaign for the Presidency. In a time and place when pioneer conditions prompted most men to grow beards, Thomas Lincoln, the father of Abraham Lincoln, was always clean-shaven. And in this habit, as in others, the son during most of the years of his life followed the example set him by his father. But in October, 1860, he began to grow a beard. Perhaps a letter written him by eleven-year old Grace Bedell, of Westfield, New York, may have influenced this departure. "I have got 4 brothers," she told him, "and part of them will vote for you any way and if you will let your whiskers grow I will try and get the rest to vote for you; you would look a great deal better for your face is so thin." Mr. Lincoln made prompt reply to the letter of the West-field lass, concluding with this question: "As to the whiskers having never worn any, do you not think people would call it a piece of silly affectation if I were to begin it now?"

In the end, however, Mr. Lincoln accepted the advice of his youthful correspond-ent. A photograph of him taken at Chicago in the late November of 1860 and now owned by Herbert W. Fay, custodian of Lincoln's Tomb at Springfield, shows him, the first of many to do so, with a short crop of beard. And when on a February day in 1861 the train carrying Mr. Lincoln and his party to Washington halted at West-field the President-elect announced to the welcoming crowd: "I have a little corre-spondent in this place, and if she is present will she please come forward."

"Who is she? What is her name?" demanded a chorus of voices.

"Grace Bedell," was Mr. Lincoln's response.

The friend who had escorted the Bedell family to the station led Grace to a low platform beside the train, and Mr. Lincoln stepping down from the car, shook her hand and kissed her. "You see," he said, indicating his beard, "I let these whiskers grow for you."

Grace Bedell, who in due course became Mrs. George N. Billings, died a few years ago at Delphos, Kansas, at the ripe age of eighty-nine. Her most cherished memory until the end of her days was her meeting with Mr. Lincoln. It must be noted, how-ever, as a part of the record, that not a few of his friends deprecated the decision that caused him to grow a beard. "It was ill advice," writes Charles A. Barry, the artist, "that caused the growing of whiskers on Lincoln's face, for they utterly destroyed the harmony of his features, and added not a little to the melancholy of his coun-tenance when in repose."

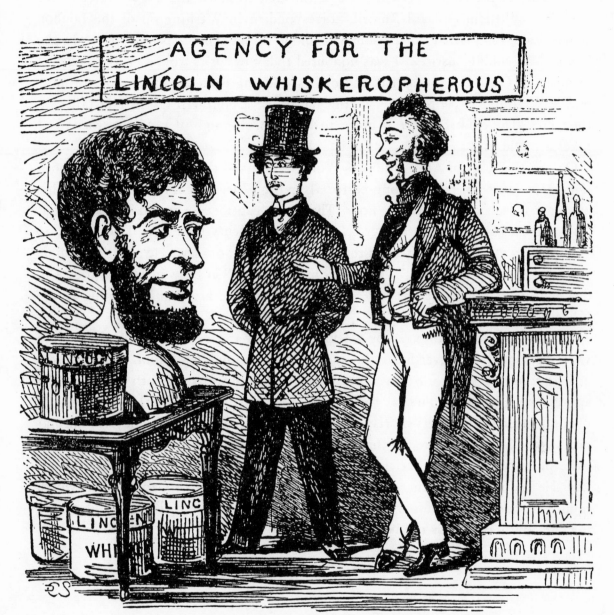

PLATE No. 56 Mr. Lincoln Sets a Style, Vanity Fair, March 16, 1861

PLATE NO. 57

The cartoon Prof. Lincoln in His Great Feat of Balancing drawn by Stephens appeared in Vanity Fair on March 23, 1861, at a time when it devolved upon Mr. Lincoln to fix the course he was to steer through troubled and angry waters. Five days later William Howard Russell, correspondent in Washington of the London Times wrote his journal, in the summary mood of one who dispenses the high, the low and the middle justice: "I was honoured today by visits from a great number of members of Congress, journalists and others. Judging from the expressions of most of the Washington people they would gladly see a Southern Cabinet installed in their city. The cold shoulder is given to Mr. Lincoln, and all kinds of stories and jokes are told at his expense."

On the third day of April, the New York Herald and the New York Times, both important journals, printed long editorials calling Mr. Lincoln to account for his apparent indecision in a critical hour. The Times captioned a two-column editorial "Wanted—a Policy," and without delay its editor, Henry J. Raymond, journeyed to Washington to secure at first-hand the President's point of view. He got it in a single sentence. "I am like a man," Mr. Lincoln told him, "so busy in letting rooms in one end of his house that he can't stop to put out the fire that is burning in the other."

But the President, hampered by a divided Cabinet and a confusion of advice as to what he should do, nevertheless knew how to shape public opinion in the North, and he shrewdly saw to it that at the parting of the ways the South should be the aggressor. "Lincoln's course as to Sumter," declared the late Charles W. Ramsdell of the University of Texas shortly before his death, "was from the outset aimed at getting the Confederates to fire the first gun." "In so doing," adds Avery W. Craven, "the plain citizen of the prairies had seen deeper and farther than any man of his day. He had understood that a Union dedicated to the hope of mankind was worth saving even at the cost of four long and bitter years of civil war. By this understanding the South as well as the North was to profit."

PLATE No. 57   Prof. Lincoln in His Great Feat of Balancing, Vanity Fair, March 23, 1861

[115]

The cartoon, Winding Off the Tangled Skein, appeared in Harper's Weekly on March 30, 1861. Then Mr. Lincoln had been less than four weeks in the White House, but had already discovered that the task passed onto him by President Buchanan was of a sort to sorely tax all of his mental and moral resources. Indeed, since the closing hours of November 6, 1860, when the wires informed him and a group of friends gathered in the telegraph office at Springfield that he had triumphed at the polls, he had been made aware in grim and steadily increasing measure of the weight of the burden soon to be placed on his shoulders.

Shortly after Christmas in 1861 Joseph Gillespie, an old and trusted friend of the President-elect—their close and trustful intimacy dated from the coming of both of them to Illinois thirty years before—passed a night in the Lincoln home. In old age Judge Gillespie put on record his memories of eventful hours. "Joe," said Mr. Lincoln when at the end of the evening the family had retired and he was alone with his guest, "I would willingly take out of my life a period equal to that which separates me from my inauguration to take the oath of office now. Every hour adds to the difficulties I am called upon to meet, and the present Administration does nothing to check the tendency toward dissolution. Do you remember that trial down in Montgomery County when the lawyer associated with you gave away the whole case in his opening speech. I saw you signaling to him, but you couldn't stop him. That's just the way with me and Buchanan. He is giving away the case, and I have nothing to say, and can't stop him."

Mr. Lincoln's moods of despondency, however, were passing ones. "I parted with him," adds Judge Gillespie, "a few days before his departure for Washington. 'I only wish,' said he, 'that I could have got there to lock the door before the horse was stolen. But when I get to the spot I can find the tracks'." Nor did his self-reliance fail him after he became President. When on the first day of April, 1861, Secretary Seward submitted to Mr. Lincoln an extraordinary letter captioned Some Thoughts for the President's Consideration—a letter which intimated that the emergency demanded a leader and that he was the man for the task—his chief found a way to put Seward in his place, making him at the same time a loyal and willing right-hand.

And so effectively did Mr. Lincoln meet and master each new situation that when in April, 1865, Jefferson Davis, fleeing from his fallen capital, was told of Wilkes Booth's foul deed, he did not fail to pay instant and grateful tribute to the dead man's worth. "I am sorry," said he to Stephen R. Mallory, one of the members of his cabinet. "We have lost our noblest and best friend in the court of the enemy."

PLATE No. 58   Winding Off the Tangled Skein, Harper's Weekly, March 30, 1861

The cartoon, Old Abe Invokes the Spirit of St. Patrick appeared in one of the issues of the Phunny Phellow of New York for March, 1861, that being the month in which falls the feast day of Saint Patrick, the apostle of Ireland. Legend has it that it was in the opening decades of the fifth century that Saint Patrick drove the snakes from that island. Fourteen centuries later the artist depicts an American President appealing to the Irish saint to free him from a less dangerous but equally annoying pest—an army of importunate office-seekers. The day after his election applicants for place laid seige to Mr. Lincoln in Springfield; and until the end of his days he was never free from them.

Some of the visitors, however, at Springfield, were of a different sort. Thomas D. Jones, who in the opening weeks of 1861 executed from life his well-known bust of Mr. Lincoln, has drawn an amusing picture of one caller who came to bestow and not to receive. "One of those friends," writes Mr. Jones, "appeared one morning at my studio (in a Springfield hotel). He wore a bottle-green coat and had a pair of grasshopper legs. I requested him (at the door) to wait in the reading room as Lincoln would soon go downstairs, and he could meet him there. Lincoln seemed annoyed that I did not show him in, and on going downstairs sought the gentleman I had described to him. Not finding him he concluded to read the morning papers. When he finally looked up there stood the bottle-green specter in front of him.

" 'What can I do for you?" inquired Mr. Lincoln.

" 'Don't you know me?' said the emerald individual.

" 'I may have met you before, as I have thousands, but I cannot recall your face at present.'

" 'Yes, we met fifteen years ago. I have been in California ever since and have brought you this red wood gold-mounted cane as a slight token of our second meeting.'

"The body of the cane was of California red wood. The handle or head of generous proportions, was composed of quartz and gold, highly artistic and in excellent taste. This was only one of the many incidents that occurred almost daily until Lincoln left for Washington. The bottle-green imp remained in Springfield until he could accompany him."

Mr. Lincoln found a throng of eager place hunters awaiting him in Washington, and thereafter his morning, afternoon and evening hours were seldom free from them. Be it recorded that what was probably his last official act on April 14, 1865, was to see to it that a Negro woman who had appealed to him should receive the overdue pay of her husband, a volunteer serving in the Army of the Potomac.

PLATE No. 59   Old Abe Invokes the Spirit of St. Patrick, Phunny Phellow, New York, March, 1861

The cartoon, Dr. Lincoln's Homeopathic Treatment, appeared in one of the March, 1861, issues of Yankee Notions of New York. Dr. Lincoln is represented as telling a downcast patient: "Now, Miss Columbia, if you will follow my prescriptions, which are of an extremely mild character, but which your old nurse, Mrs. Buchanan, seems to have been so averse to, I have no doubt but that the Union will be restored to position, health and vigor." In the background Mrs. Buchanan listens with manifest disapproval to the assurances of the new physician.

Buchanan, no doubt, wished to see the Union preserved, if this could be effected without a resort to force; but he was not without the usual regrets and envies which afflict those who have tried and failed, and in his first months of retirement at Wheatlands he found no small degree of satisfaction in the letters that came to him from friends who informed him that Mr. Lincoln was facing his problems in an aimless and futile way. One of the correspondents who did not fail to promptly and regularly advise him of the situation developing at Washington was Edwin M. Stanton who had served him as attorney general in the last months of his administration, and who had now returned to the private practice of law at the capital.

As yet Stanton could see nothing to commend in Mr. Lincoln or in his handling of a difficult situation. "The dreadful disaster of Sunday," he wrote Buchanan on the morrow of Bull Run, "can scarcely be mentioned. The imbecility of this administration culminated in that catastrophe; an irretrievable misfortune and national disgrace never to be forgotten are to be added to the ruin of all peaceful pursuits, and national bankruptcy, as the result of Lincoln's 'running the machine' for five months. The capture of Washington seems now to be inevitable."

Stanton in after days had abundant cause to regret this and other letters to Buchanan, for on January 20, 1862 he became secretary of war, and thereafter gave effective if not always loyal service to a chief whom ere long he grew to honor above all other men.

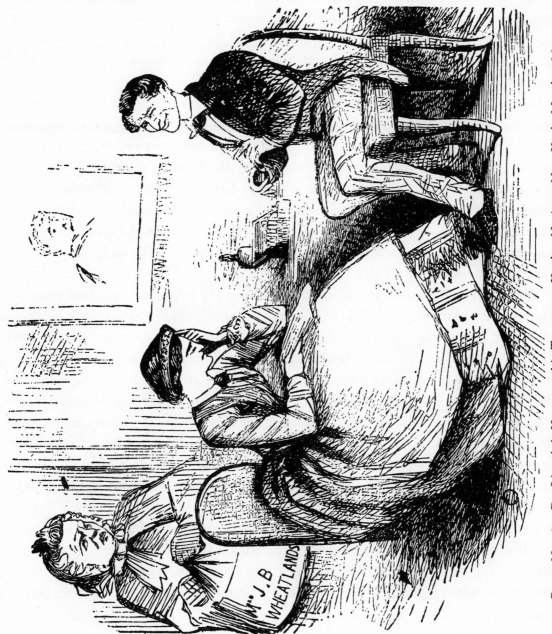

PLATE No. 60 Dr. Lincoln's Homeopathic Treatment, Yankee Notions, New York, March, 1861

PLATE NO. 61

The poster cartoon, The Schoolmaster Abroad at Last, was distributed by a New York printer in late March, 1861, when seven of the Southern States had seceded, but the clash of arms was still in the future. Schoolmaster Lincoln in the role of Uncle Sam stands on the shore of a pond labelled Secession and thus addresses a group of four truants who are swimming in it and an equal number who are making ready for a plunge into its waters: "Come, Boys! they are all waiting for you—you have stayed there long enough! I will forgive you this time if you will try to do better in the future."

In real life, Mr. Lincoln was never the master of unruly pupils, and had only a few months of schooling in what he once described as the "pretty pinching times" of his boyhood; but he brought away from those few months more than one amusing memory of which he made effective use in after life. Witness the story he told John B. Henderson when on a Sunday afternoon in the early summer of 1862 the Missouri senator called on him at the White House. Among other things he related to Henderson how he was being steadily urged by Henry Wilson, Charles Sumner and Thaddeus Stevens to emancipate the slaves, although his better judgment told him that the time was not yet ripe for such action.

Then the President rose from his chair, crossed the room to a window that commanded the approach to the White House, and calling his visitor to his side pointed to Wilson, Sumner and Stevens advancing from Pennsylvania Avenue. "Henderson," said Mr. Lincoln with a smile, after a moment's silent inspection of the approaching trio, "what little schooling I got in early life was at an old blab school in Indiana. All our reading was done from the Bible. We stood in a long line and read in turn from it. One day our lesson was the story of the three Hebrew children who escaped from the fiery furnace. A little tow-headed fellow who stood next to me read for the first time the verse with the unpronounceable names. He made a mess of Shadrach and Meshach, and went all to pieces on Abednego. The master boxed his ears until he sobbed aloud. Then the lesson went on, each boy reading a verse in turn. The tow-headed boy stopped crying, but when he fixed his gaze upon the verses ahead set up a yell of alarm. The master demanded the reason for this outbreak. 'Look,' said the boy, and he pointed at the verse he shortly would be expected to read, and at the proper names contained in it. 'There comes them same damn three fellows again!'"

PLATE No. 61   The Schoolmaster Abroad at Last, Poster Cartoon published in New York, March, 1861

The cartoon Consulting the Oracle appeared in Harper's Weekly on April 13, 1861, the day before the firing on Sumter. Mr. Lincoln, the Chicago Platform protruding from the tall hat he has placed on the floor behind him, faces the American eagle, and Columbia, who wears a Liberty cap and holds out to him a Constitution Amended. "And what next?" asks the President, to which Columbia makes answer: "First be sure you are right; then go ahead."

There was no doubt need to consult oracles during Mr. Lincoln's first day in office; but we know now that it was his custom, when faced with a difficult problem to take counsel with his conscience, and leave the issue to a higher power. Lucius E. Chittenden, Register of the Treasury during the Civil War, offers in his Recollections impressive testimony to the President's reliance on that higher power. He writes that opportunity offering in the summer of 1864 he made bold to ask Mr. Lincoln how far and in what measure he believed that the Almighty directed human affairs. The President was silent for a time, and then made answer:

"The Almighty does make use of human agencies. I have had so many evidences of his direction, so many instances when I have been controlled by some other power than my own will, that I cannot doubt that this power comes from above. I frequently see my way clear to a decision when I am conscious that I have no sufficient facts upon which to found it. But I cannot recall one instance in which I have followed my own judgment, founded upon such a decision, where the results were unsatisfactory; whereas, in almost every instance where I have yielded to the views of others, I have had occasion to regret it. I am satisfied that when the Almighty wants me to do or not to do a particular thing, he finds a way of letting me know it. . . .

"At first, when we had long spells of bad luck, I used sometimes to lose heart. Now I seem to know that Providence has protected and will protect us against any fatal defeat. All we have to do is to trust the Almighty and keep right on obeying his orders and executing his will."

PLATE No. 62 Consulting the Oracle, Harper's Weekly, April 13, 1861

[125]

PLATE NO. 63

The cartoon The Last Advice appeared in Vanity Fair on April 20, 1861. It shows Mr. Lincoln and Jefferson Davis as schoolboys about to fight when Uncle Sam, a very different figure from the one with which present-day Americans are familiar, interposes and this dialogue ensues:

Uncle Sam—"Here! here! What's this mean?"

Master Lincoln—"Why, this here Jeff Davis and his fellers been a crowin' over us long enough, and now there's going to be a row."

Uncle Sam—"Well, now! If you are going to fight, mind you fight like your father—go!"

This cartoon appeared in a critical hour for Mr. Lincoln and the Union cause. Sumter fell on April 14, and on the morrow came the answer of the North to this appeal to force. Mr. Lincoln by proclamation called for 75,000 volunteers, and before the end of the day on which this call was issued quick and eager responses showed that the fall of Sumter had made a unit of the North. It had, on the other hand, done no less for the South. It silenced protests against secession and brought doubting ones to the support of the Confederacy. On April 17 Virginia, until then wavering between loyalty and disunion, passed an ordinance of secession, and her example was speedily followed by North Carolina, Arkansas and Tennessee; Richmond was made the Confederate capital, and a call from President Davis for volunteers was obeyed as eagerly as Mr. Lincoln's had been in the North.

Washington, meanwhile, underwent a brief period of isolation and seeming peril. The Sixth Massachusetts reached the capital on the evening of April 19, but it had been attacked by a mob and some of its members killed and wounded during its passage through Baltimore, and during the next two days the pro-slavery element in Maryland, to prevent the further passage of troops through that State, tore up railroad tracks, destroyed bridges, and cut telegraph lines, thus completely severing Washington from communication with the North. The President during these trying days was the most collected man in his capital, but the suspense of isolation and the non-arrival of expected troops proved a sore strain to even his strong fibre, and pacing the floor of his office he was more than once heard to exclaim to himself: "Why don't they come! Why don't they come!"

This question was happily answered on April 25, when the Seventh New York and the Eighth Massachusetts, building bridges and laying track as they advanced, arrived inWashington. The following day brought the First Rhode Island. Before the end of the week seventeen thousand volunteers were in Washington, and the safety of the capital was assured.

PLATE No. 63 The Last Advice, Vanity Fair, April 20, 1861

The cartoon, Lincoln and the Negro Question, appeared in one of the April, 1861, issues of the Kladderadatsch, a comic journal of Berlin, and was drawn by William Scholz, then the most widely known caracaturist in Germany, and an undisputed force in shaping public opinion. Accompanied by this bit of dialogue, it reflects Europe's interpretation of the drama at that time developing in America:

Negro: "May I be so bold—"

Lincoln: "Step nearer, my friend."

Southern Statesman: "Then I beg to be excused." (He secedes from the Union.)

All of which confirms the fact that both in Europe and America there was in April, 1861, only dim and faulty perception of the truth that the initial and primary purpose of Mr. Lincoln, a purpose slowly and inevitably altered by the pressure of events, was not to abolish slavery but to preserve the Union. The radical leaders of the South were resolved on secession and the erection of a confederacy pledged to the protection of an institution which they affected to believe to be threatened by the North; and the sequel proved that only a resort to force could thwart their purpose.

The Peace Convention of futile purpose adjourned on February 27 after adopting a report addressed to Congress which favored, among other things, the extension by constitutional amendment of the Missouri Compromise line to the Pacific; that no new territory acquired should be acquired by the United States, unless approved by the Senate by a majority vote of senators from both sections, and that the protection of slavery within the Slave States against future adverse action by Congress should be assured by an amendment to the Constitution; but Southern senators refused to carry out these recommendations, which went too far to suit the North and not far enough for the South, and the Senate after angry debate rejected them by one less than a two-thirds vóte. Instead in its last hours it accepted a resolution previously adopted by the House referring this constitutional amendment to the States:

"Article 13. No amendment shall be made to the Constitution which will authorize or give to Congress the power to abolish, or interfere, within any State, with the domestic institutions thereof, including persons held to labor or service by the laws of said State."

In the turmoil and rising passions of the spring and early summer of 1861 this proposed amendment to the Constitution, ignored and forgotten, was never passed upon by the State legislatures. Less than a year later came, as a war measure, announcement of the proposed emancipation of the slaves. Mr. Lincoln was wholly right when he later declared that he had not guided events, but that events had guided him.

Plate No. 64   Lincoln and the Negro Question, Drawing by William Scholz, April, 1861

PLATE NO. 65

The cartoon The Spirit of '76 appeared in Vanity Fair on May 4, 1861. It shows the President watering a flower bed with the Spirit of '76, and remarking to Columbia, who is watching his work: "Arn't there a nice crop. There's the hardy Bunker Hill flower, the Seventh Regiment pink, the fireboy tulip. That tri-colored flower grows near Independence Hall. The western blossoms and prairie flowers will soon begin to shoot."

Columbia—(Pointing to a miniature gallows) "What charming plant is this?"

Lincoln—"That is rare in this country. It will blossom soon and bear the Jeffersonia Davisiana."

The spirit of this cartoon was in keeping with the flow of events. The day before it appeared Mr. Lincoln issued a call for volunteers to serve three years, ordered the regular army to be increased, and directed the enlistment of additional seamen. Just three weeks later, on May 24, occurred the death of Colonel Elmer E. Ellsworth, the first officer casualty on the Virginia front—an incident charged for the President with an intimate and poignant sense of loss. A young man of twenty-four, Ellsworth just before 1860, had brought together in Chicago, where he was preparing for the bar, a company of Zouaves which attracted much attention when it toured the North giving exhibition drills. When war began he recruited a regiment among the volunteer firemen of New York City and dressed and drilled them in the Zouave manner.

In the early morning of May 24 Ellsworth and his regiment took part in the capture of Alexandria. The Marshall House, a second-class hotel, was found flying a Confederate flag from its roof. Followed by a few friends, Ellsworth sprang up the stairs to the third floor. Then with a ladder he mounted to the roof and cut down the flag, but as in descent he reached the first-landing place, he was shot and killed by the lurking landlord, who in the same instant was slain by a corporal of Zouaves. The young colonel's death shocked the North, and quickened enlistments in the Union army.

It was also deeply mourned by Mr. Lincoln. Two callers at the White House in the afternoon of May 24 found the President standing at a window looking out across the Potomac. "Excuse me, but I cannot talk," said he to his visitors, and then burst into tears. "I make no apology," he continued, when he had in part recovered his composure. "I knew poor Ellsworth well and held him in high regard. Just before you entered the room Captain Fox had given me the painful details of his death. Poor fellow, it was doubtless an act of rashness, but it shows the heroic spirit that animates our soldiers. One fact has reached me which is a great consolation. When the Stars and Stripes were raised again in Alexandria many of the people wept for joy. All the South is not secessionist."

PLATE No. 65   The Spirit of '76, Vanity Fair, May 4, 1861

PLATE NO. 66

The cartoon The American Difficulty appeared on May 11, 1861 in London Punch which then caricatured Mr. Lincoln for the first time. Tenniel, the artist, no doubt as yet in ignorance of the fact that the new President in recent months had grown a beard shows him without one, an error he did not repeat in subsequent drawings. Now a beardless Lincoln, as poker in hand he contends with the cloud of smoke charged with inky specks issuing from a White House fireplace, is represented as exclaiming: "What a nice White House this would be, were it not for the Blacks."

What was to be Mr. Lincoln's policy toward the Blacks and what the measure of success that would attend the efforts of the Confederate leaders to destroy the Union, were in 1861 and the three ensuing years causes for angry debate and sharp differences of opinion among the English people. An influential element which included most of the nobility and the men then charged with rule in England earnestly hoped for the success of the Confederate cause, and for a long period sought in every way short of open hostility to make the path of Mr. Lincoln a thorny and troubled one. On the other hand the mass of the English people were not slow in recognizing that the Union cause was the cause also of universal liberty and the rights of the common man; and this conviction found eloquent and telling expression in the speeches and writings for the press of such noble and intrepid spirits as John Bright, Richard Cobden, John Stuart Mill and Goldwin Smith.

So great a man as Gladstone, for the moment blind to the larger truths, sinned against the light and reckoned the days of the Union numbered ones; but Quaker John Bright, first and foremost in a mighty struggle, saw clearly what was at stake, and, rousing the English masses, then without a vote, to proclaim their sympathy with freedom across the Atlantic, did more than any other man not an American to prevent a war between the United States and Great Britain, a war that would have turned the world's course into new and evil channels.

"If we interfere," Bright wrote Cobden in October, 1861, "we shall not only create a great slave nation, but be compelled to guarantee its permanence." And speaking in the House of Commons in June, 1863, he reminded that body that in the Slave States every year were "150,000 children born into the world—born with the badge and doom of slavery—born to the liability by law, and by custom, and by the devilish cupidity of man, to the lash, the chain and the branding iron, and to be taken from their families and carried they know not where." By such appeals Bright, and those who labored with him, changed the drift of public opinion in England and, making a full half of its people see the truth as they saw it, helped Mr. Lincoln to end slavery and preserve the Union.

PLATE No. 66   The American Difficulty, London Punch, May 11, 1861

The cartoon, Robbery of the National Orchard, appeared in Harper's Weekly on May 18, 1861, accompanied by this exchange between Mr. Lincoln and Jefferson Davis:

President Lincoln—"I say, Jeff, this thing has been going on, long enough. Suppose you drop these apples now and come down."

Jeff Davis—"Please don't shoot, Mr. Lincoln. All I want is to be let alone."

Mr. Davis with good reason requested to be let alone, for when this cartoon appeared not only had the Confederate leaders without compunction robbed the national orchard in the shape of the seizure of Federal property located in the South, but were now taking steps to legally absolve their people from debts owed by them to merchant and other creditors in the North. Thus during the month of May, 1861, the Confederate Congress passed an act authorizing all persons who owed debts in the United States, except in the States of Delaware, Maryland, Kentucky and Missouri and in the District of Columbia, to pay it into the Confederate Treasury. About the time this act was passed a commercial agency reported that the South owed Northern merchants upward of $210,000,000, four-fifths of which was due in New York City, which, be it said in passing, housed a small army of Southern sympathizers.

Nevertheless from first to last the Confederacy was desperately short of funds. Indeed it has been shrewdly contended by students of a vexed subject that had Davis and his advisers instead of looting Northern men and concerns of what was justly due them, at the outset seized the baled cotton of the South and made it a basis for European loans, they would have been able to wage a longer, albeit losing, war. What they did was to refuse to sell cotton to England and France in the hope that by so doing they would force those countries to use their navies to break the Union blockade of Southern ports, and in the end grant full recognition to the Confederacy. This hope proved a disappointing one, and when in 1863 the Confederate treasury, with much difficulty and on prohibitive terms, floated a loan of $15,000,000 in London the returns were employed in a way that in the last analysis afforded no help to a losing cause. The belief fondly cherished in the South that cotton was king, a belief termed by a later economist the "grandest of delusions," and the attempt of the Confederate leaders to make cotton an engine of coercion, in the end helped Mr. Lincoln to preserve the Union.

PLATE No. 67   Robbery of the National Orchard, Harper's Weekly, May 18, 1861

The poster cartoon, Caving in, or a Rebel "Deeply Humiliated," was drawn by Benjamin Day and distributed by a New York printing house in June, 1861. It shows Lincoln and Davis engaged in a prize fight in which the former clearly has the best promise of emerging the winner. "Now, you scoundrel," says Mr. Lincoln, "I have got my muscle up, and I'll put in the blows till I finish you!" And Davis, already much the worse for wear, replies: "Oh! Mr. Lincoln I abandon the 'Defensive Policy'. I see that I have undertaken more than I can accomplish."

The group gathered to witness the contest includes the king of Prussia, the third Napoleon and John Bull, who comment in this wise:

King of Prussia—"Go it, Lincoln. I knew he'd be obliged 'to Cotton' ".

Napoleon—"I will say nothing just yet."

John Bull—"Ho my! I begin to feel queer. H'im afraid when he has finished Jeff he'll pitch into me."

The prize fight, with Lincoln and Davis as the contenders, was a motive often made use of by artists in the opening days of the Civil War. Among the prized possessions of Mr. George N. Malpass, an East Rochester, New York, philatelist, untiring in his search for rare and curious things, is a set of five cartoon envelopes which depict with humorous zest the several stages of a Championship Prize Fight Between Lincoln and Davis in Five Rounds.

The face of each envelope is devoted to a round of a contest, the end of which, it is clear from the first, will show Mr. Lincoln the winner. In the fifth and last, his opponent mastered and no longer equal to a defense of any sort, the President is shown as champion receiving the plaudits of his friends. It is an occasion for real regret that difficulties in reproduction forbid the inclusion of this unique series in the present collection.

Recurring to the Day drawing here under consideration it may be noted in passing that Mr. Lincoln's prowess as a fighter was long kept in memory by those who knew him as a youth in Indiana. One of the stories told again and again by Dennis Hanks in garrulous age had to do with a fight between Lincoln then sixteen and William Grigsby. "The fight," as Hanks recalled it, "arose over a pup which Abe and Bill each claimed Dave Turnham had promised him. Abe who knew he could whip Bill, proposed that Jack Johnston, his stepbrother and a more equal match for Bill, should take his place. This offer was accepted, but it was soon seen that Jack was no match for Bill; so Abe seized Bill and threw him over the crowd. He then called on Bill's friends to take a hand, but they had no stomach for it. The pup, you see, really belonged to Abe, and that was why he jumped in when he had agreed to let Bill and Jack fight it out."

CAVING IN, OR A REBEL "DEEPLY HUMILIATED".

Plate No. 68   Caving in, or a Rebel "Deeply Humiliated" Currier and Ives, June, 1861

The cartoon The Situation appeared in Harper's Weekly on July 13, 1861. It shows Officer Lincoln arresting the outlaw Jeff Davis bent upon looting the Federal Treasury. "I guess I have got you now, Jeff," says Officer Lincoln, and his prisoner replies: "Guess you have—well now let us Compromise." This exchange, however, was a misleading forecast of the immediate future of the Union cause, for on Sunday, July 21 was fought the first battle of Bull Run where an army of 31,000 men under McDowell was beaten and put to flight by 22,000 Confederates led by Beauregard and Jackson, who there won the name of Stonewall.

The capital, swarming with fugitives, for the moment appeared doomed to capture. Robert L. Wilson, a trusted friend of Mr. Lincoln dating from New Salem days, chanced to be in Washington at the time and sought news of the battle from the President. "Grasping my arm," writes Wilson, "he leaned over and said, in a shrill and subdued voice: 'It's damned bad.' It was the first time I had ever heard him use profane language, but under the circumstances no other term would have qualified."

Horace Greeley needed more words in which to phrase his despairing reaction to the Bull Run defeat. At midnight of July 29, "in strict confidence and for your eye only" he wrote Mr. Lincoln: "This is my seventh sleepless night—yours, too, doubtless—yet I think I shall not die, because I have no right to die. I must struggle to live, however, bitterly. But to business. You are not considered a great man and I am a hopelessly broken one. You are now undergoing a terrible ordeal, and God has thrown the gravest responsibilities upon you. Do not fear to meet them. Can the rebels be beaten after all that has occurred and in view of the actual state of feeling caused by our late awful disaster? The gloom in this city is funereal—for our dead at Bull Run were many, and they lie unburied yet. On every brow sits sullen, scorching, black despair."

Mr. Lincoln made no reply to a letter which in its closing sentences revealed the editor of the Tribune as prepared for peace at any price, but he termed it "pusillanimous" when he talked to young John Hay about it. Abraham Lincoln had no occasion to seek wisdom and courage from Horace Greeley when facing a weighty task. The second night after Bull Run found him, ever confident of ultimate victory, calmly shaping new plans for the defeat of the Confederacy and the restoration of the Union.

PLATE No. 69   The Situation, Harper's Weekly, July 13, 1861

The cartoon, The Comedy of Death, distributed from Baltimore in July or August 1861, is another of the engravings, charged with bitterness and gall, in which Adalbert Volck ridiculed Mr. Lincoln and the other leaders and defenders of the Union cause. To a stage which has a death's head for its chief decoration comes the President, garbed as a clown, to enact with his players "a pleasant comedy, a kind of history." Gideon Welles, secretary of the navy, who rows a boat at the rear of the stage, was to prove the only one of the players to keep Mr. Lincoln company, and render him service of a quiet yet always effective sort until the fatal fourteenth of April, 1861.

John C. Fremont who with Scott and McClellan holds the front of the stage, by his initial clashes with and later open but futile opposition to Mr. Lincoln and his policies, was to prove to the thoughtful that he was never other than a second-rate man. General Scott, weighed down by the years, passed into honored retirement in the closing weeks of the first war year. Retirement from service, but for very different reasons, was also to be the lot of Scott's successor, General McClellan who in unwelcome inactivity was to see his unfinished task taken up and carried to success by the modest captain from Galena, Grant, a man who had the defects of his qualities but who never over-estimated the size and prowess of the enemy.

Simon Cameron, Mr. Lincoln's first secretary of war, in the Volck engraving under consideration is the puppet whose wire runs through the highest hole and makes him a hapless companion of the majestic Chase. With no one of the players here portrayed had Mr. Lincoln more singular relations than with Cameron. Reluctantly compelled, in order to redeem convention pledges made by his managers without his knowledge or consent, to make Cameron secretary of war, the latter's faulty direction of the affairs of that office, forced Mr. Lincoln early in 1862 to send him into exile by way of our embassy to Russia. Cameron returned ere long to the United States and to private life for the period required to make possible a return to his old seat in the Federal Senate. However, never for a moment did he cease to be the friend of Mr. Lincoln and a defender of the latter's policies, and in 1864 his shrewdness as a political manager contributed in rounded measure to his former chief's nomination and election for a second term.

In a talk with the writer Simon Cameron in extreme old age had but one reproving thing to say about Mr. Lincoln and that was that he had put aside investments suggested by his secretary of war which, without any hint of sharp practices, would have made him a rich man. Few men have been more loyal to their friends than was Simon Cameron.

PLATE No. 70   Comedy of Death, Drawing by Volck, July, 1861

The cartoon, Dictator Greeley Dismisses the Cabinet, and Warns Mr. Lincoln that he will stand no more Nonsense, appeared in Harper's Weekly on August 10, 1861, and bears witness to the hasty and short-sighted ways in which the editor of the New York Tribune contributed to Mr. Lincoln's worries during the hectic first months of the war between the sections. "A decimated and indignant people," he declared in his journal on July 23, 1861, the morrow of Bull Run, "demand the immediate retirement of the present cabinet from the high places of power, which, for one reason or another, they have shown themselves incompetent to fill. The people insist upon new heads of Executive Departments."

Mr. Lincoln did not remake his cabinet at the command of the editor of the Tribune, and the latter continued a thorn in the flesh of a sorely tried President. Greeley would have more effectively served the Union cause had it not been for his own insatiable hunger for what he termed the "high places of power." As editor of the Tribune he exercised a political and moral influence of the first order, but, not content with the great role a kindly Providence had assigned him, he labored under the belief that he was also better fitted than most of his compeers for the right conduct of public affairs. Greeley's own estimate of his capacity for a wide range of service was a sadly mistaken one. "While I had a high opinion of Greeley as a journalist, I don't think he has ever had his equal in that capacity in this country" writes Beman Brockway, an early associate and lifelong friend of the Tribune" editor, "I never could see any sensible reason for his wanting an office. He was a failure as a representative in Congress, and he would have been a failure in the Senate had he been chosen to a seat in that branch of the national legislature. Just what he would have done as an executive, of course, no one knows, but I do not imagine he would have been a brilliant success." Brockway adding that few are capable of discharging the duties of a first-class editor, declares "there was no man in the country competent to take Mr. Greeley's place."

It is good to record that there came a time when with mistaken fault-finding a part of the past, Horace Greeley could pay generous, if discriminating, tribute to the greatness of Abraham Lincoln. "Looking back," he wrote in 1868, "through the mists of seven eventful, tragic, trying, glorious years, I clearly discern that the one providential leader, the indispensable hero of the great drama—faithfully reflecting even in his hesitation and seeming vacillations the sentiments of the masses —fitted by very defects and shortcomings for the burden laid upon him, the good to be wrought through him, was Abraham Lincoln. His true career was just opening when an assassin's bullet quenched his light of life."

PLATE No. 71   Dictator Greeley Dismisses the Cabinet, Harper's Weekly, August 10, 1861

This poster cartoon, The Bark of State with Long Abe at the Helm, put out in the late summer of 1861 pleasantly recalls Mr. Lincoln's early experiences as a flatboat man, and ties them up with the achievements of the Congress which assembled on July Fourth of that year. Mr. Lincoln in his youth made three trips down the Ohio and Mississippi to New Orleans. One of them, while he was still in his teens and a resident of Indiana, brought him for the first time in sobering contact with the evil effects of slavery. The third and last ended in his eventful residence at New Salem. Reminders of all three had a picturesque part in the campaign which made him President.

The outstanding accomplishments of Mr. Lincoln's first Congress—termed by one of its members "a giant committee of ways and means"—included besides generous appropriations for the conduct of the war, the passage of bills reforming the administration of the postoffice department, making a protective tariff the declared policy of the Republican party and providing for the construction of a railway to the Pacific Coast. And it also cleared the way for the passage of the homestead law, one of the most potential pieces of legislation ever placed on the federal statute books, which was signed by Mr. Lincoln on May 20, 1862. Credit for the passage of the homestead law belongs in the main to Galusha A. Grow of Pennsylvania, who served as speaker of Mr. Lincoln's first Congress.

Half a century ago it was the writer's privilege to receive from Mr. Grow an account of the events which caused him to be hailed as father of the homestead law. "I early came to believe," said he, "that the government should bestow the public domain in small homesteads on those without land for settlement and cultivation. My first speech in Congress was made in support of a bill embodying this doctrine. The leaders of the slavocracy did not care to see the territories settled by small farmers from the free States, and their opposition defeated the passage of the homestead law until secession split the Union. I introduced five bills at five different sessions of Congress before one was finally passed and became a law. It was one of the most gratifying moments of my life when as speaker I had the pleasure of signing the bill. The two questions which gave the Republican party its ascendancy was its policy on slavery and the public lands. Non-extension of slavery appealed to the conscience of the whole North; its policy of homesteading and securing the public lands to actual settlers appealed to the convictions and interests of the new States and especially the territories, so that all of the States admitted since the foundation of the Republican party have been Republican in politics."

PLATE No. 72   The Bark of State with "Long Abe" at the Helm, Poster Cartoon, September, 1861,
Redrawn by Elbert W. Ryerson

The poster cartoon The Fate of the Rail Splitter—Abe Lincoln, reproducing a crude engraving on wood, was put out at Richmond in October, 1861, and reflects the animosity and bitterness with which many of the people of the South regarded Mr. Lincoln both during and long after his Presidency. In the autumn days of 1861 rough-and-ready spirits in the North were boasting in song that they "would hang Jeff Davis to a sour apple tree," and a like element in the South were prompt to consign Mr. Lincoln to a similar fate. Indeed, he was regarded by all classes below Mason and Dixon's Line as the chief begetter of the throng of ills which confronted the Confederacy from its inception until Lee surrendered to Grant at Appomattox.

One has only to examine the files of Southern newspapers of the period to find sobering confirmation of this statement. "Mr. Lincoln vainly imagines," declared the Nashville Union and American two days after he took office, "the government of this Union has come into his hands unbroken. He talks boastingly of enforcing laws in States which have proclaimed and established a separate government. He will shed no blood unless it is forced on him. By this he probably means that he will not use force, if every demand he makes is tamely complied with and every right claimed by the Confederate States is surrendered. Great God! has it come to this? And are there any Southern men that are so base as to lick the hand that smites them to the earth?"

And soon the Richmond Examiner was urging the capture of Washington "at all and every human hazard. The filthy cage of unclean birds must and will be purified by fire," it declared. "Our people can take it, and Scott, the arch-traitor, and Lincoln the Beast, combined, cannot prevent it. The just indignation of an outraged and sorely injured people will teach the Illinois Ape to retrace his journey across the borders of the Free negro States still more rapidly than he came. Many indeed will be the carcasses of dogs and caitiffs that will blacken the air on the gallows before the great work is accomplished. So let it be."

But Sumter and Bull Run were followed by four battle summers which took heavy toll of the nation's youth. Slowly yet sternly the North wore down the Confederate armies, and month after month brought inevitably nearer the day of surrender. Then at long last the moderate leaders of the South, their vision cleared by coming defeat, recognized the South's best friend in the wise and patient man in the White House, whose triumphant resolve that the Union should be preserved was now tempered by mercy and pardon for a lost cause and its leaders. "God help us" remarked Clement Clay of Alabama, when he heard of Mr. Lincoln's death. "If that be true, it is the worst blow that yet has been struck at the South."

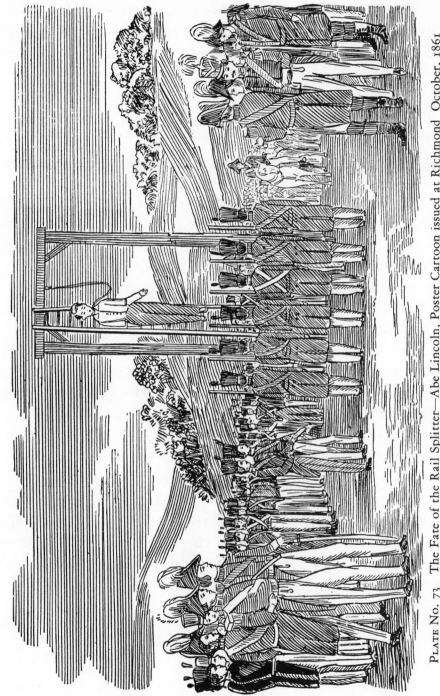

PLATE No. 73   The Fate of the Rail Splitter—Abe Lincoln, Poster Cartoon issued at Richmond October, 1861

[147]

The cartoon Got the Right Weapon at Last was published in Harper's Weekly on October 19, 1861, and was one of the earliest of the Lincoln caricatures by twenty-one year old Thomas Nast to appear in that journal. President Lincoln is shown with a five hundred million dollar loan (in the form of what were known as five-twenty bonds) as a weapon reaching across the Potomac to batter down the house of cards lately set up at Richmond by the Confederate leaders. As a matter of fact, however, when young Nast made his drawing the act authorizing the loan in question was still in the future, for it was not passed by Congress and signed by the President until the last days of February, 1862.

Nor did it become an effective weapon for waging war, the banks of the North being slow and faulty in their support of the government, until Secretary Chase wisely determined not to rely longer upon their uncertain help, but to put the sale of bonds in exclusive charge of a general agent. That decision was duly translated into action, and Jay Cooke named as such agent. Cooke, a man of great energy who knew better than any of his contemporaries how to reach the pocketbooks of the masses, quickly established local agencies of his banking house in all parts of the North. Soon thereafter a steady stream of the people's money began to flow in to the treasury, and in such volume that, although Cooke's commission was only three-eights of one per cent, of which the banks and others who aided him received one-fourth of one per cent, his earnings from this source before the end of 1864 made him a millionaire. But partisans who charged Jay Cooke with profiteering, as some of them did, had to admit that he was one of the men who saved the Union.

Nor was Secretary Chase, who, despite his great ability, had too many untimely sneers for his chief, slow in criticising the use made of the funds raised by Cooke and his agents. "It seems as if there were no limit to expense," he wrote to a youthful admirer. "Contrary to all rules the spigot in Uncle Abe's barrel is made twice as big as the bung-hole. He may have been a good flat-boatman and rail-splitter, but he certainly never learned the true science of cooperage." All of which in the light of after days did Secretary Chase no particular credit.

PLATE No. 74   Got the Right Weapon at Last, Harper's Weekly, October 19, 1861

PLATE NO. 75

The cartoon, Lincoln Guarding the Trout Pond appeared in Vanity Fair on November 16, 1861. It had for its subject the Union's relations with foreign countries, which at the time were assuming new and perplexing phases, and shows Mr. Lincoln guarding with sword and cannon a pond filled with trout (the Confederacy) in which three boys—England, France and Spain—are keen to cast their lines. To his left and rear a structure captioned Mexico recalls the part that country, much against the will of its people, was about to play in the international system. "Boys, I reckon I wouldn't," is his significant comment.

That the North had the better cause, with men and means to uphold it, in the end prompted England and France to reluctantly forego recognition of the Confederacy, but the interference of France in Mexico, in which it was joined for a time by England and Spain, proved another and different affair. The third Napoleon had a fondness for mixing in other people's concerns that was never hampered by a keen sense of right and wrong. In 1861, on account of a money dispute France, Spain and Great Britain sent an armed expedition to Mexico, but early in 1862 Great Britain and Spain withdrew their forces, and Napoleon, thus permitted to play a lone hand, set out to conquer Mexico and place a European monarch on its throne.

The Archduke Maximilian of Austria accepted Napoleon's invitation to become emperor of Mexico and in 1864 sailed for that country. But his venture proved a failure from the start and only the support of a French army kept him on his throne. Mr. Lincoln and Secretary Seward handled a delicate situation with a patience and discretion that enabled them to preserve peace with France during a critical period. When the Civil War came to an end Napoleon prudently withdrew his troops from Mexico, and Maximilian was left to his fate. Driven from the Mexican capital by a liberal army under Juarez, he was beseiged, captured and shot at Queretaro; and an army under Sheridan freed from further conflict with Confederate forces was also spared the task of restoring order in Mexico.

PLATE No. 75   Lincoln Guarding the Trout Pond, Vanity Fair, November 16, 1861

PLATE NO. 76

Tenniel's cartoon Up a Tree—Colonel Bull and the Yankee 'Coon which appeared in London Punch on January 11, 1862, one of his first caricatures of the President, was prompted by an incident which for a time threatened an end to peaceful relations between the United States and Great Britain. The artist inspired by the summary and as it proved unwarranted capture by Commander Wilkes of the Confederate envoys Mason and Slidell, bound for England and France on a British vessel, and having in mind Davy Crockett's familiar story of Colonel Scott and the 'Coon, depicts that animal with the head of Mr. Lincoln crouched on the limb of a friendly tree, and gazing furtively down on John Bull, armed with a blunderbuss and about to fire, when the following dialogue ensues:

'Coon—"Air you in arnest, colonel?"

Colonel Bull—"I am."

'Coon—"Don't fire—I'll come down."

The point of view of this cartoon is one of contemptuous ridicule but as a matter of fact the wise and ample apology which Mr. Lincoln, moved by a sense of what was fair and right, wrung from a short-sighted and reluctant cabinet, softened asperity and cleared the way to an understanding of a becoming sort; and it is pleasant to recall that the issue of Punch in which Tenniel's savage caricature appeared also included a group of verses charged with good nature and lively hope for an early settlement of the pending dispute.

PLATE No. 76 Up a Tree-Colonel Bull and the Yankee Coon, London Punch, January 11, 1862

The cartoon, Jemmy Twitcher Floyd which held the first page of the issue of Vanity Fair for March 15, 1862, celebrates the disappearance of a shabby figure from public life and the emergence of a nobler one—in the persons of John B. Floyd and Ulysses S. Grant—this thanks to their widely contrasting parts in the capture of Fort Donelson, on February 16. Gay in The Beggar's Opera had made Jemmy Twitcher, a knave always ready to betray a leader or cause, a familiar figure to several generations of music lovers. Now Jemmy Twitcher Floyd, whom an angry President, whip in hand grasps by the ear, true to a sorry role, plaintively protests: "Well, if I didn't steal your guns, I didn't fire 'em."

John B. Floyd, a Virginia lawyer and politician who had been governor of his State, in 1857 became secretary of war in Buchanan's cabinet with unhappy results to himself and his chief. When in December, 1860, Major Anderson removed his command from Fort Moultrie to Fort Sumter in Charleston Harbor in order to retain its control, Floyd declared the act contrary to his orders, and, when Buchanan would not allow him to direct Anderson to return to Fort Moultrie, he made the President's refusal a pretext for resignation from the cabinet.

At the same time Floyd bred anger in the North because as secretary of war he sold to Southern States large quantities of arms. It is now, however, agreed that these were old arms replaced in Northern arsenals by new and more efficient ones; that Floyd did not personally profit by his acts as secretary, and that incompetence of a very hopeless sort was the only crime that could be fairly charged against him. When war came he entered the Confederate Army and was in command at Fort Donelson when Grant laid seige to it. But fearing that if he fell into Union custody he would be held to stern account for his conduct while in Buchanan's cabinet, he passed the command on first to Pillow and then to Buckner, who had been with Grant at West Point, and who now reluctantly yielded to his old classmate's demand for unconditional and immediate surrender. Jefferson Davis, who nursed an old quarrel with Floyd, at once removed him from command, and he died a year later a broken and discredited man.

In the capture of Donelson, on the other hand, Grant first gave shining proof of the qualities that were to win him first place among Union captains. "The blow was most disastrous," wrote Albert Sidney Johnston to Davis, "and almost without remedy." Johnston told less than the truth. Grant's victory saved Kentucky to the Union, assured a firm foothold in Tennessee, and cleared the way for Union forces to advance two hundred miles into enemy territory. Mr. Lincoln promptly made Grant a major general, and thus the latter's feet were firmly planted in the path that, despite intrigue and slander, was to lead him two years later to command of all the Union armies and to final victory for the Union cause.

PLATE No. 77   Jemmy Twitcher Floyd, Vanity Fair, March 15, 1862

PLATE NO. 78

The cartoon by Tenniel, Oberon and Titania, appeared in London Punch on April 5, 1862. Mr. Lincoln garbed as Oberon is represented as thus supplicating Virginia, who as Titania holds a negro child by the hand:

Oberon—"I do but beg a little nigger boy to be my henchman."

Titania—"Set your heart at rest. The northern land buys not this negro child from me."

Tenniel's drawing reflects British reaction, cynical and shortsighted, to Mr. Lincoln's patient and persistent efforts to end the conflict between the sections by purchase at a fair price of all the slaves owned in the South, which he argued, in conferences with Union leaders and in messages to Congress, would assure the saving of unnumbered lives and dollars. He first urged such a measure on the slave holders of the Border States, and in April, 1862, induced Congress to pass a joint resolution approving his plan in principle, and pledging pecuniary aid to any State that would adopt gradual abolishment of slavery. But, as his secretaries phrase it, the attitude of Union leaders in the Border States, was "one of doubt, of qualified protest, and of apprehensive inquiry"; and, due to a miscarriage of plans by the lawmakers regarding Missouri, no grant of money to any State was ever made by Congress to aid in the purchase of slaves.

Slavery, however, was abolished in the District of Columbia with reasonable payments to owners, and even after he issued the Emancipation Proclamation, Mr. Lincoln continued to labor valiantly but in vain for compensation to Southern owners as in his belief a prompt and fair solution of the slavery issue. Alexander H. Stephens reports that at the Hampton Roads Conference in February, 1865, he declared that he "would be willing to be taxed to remunerate the Southern people for their slaves"; that he believed that "the people of the North were as responsible for slavery as the people of the South," and that he would favor "the Government paying a fair indemnity for the loss to the owners."

And Gideon Welles, records in his Diary that on the morrow of his return from Hampton Roads, Mr. Lincoln in "an earnest desire to conciliate and effect peace," proposed to his cabinet that four hundred million dollars—the cost of two hundred days of war—be paid to the Southern States "for the extinguishment of slavery, or for such other purpose as the States were disposed. It did not meet with favor," Mr. Welles concludes, "and was dropped." It was not the fault of Mr. Lincoln that the people of the South faced bankruptcy at the end of the war.

PLATE No. 78 Oberon and Titania, London Punch, April 5, 1862

PLATE NO. 79

The cartoon Cooperation appeared in Vanity Fair on April 12, 1862 and reflects the problems Mr. Lincoln was compelled to face in the last days of the first year of war. A Zouave who may be doing duty for General McClellan, in whom at the moment Union hopes of an early victory mainly centered, holds a bundle of staves each representing a seceded State which he hands one by one to Cooper Lincoln who is seeking to repair a barrel apparently broken past mending.

The events of the immediate future were to confirm this gloomy prospect. In his December, 1861, message to Congress Mr. Lincoln made it clear why McClellan had been given high command, pointing out that General Scott, before going into retirement, had repeatedly declared the young general the proper man to succeed him. But it was not long before McClellan began to treat in an indifferent way Mr. Lincoln's earnest desire for action, and in a brief note curtly dismissed all of his suggestions looking for a forward movement of the Union forces. At the same time, guided by misleading reports, he multiplied the strength of the enemy and incessantly called for more troops, one of these calls prompting Mr. Lincoln's somber observation that sending more troops to McClellan was "like shovelling fleas in a barnyard."

The troubled and anxious spring and summer of 1862 yielded the seven days of battle of the Peninsula, second Bull Run with its inglorious ending, and Antietam, which brought to a disputed close McClellan's career as a commander. Generals came and went in those clouded days, but Mr. Lincoln, steadfastly facing each fresh disappointment, kept the faith. Witness the letter he wrote to Seward on June 28, 1862, to be shown by his secretary of state to men of influence and power in New York City. "I expect," he said, "to maintain this contest until successful, or till I die, or am conquered, or my term expires, or Congress or the country forsake me."

And so while McClellan on September 18, 1862 permitted Lee to retreat from Antietam with his beaten army intact, six days later that battle had a brave sequel in Mr. Lincoln's stout-hearted emancipation of the slave.

PLATE No. 79 Cooperation, Vanity Fair, April 12, 1862

PLATE NO. 80

One of the most trenchant cartoons of Mr. Lincoln drawn by Frank Bellew appeared in Frank Leslie's Illustrated Newspaper on May 3, 1862 with the title Sinbad Lincoln and the Old Man of the Sea. It showed the President as Sinbad carrying on his shoulders the Old Man of the Sea—Gideon Welles, whose course as secretary of the navy was then the cause in certain quarters of much ill-natured comment. There was, however, as the sequel proved, no real cause for criticism of Mr. Welles, who, not given to self-advertising, was nevertheless in all important ways wholly equal to the heavy demands made upon him. He transformed a small and outmoded navy into a first-class fighting force, and in sponsoring the construction of John Ericsson's Monitor helped to work an instant and complete revolution in sea-fighting.

"Welles was a curious looking man," wrote Charles A. Dana in old age. "He wore a wig which was parted in the middle, the hair falling down on each side, and it was from his peculiar appearance, I have always thought, that the idea that he was an old fogy originated. Nevertheless" adds Mr. Dana, "he was a wise, strong man. There was no noise in the street when he went along, but he understood his duty and did it. We had no navy when the war began, and he had to create one; but he was patient, laborious and intelligent at his task." Mr. Dana speaks with the authority of first-hand knowledge. Than Gideon Welles, Mr. Lincoln had no more loyal or efficient helper. The same cannot be said of some of the other members of his cabinet of whom the often acid pages of Mr. Welles' Diary afford revealing glimpses.

PLATE No. 80 Sinbad Lincoln and the Old Man of the Sea, Frank Leslie's Illustrated
Newspaper, May 3, 1862

PLATE NO. 81

The cartoon, The New Orleans Plum, which appeared in London Punch on May 25, 1862, was suggested by the capture the preceding month of New Orleans by Union naval and land forces under Farragut. The artist borrowing from an old nursery tale, shows Lincoln seated in a corner and plucking a plum from the generous pudding in his lap. Possibly for fear that his caricature might not be perfectly clear to the British mind he appended to it these informing words: "Big Lincoln, up in a corner, thinking of humble pie, found under his thumb a New Orleans plum and said 'What a cute Yankee am I.'"

The capture of New Orleans, a city of 168,000 and the largest seaport of the South, was the first great naval victory of the war, and made Farragut, a native of the South who had remained loyal to the Union cause, a master and directing spirit in all major operations at sea during the remainder of the conflict. Mr. Lincoln at once advanced him to the rank of rear admiral, and thereafter gave him his confidence in full and unstinted measure. And the President made no mistake in honoring and trusting Farragut, for the latter's capture of New Orleans was an event of present and future import in a troubled period. A little more than a year later after a long and stubborn siege a Union army under Grant and Sherman, aided by Farragut and his fleet, compelled the surrender of Vicksburg, sundering the Confederacy in twain, and in another month a President, confident of the future, could write old friends in Springfield: "The Father of Waters again goes unvexed to the sea."

PLATE No. 81   The New Orleans Plum, London Punch, May 25, 1862

The cartoon, "Norfolk is Ours!" (Frisky Manner in which the news was received by the President and Secretary of War) appeared in Vanity Fair on May 31, 1862. Early in the month named, Mr. Lincoln, with a party that included Secretaries Chase and Stanton, made the first of his many memorable visits to Fortress Monroe, then commanded by Major General John E. Wool, a zealous supporter of the Union cause, but one whom the years had shorn alike of the capacity for well-directed planning and effective action.

Thus Mr. Lincoln and his secretaries found a condition of affairs at and around Fortress Monroe not at all to their liking, and as a result of the prompt measures taken to mend them, Norfolk, the most important port on the South Atlantic coast, along with its great navy yard, which in April, 1861, had been captured by the Confederates, now fell like a ripe apple into Union hands. The veteran Wool, lagging superfluous on the stage, was marked for early retirement, and General Egbert L. Viele, a younger officer with a will to do things who had kept the President company from Washington, was now left behind as military governor of Norfolk.

But for students of Mr. Lincoln's career perhaps the most significant incident of his first visit to Fortress Monroe was a revealing talk he had with Colonel Le Grand B. Cannon, then on the staff of General Wool. "The President," begins the story Colonel Cannon delighted to tell in old age, "occupied my office, and spent the morning (after his arrival) reading Shakespeare. After the lapse of several hours he got up from his reading, and said to me:

" 'You have been busy, Colonel. Sit with me and rest, and I will read you some passages from Shakespeare.'

"He commenced by reading from Macbeth, then from King Lear and then from King John. As he read that part of King John where Constance bewails the loss of her son, his voice became tremulous, and he seemed to be deeply moved. When he reached the end he closed the book, and said:

" 'Did you ever dream of some lost friend, and feel that you were having a sweet communion with him, and yet conscious that it was not a reality?'

" 'I think we all have some such experiences,' I replied, deeply moved by his manner and the circumstances.

" 'That is the way I dream of my lost boy Willie,' said Mr. Lincoln. (He had just lost his boy, who was his idol.) Then he broke down in most convulsive weeping. Sympathetically moved, I too broke down utterly. He sat with head bowed down on the table, and I quietly left the room. He never alluded to this incident afterward, but treated me always with the most genuine affection. He had given me a sacred confidence, and I grew to have a most intense affection for him."

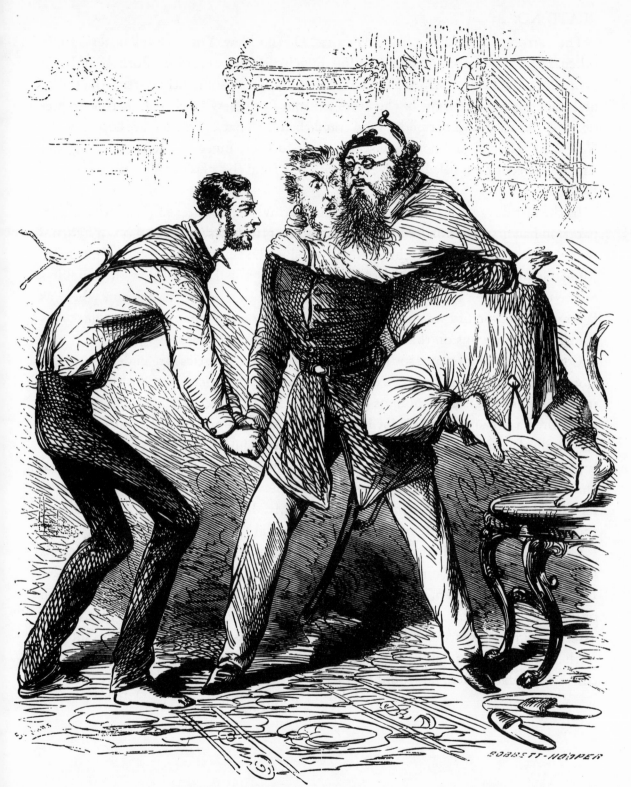

PLATE No. 82   Norfolk is Ours, Vanity Fair, May 31, 1862

PLATE NO. 83

The cartoon, The Latest from America; Or the New York "Eye-Duster" to be taken Every Day, appeared in London Punch on July 26, 1862. Both brutal and cynical this caricature, which may have been drawn by some other artist than Tenniel, seeking to make light of the news sent out from New York at that time, represents Mr. Lincoln as a bartender who stands behind a bar, on which are copies of the New York Herald, and bottles inscribed Soft Sawder, Bunkum, Bosh and Brag, and shifts a concoction labeled The New York Press from the glass of Victory to that of Defeat.

In the last days of July, 1862, McClellan's army, which after nine months of preparation had first come under fire the preceding April, had seen seven days of fighting in an attempt to capture Richmond and subdue the Confederate forces, first under Johnston and then under Lee. Once the Union troops had advanced to the outskirts of the Confederate capital but the courage of their commander failed him when, as is now known, victory was within his grasp, and soon the Army of the Potomac was back in its old camps on that river, within sight of the Capitol.

Contrary to the inference sought to be conveyed in the caricature under consideration, neither the journals of New York nor those of any other Northern city, essayed in their news or editorial columns to foster a belief that McClellan's series of battles had scored a decisive triumph for the Union cause. As a matter of fact at no time in its troubled course did the Lincoln administration, with two exceptions, receive support of the right sort from the New York press. It had a stout and unfailing champion in the Evening Post, whose editor, the venerable William Cullen Bryant, had made early and convincing discovery of Mr. Lincoln's sterling qualities, and the same was true of the Times, edited by Henry Jarvis Raymond.

On the other hand Horace Greeley's Tribune was constantly seeking new reasons for censuring or questioning Mr. Lincoln and his ways; the Herald under the elder Bennett, long a Southern sympathizer, until the war was nearing its end gave him only grudging support, and the World edited by Manton Marble, from first to last assailed him in unsparing and wholly unwarranted fashion. It was not the support of the Northern press, but his own steadfast spirit that in the end brought Mr. Lincoln to the place where he would be.

PLATE No. 83   The Latest from America, London Punch, July 26, 1862

PLATE NO. 84

The cartoon, After His Last Run, appeared in London Fun on August 2, 1862, and was the first of the London caricatures which Matt Morgan contributed to that journal. It shows General McClellan soaking his travel-spent feet in a basin of hot water while Doctor Lincoln, a copy of the New York Herald protruding from one of his pockets, anxiously inquires: "Well, Well, McClellan, and how are your feet?"

After the lapse of years the story of McClellan and the army he commanded in the spring and summer of 1862 does not make pleasant reading. On May 5, 1862, McClellan at the head of one hundred and twenty thousand men—despite his fears to the contrary his army from first to last outnumbered that of the enemy's maximum ninety thousand by from thirty to forty thousand—left his defenses at Yorktown, fought a rear guard action at Williamsburg, advanced to White House Landing, and then, changing his base to the James, twenty miles from Richmond, in a series of battles pushed his troops to a point within four miles of the Confederate capital, all the way steadily imploring the War Department and the President for more men and guns. "I have seen too many dead and wounded comrades," he wired Secretary Stanton, after the first of seven days of battle, "to feel otherwise than that the government had not sustained this army. If you do not do so now the game is lost."

"Save your army at all costs. We will send reinforcements as fast as we can," was Mr. Lincoln's reply to this telegram; and he was as good as his word. But the President's grim remark to those about him was "he has the slows," and when another request came for more men he said: "If I gave McClellan all the men he asks for they could not find room to lie down. They'd have to sleep standing up." And so McClellan, believing he was a loser when he was not, failed to command success. In the end his army was brought back to its old camping grounds on the Potomac; then, to reinforce another commander, reduced to a fraction of its original strength, after which its head was relieved of command in the field and told to report for orders at Alexandria.

But the worst was yet to come, and in a still darker hour Mr. Lincoln proved his greatness. Late in August, 1862, the army which had been assembled under Pope, who in an anxious search for the right man had been called from the West to prove his caliber, faced defeat at Second Bull Run. Lee threatened Washington and a new commander had to be found without an hour's delay. McClellan still enjoyed the trust of the men in the ranks, and Mr. Lincoln who always knew when to be firm, ignoring the angry protests of his cabinet, restored him to command. A few weeks later McClellan performed his last and greatest service to the Union cause by stopping Lee at Antietam and forcing him back into Virginia. And the sequel of Antietam, as already recorded in another place, was emancipation.

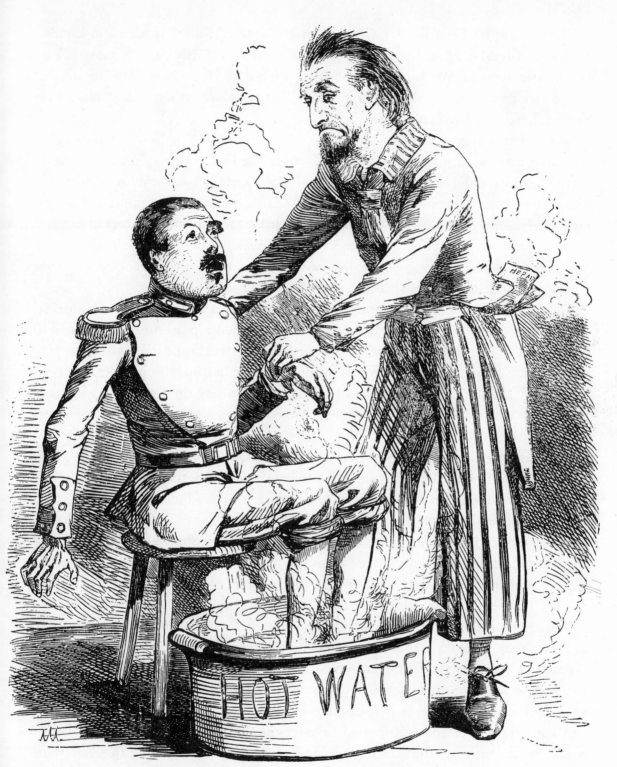

PLATE No. 84   After His Last Run, *London Fun*, August 2, 1862

The cartoon by Tenniel, One Good Turn Deserves Another, appeared in London Punch on August 9, 1862. It reflects more humor and less malice than do most of Tenniel's caricatures of Mr. Lincoln, who, here garbed as Uncle Sam, hands a musket and cartridge box to Sambo, saying "Why, I du declare, it's my dear old friend Sambo. Lend us a hand, old hoss, du."

Nor was this appeal a vain one. Between 1863 and 1865 one hundred and eighty thousand men of African descent enlisted under the Union flag to prove "brave in action, patient under dangerous and heavy labors, and cheerful amid hardships and privations." Mr. Lincoln early advocated the raising of colored troops, but at first faced determined opposition to such a measure from some of the members of his cabinet, likewise from some of his generals; and it was not until after the capture of Vicksburg and the opening of the Mississippi made the time ripe for action, that colored enlistments were pushed in a systematic and substantial way.

Then the President had the earnest support of General Grant who on August 23, 1863, wrote him: "By arming the negro we have added a powerful ally. They will make good soldiers, and taking them from the enemy weakens him in the same proportion they strengthen us." Events confirmed this prediction. Not only in and about Vicksburg, and in the capture of Port Hudson, but all along the Union front east and west the negro soldier fought bravely, nor did enlistments cease so long as there was need for them.

No doubt the colored regiment that will live longest in history was the one that was first to go to war. This was the Fifty-fourth Massachusetts Volunteers recruited in and about Boston in the opening weeks of 1863 and which had Robert Gould Shaw of immortal memory for its colonel. When in an attempt to capture Charleston in the following July, an assault was made on Fort Wagner Shaw and his men headed the storming column. They charged with spirit, and, despite a fire that made great gaps in their ranks, planted their flag on the parapet, Shaw waving his sword and crying, "Onward, boys!" But they could not retain their hold, and were forced to retreat. Shaw was among the fallen and was buried with his men.

Thirty-four years later there was erected on Boston Common a monument by St. Gaudens which portrays Shaw and his soldiers marching to Battery Wharf to take the steamer for the South. Across its base is inscribed these words of Lincoln: "And there will be some black men who can remember that with silent tongue and clenched teeth and steady eye and well-poised bayonet they have helped mankind on to this great consummation." that consummation being proof "that among free men there can be no successful appeal from the ballot to the bullet."

PLATE NO. 85   One Good Turn Deserves Another, London Punch, August 9, 1862

The cartoon, Angling for Recruits (Recruiting ala Mode) drawn by Morgan appeared in London Fun on August 23, 1862. It shows Mr. Lincoln, in the role of Uncle Sam, with his secretary of the treasury, making ready, with postage stamps for bait, to angle for recruits for the Union Army in a body of water labeled Bondey River, all of which, while doing violence to the truth, calls to mind what, after the first rush to volunteer had come to an end, was to prove until Lee's surrender one of Mr. Lincoln's principal causes for anxiety—the need of more fighting men for the Union armies.

Due to overconfident belief as to what was to be accomplished by the Army of the Potomac under McClellan recruiting was ordered suspended in April, 1862, Secretary Stanton mistakenly assuming that the forces already in the field were enough to win the war. But soon there was a sharp awakening to a contrary condition of things, an awakening made all the sharper by McClellan's campaign before Richmond and Second Bull Run. A call on July first, 1862, for three hundred thousand three-year men met with a disappointing response because of McClellan's handling of his army, and on August 4, the President issued a second call for a like number of men.

Once more the President's hopes proved disappointing ones, and when in June, 1863, he issued a third call, this time for a hundred thousand six-months men to help repel the Confederate invasion of Pennsylvania only a fraction of that number came forward to enlist. In the end it became clear that only by compulsion could men be found to fill the ranks of steadily dwindling armies, and on March 3, 1863, the President approved a Conscription Act passed by Congress, which, replacing previous machinery for raising troops, operated directly on the people of the nation instead of through the medium of the States, which had been the practice up to that time.

The several calls for troops under the Conscription Act, the last made in December, 1864, added a little more than seven hundred thousand men for longer or shorter periods to the Union armies. A drafted man, if he so desired, could secure exemption from service by paying three hundred dollars to the government or hiring a substitute. In April, 1864, John Summerfield Staples, a nineteen-year-old Pennsylvania lad, agreed to become a substitute for Abraham Lincoln, at the latter's request, and until his honorable discharge in September, 1865, served as a private in the Second District of Columbia Volunteers. Staples passed his latter years at Stroudsburg in his native State, and his grave in one of the burial grounds of that town is paid especial honor on each returning Memorial Day.

PLATE No. 86   Angling for Recruits (Recruiting a la Mode) London Fun, August 23, 1862

The cartoon, Lincoln's Two Difficulties, drawn by another hand than Tenniel, appeared in London Punch on August 23, 1862. The President, again in the guise of Uncle Sam, with hands in pocket and a perplexed expression on his face, exclaims to a tax collector on his right and to a soldier on his left: "What? No money! No men!" The men who made up the ruling class of England were, as events proved, sadly at fault in weighing the moral forces behind the Union cause; they were also sorely in error when, until the war was in its final stages, they over-estimated the Union need for men and money with which to wage a winning contest.

Volunteer enlistments and then conscription solved the first, and the sale of bonds, in steadily increasing volume the second of these problems. It is true that for a short but anxious period during the last weeks of 1862 and the first of 1863 the Union finances were at a low ebb. Due to faulty methods Government bonds were not selling, and many million dollars back pay were due the men of the army and navy. But there followed a quick and welcome change. Jay Cooke and his agents found ways to induce the people to lend large sums of money to the government, and by early July of 1863 Secretary Chase, well content with results, could declare the popular loan he had devised an assured success, bond purchases then averaging over three million dollars a day.

And news of these changed conditions were promptly reported to those in high places in England. "The secretary of war told me yesterday," Charles Sumner on April 26 wrote to the Duchess of Argyll, "that our rolls showed eight hundred thousand men under arms—better clothed and better fed than any before. —Besides our army, we have a credit which is adequate to all our needs; and we have powder and salt-petre sufficient for three years, even if our ports should be closed, and five hundred thousand unused muskets in our arsenals, and the best armorers of the world producing them at the rate of fifty thousand a month."

In a measure the soldiers produced by the draft were in some ways inferior to those who had volunteered in 1861 and 1862, but only in a measure. Brawny men from Canada, and sturdy newcomers from Europe entered the Union army in 1863 and 1864, drawn by the high wages offered for military service, and these proved fighting men of the first-class. "I will see," wrote General Sherman to his brother in April, 1864, "that by May first I have on the Tennessee one of the best armies in the world." This promise had splendid fulfilment in the months that followed, while in Virginia soldiers of like training and quality enabled Grant to battle Lee to a standstill.

PLATE No. 87   Lincoln's Two Difficulties, London Punch, August 23, 1862

PLATE NO. 88

The cartoon, The Overdue Bill, similar in spirit to the one just described, appeared in London Punch on September 27, 1862—five days after Mr. Lincoln gave the Emancipation Proclamation to the country, an edict which opened a new era in the world's history. The drawing shows Mr. Lincoln seated at a desk, with hands, as usual, thrust into his pockets, glancing uneasily at a paper inscribed, "I promise to subdue the South in ninety days—Abe Lincoln," held out to him by a Confederate soldier, who says: "Your ninety days' promissory note isn't taken up yet, sirree!"

Perhaps it would have been more fitting had Punch made the always hopeful Seward the central figure in this cartoon, for it was Mr. Lincoln's secretary of state, and not the President himself who in 1861 was loudest in proclaiming that the war would end within three months. It is due to Seward to record that when in after years he was questioned by a friend as to the reasons which prompted this famous prediction of his, he at first declined to give an answer, but finally said with some reluctance that he believed at the time that if the South did not yield in ninety days the North would!

As a matter of fact the belief that the North would quickly master the South was one confidently cherished by many of Mr. Lincoln's supporters in the first days of the war. Union defeat at Bull Run, unexpected and disastrous, was the first blow to this belief. It was further impaired in 1862 by McClellan's luckless campaign before Richmond and by Second Bull Run. Meanwhile, Mr. Lincoln pushed his patient, determined search for a general who could compel success, a general on whom he could rely and on whom he could throw the full responsibility of operations in the fields. Scott, whose past had been a glorious one, failed him because he was old and infirm; McClellan failed him because, although a masterly maker of armies, he faced the enemy with fear and reluctance, and Halleck, when summoned from the West as the right man for the place avoided responsibility as he would the plague, and speedily proved that he was little more than a capable clerk, who could take but could not give orders.

The war, however, went on and in March, 1864, the appointment to supreme command of General Grant, a man who said little but did things, cleared the way for Appomattox and final victory.

PLATE No. 88   The Overdue Bill, London Punch, September 27, 1862

PLATE NO. 89

This cartoon, Breaking the "Backbone," drawn by Benjamin Day, an artist of exceptional force and directness, and put out by Currier and Ives in September 1862, bears striking witness to the fact that the second summer of the Civil War was a trying and uncertain season for the people of the North. The draft law of 1862, Stanton's favorite weapon, while a greatly needed one was yielding results of less than a satisfactory sort. The skill of Halleck and the strategy of McClellan had both proved of a most disappointing order. Indeed it was already clear that in making Halleck his chief military adviser Mr. Lincoln had chosen an inept and useless helper.

On the other hand, the Army of the Potomac under McClellan, victim of his own delusions, had fallen back from its costly campaign to win Richmond, and was once more occupied with the defence of its old lines in front of Washington. Then on August 29–30, 1862, came Pope's disastrous defeat at Second Bull Run and its proof of the utter incapacity of another Union general. The Southern "gyascutis," viewed with manifest approval by Jefferson Davis in Mr. Day's drawing, was proving a doughty foe, and how to break its backbone remained the baffling problem of the Union leaders. Mr. Lincoln, however, had at his command a most effective weapon— the emancipation of the slaves—and now he made ready to use it. On July 13, 1862, he informed Secretaries Seward and Welles that he had resolved to issue a decree of emancipation as the only sure means of saving the Union. A draft of such a decree was prepared, but on second thought laid aside until it could have behind it the moral force of a victory of the Northern armies. Quickly followed Lee's invasion of Maryland and his repulse at Antietam on September 14. Eight days later, September 22, Mr. Lincoln issued the Emancipation Proclamation, effective January 1, 1863. This great document had three results: it renewed in the North the will to victory; appealing to the friends of the Union in England and France, it removed foreign intervention from the list of possibilities, and last but by no means least it convinced a growing minority in the South that only defeat awaited them, thereby shortening the period of conflict. Thus Mr. Lincoln with his pen, putting into action his remark to Stanton in the Day drawing, finally broke the back of the "gyascutis."

PLATE No. 89   Breaking the "Backbone" Drawing by Benjamin Day issued by Currier and Ives, September, 1862

The engraving, Under the Veil, made by Adalbert Volck of Baltimore at the time of the Emancipation Proclamation in September, 1862, was one of the caricatures which brought trouble and thwarted plans to an artist of parts. Volck began his war etchings at Baltimore in 1861 and there worked on them at intervals for two years but when he had put out ten of them their animus caused their publication to be suppressed by the Federal Government. Then the artist fled to Europe and there continued his work, sending his later output back to America by a blockade runner, only to have his plates captured and destroyed before they could secure distribution. Volck returned to America in 1864, and under a London imprint, as elsewhere recorded, issued a small edition of a portfolio containing twenty-nine plates to which he gave the title Confederate War Etchings; but feeling against the South was still strong in the North, and the artist shortly deemed it best to withdraw the portfolio from circulation.

The plate Under the Veil was not included in this portfolio and has only come to light in recent years. Mr. Lincoln is disclosed as a negro when the veil is lifted, a bit of savagery based on the unfounded rumors then in circulation in the South concerning the lineage of the President. Mr. Lincoln's political followers were for long referred to in the South not as Republicans, but as Black Republicans, and from this practice may have sprung the rumors which gave Volck a motive that appealed to him. The evil-minded reports that Mr. Lincoln's mother, Nancy Hanks had been born out of wedlock probably had their origin with William Henry Herndon, his longtime partner.

What Herndon had to say about Mr. Lincoln's ancestry and origin took final form in 1888 in his life of Lincoln. "I remember only one time," he wrote "when Mr. Lincoln referred to the subject. It was about 1850 when he and I were driving to the Court in Menard County, Illinois. During the ride he spoke for the first time in my hearing of his mother. He said, among other things, that she was the illegitimate daughter of Lucy Hanks and a well-bred Virginia farmer or planter . . . he believed that his better nature and finer qualities—qualities that distinguished him from other members and descendants of the Hanks family—came from this broad-minded, unknown Virginian."

Be all this as it may, later research has confirmed the fact that Thomas Lincoln and Nancy Hanks were married by the Reverend Jesse Head—let it be recorded in passing a stout foe of slavery—in Washington County, Kentucky, on June 12, 1806, and that Abraham Lincoln was the second child born of this union. And so a lie bred in malice returns to confuse those with whom it had its origin.

PLATE No. 90   Under the Veil, Caricature by Volck, September, 1862

PLATE NO. 91

This caricature appeared in Harper's Weekly on October 4, 1862, but there is no means of identifying the artist who drew it. Jefferson Davis, head of the Confederacy, is depicted in sick-room garb, and as a Negro servant holds out to him a bottle labeled Last Southern Draft 5 Men, he complains of the draft from an open door, before which sits Mr. Lincoln with a huge club in his hand.

All of which bears amusing witness to the fact that, if the need for men and money made heavy demands on Mr. Lincoln's fortitude and patience it was for Mr. Davis a still more perplexing one. Added to the fact that the Union was composed of twenty-three States with twenty-two million people while the Confederacy was made up of eleven States in all with a population of nine million of whom those held in bondage formed a substantial part, Mr. Davis from first to last had to depend on the governors of the Southern States for sorely needed recruits to replenish his diminishing armies. And these governors more often than not received his requests for troops in a complaining spirit and were slow in complying with them.

This was true in continuing measure of Brown, governor of Georgia, and Vance, governor of North Carolina. As the clouds lowered Brown returned a definite refusal to the requests of Davis for troops, and Vance covertly pondered ways for withdrawing his State from the Confederacy. More than once lack of support from his own people made Davis the victim of devastating fears. He "acts as if he had not any confidence in the attainment of independence" Alexander H. Stephens confided to a friend in May, 1862, when the Army of the Potomac was advancing on Richmond and Federal gunboats reached a point only eight miles below the Confederate capital.

Crying as was the Confederate need for soldiers no less crying was its need for money with which to arm and feed them. The Union blockade of its coasts, growing steadily in scope and efficiency, deprived it of hoped-for export and import duties, and it was unable to raise any adequate amount by internal taxation. Instead it had to rely for support on its issues of paper money and the returns from bonds paid for in such currency. Before the end of 1864 the Confederate output of paper money exceeded a billion dollars, while its receipts in specie during its existence of four years fell below thirty million dollars. These conditions quickly bred inflation, and the high prices that invariably accompany it. Thus at a Richmond restaurant in January, 1864, a dinner partaken by nine men cost $631.50 in Confederate currency, and in the same year the usual dinner of Robert E. Lee, commander of the Army of Northern Virginia was "a head of cabbage boiled in salt water, sweet potatoes, and a pone of corn-bread." The student of history now knows that the Confederate cause was from the first a losing one.

PLATE No. 91   That Draft, Harper's Weekly, October 4, 1862

The cartoon, What Will He Do With Them, appeared in Vanity Fair on October 4, 1862, and records that journal's approval of Mr. Lincoln's preliminary Emancipation Proclamation. It pictures the President as a vagrom bird-peddler whom an absence of customers impels to the remark: "Darn these here blackbirds. If nobody won't buy them I'll have to open cages and let 'em fly." The processes by which Mr. Lincoln reached this state of mind hold unfailing interest for the student of history. Mr. Lincoln kept his own counsel until he was ready for action, but, keenly aware that public sentiment in the North of which he was an almost unerring judge, was setting in the direction of freedom for the slave, at last by gradual yet inevitable stages he reached the conclusion that to restore the Union he must use emancipation as a weapon.

Meanwhile, when on September 13, 1862, a delegation of Chicago clergymen called on Mr. Lincoln, and urged such action as a token of "national repentance for the sin of oppression," the President made characteristic if mildly sarcastic response to their demands. "I hope," he told his visitors, "it will not be irreverent for me to say that if it is probable that God would reveal his will to others on a point so connected with my duty, it might be supposed he would reveal it directly to me; for unless I am more deceived in myself than I often am, it is my earnest desire to know the will of Providence in this matter. And if I can learn what it is I will do it."

Ten days later, September 23, came final action and the next evening Mr. Lincoln made a short speech to a group of serenaders who approved it. "What I did," he told his visitors, "I did after a very full deliberation, and under a very heavy and solemn sense of responsibility. I can only trust in God I have made no mistake." That he had made no mistake soon became the measured verdict of history.

PLATE No. 92   What Will He Do With Them?, Vanity Fair, October 4, 1862

The cartoon, Lincoln's Last Warning, appeared in Harper's Weekly on October 11, 1862, and was one of the first drawings contributed by Frank Bellew to that journal. Mr. Lincoln is shown ready to apply the axe to the Slavery tree in which Jefferson Davis has taken refuge, but first gives this warning: "Now if you don't come down I will cut the tree from under you." Although emancipation was finally employed by Mr. Lincoln as a war measure, on August 23, 1862 he wrote Horace Greeley who had demanded immediate action: "I intend no modification of my oft-expressed personal wish that all men everywhere could be free," and there is ample evidence that during all his years as a lawyer and public man he recoiled from and hated slavery, and was quick, when occasion offered to give this hatred angry and effective expression. An incident related by Herndon afforded such occasion.

In 1854, as Herndon tells the story, "a young negro, the son of a colored woman in Springfield known as Polly, went to St. Louis and there hired as a hand on a lower Mississippi boat, arriving in New Orleans without what were known as free papers. Though born free he was subject to the tyranny of the Black Code, all the more stringent because of the recent utterances of Abolitionists in the North, and was kept in prison until his boat had left. After a certain length of time he would have been sold in slavery. The mother came to Lincoln and I and induced us to interfere in her behalf.

"We went first to the governor of Illinois, who responded that he had no right or power to interfere. Recourse was then had to the governor of Louisiana who responded in like manner. A second interview with the governor of Illinois resulting in nothing favorable, Lincoln rose from his chair, hat in hand, and exclaimed: 'By God, Governor'—one of the few instances of his resort to an oath to stress a purpose—'I'll make the ground in this country too hot for the foot of a slave whether or not you have the legal power to secure the release of this boy.'"

Having exhausted all legal means Lincoln & Herndon ceased to act as attorneys for Polly and her boy. Instead, Mr. Lincoln drew up a subscription list which his partner circulated, collecting funds enough to purchase the young negro's liberty. The money was sent to Alexander P. Field, a former Illinois lawyer then practising in New Orleans, who applied it as directed, and in due time the prisoner was restored to his mother.

PLATE No. 93 Lincoln's Last Warning, Frank Bellew in Harper's Weekly, October 11, 1862

PLATE NO. 94

The cartoon, Abe Lincoln's Last Card; or, Rouge et Noir, contributed by Tenniel to the October 18, 1862, issue of London Punch again shows how an important element in England, blind to the real trend and meaning of events, saw in Mr. Lincoln's prayerfully meditated Emancipation Proclamation only the gesture of a wily but desperate gambler driven to a last resource. It was accompanied by the following lines in which Mr. Lincoln is represented by their author as giving expression to his real thought and purpose:

> Brag's our game; and awful losers
>   We've been on the *Red*.
> Under and above the table,
>   Awfully we've bled.
> Ne'er a stake have we adventured,
>   But we have lost it still,
> From Bull's Run and mad Manassas
>   Down to Sharpsburg Hill.
>
> When luck's desperate, desperate venture
>   Still may bring it back:
> So I'll chance it—neck or nothing—
>   Here I lead THE BLACK!
> If I win, the South must pay for't,
>   Pay in fire and gore:
> If I lose, I'm ne'er a dollar
>   Worse off than before.
>
> From the Slaves of Southern rebels
>   Thus I strike the chain:
> But the slaves of loyal owners
>   Still shall slaves remain.
> If their owners like to wop 'em
>   They to wop are masters;
> Or if they prefer to swap 'em
>   Here are our shin-plasters!

PLATE No. 94   Abe Lincoln's Last Card, or, Rouge-et-Noir, London Punch, October 18, 1862

PLATE NO. 95

The cartoon The Confederate States Ajax Defying Uncle Sam Jupiter (The Penny Jupiter) drawn by Matt Morgan appeared in London Fun on October 18, 1862. The Confederate Ajax, a Southern planter, from a cotton field where a group of his slaves are toiling, defies Uncle Sam Lincoln, who, astride the American eagle, is about to launch his Emancipation thunderbolt from the skies.

In this drawing the artist voices the beliefs and hopes of an influential element in England which for a time regarded the Emancipation Proclamation as the futile gesture of the reckless and despairing leader of a cause doomed to failure. And on this side of the Atlantic there were troubled hours in the spring and summer of 1862 when Mr. Lincoln himself questioned the efficacy of the step demanded of him by the champions of abolition. "My paramount object," he wrote Horace Greeley in July, "is to save the Union and is not either to save or destroy slavery." And he made like answer to the members of a committee of clergymen who, as related in another place, called on him a few weeks later, bringing with them a memorial in favor of national emancipation which had been adopted at a public meeting of Christians of all denominations in Chicago.

And it is now known that when the Emancipation Proclamation was finally made public Mr. Lincoln was keenly disappointed by the lack of warmth with which it was received in the North. "While I hope something from the proclamation," he wrote Vice President Hamlin in a "strictly private" letter on September 28, 1862, "my expectations are not as sanguine as are those of some friends. The time for its effect southward has not come; but northward the effect should be instantaneous. It is six days old, and while commendation in newspapers and by distinguished individuals is all that a vain man could wish, the stocks have declined and troops come forward more slowly than ever. This, looked soberly in the face, is not very satisfactory. The North responds to the proclamation sufficiently in breath, but breath alone kills no rebels."

What with a depleted treasury, a crying need for more soldiers, and half a dozen States which had cast their electoral votes for Mr. Lincoln declaring against his party in the October and November elections, the last quarter of 1862 was, indeed, a gloomy period for the Union cause; but a new year brought a change for the better, a change underscored in July by Gettysburg and Vicksburg, and by growing proof that in Grant the North had found a general who could compel success. Thereafter even the faint-hearted could not deny that freedom for all men was on the way to become an assured and inalienable part of the federal system.

PLATE No. 95   Confederate States Ajax Defying Uncle Sam Jupiter (The Penny Jupiter), Matt Morgan in
London Fun, October 18, 1862

PLATE NO. 96

The engraving, Writing the Emancipation Proclamation, put out at Baltimore in October, 1862, was, in its manifest unfairness, one of the ugliest of Adalbert Volck's caricatures of Mr. Lincoln. On the wall of the room he draws, hangs a portrait of John Brown as Saint Ossawatamie and a canvas depicting the riot and bloodshed that followed the abolition of slavery in San Domingo. Mr. Lincoln, with one foot on a bound copy of the Constitution and the other sprawling on the floor in his rear, now and again dips into a devil's ink-pot the pen with which he is writing the Emancipation Proclamation.

Contrast with the malignancy of this suggestion of grave injustice done the South the spirit reflected in Secretary Chase's account of Mr. Lincoln's first reading of the proclamation to his cabinet, on September 22, 1862. Mr. Chase reports the President as reading a chapter from a book he had just received from Artemus Ward, High-handed Outrage at Utica, which, he observes, was enjoyed by all the members except Stanton. Then Mr. Lincoln took a graver tone and said:

"Gentlemen, I have as you are aware, thought a great deal about the relation of this war to slavery. My mind has been much occupied with this subject, and I have thought all along that the time for acting on it might very probably come. I think the time has come. When the rebel army was at Frederick, I determined, as soon as it should be driven out of Maryland, to issue a Proclamation such as I thought most likely to be useful. I said nothing to anyone, but I made the promise to myself, and —to my Maker. The rebel army is now driven out, and I am going to fulfil that promise. I have got you together to hear what I have written down. I do not wish your advice about the main matter—for that I have determined for myself.

"What I have written is that which my reflections have determined me to say. If there is anything in the expressions I use, or in any other minor matter which any one of you think had best be changed I shall be glad to receive the suggestions. Though I believe I have not so much of the confidence of the people as I had some time since, I do not know that, all things considered, any other person has more; and, however this may be, there is no way in which I can have any other man put where I am. I am here. I must do the best I can, and bear the responsibility of taking the course which I feel I ought to take."

Then the President read the proclamation to his cabinet, promptly accepting slight verbal changes in the document suggested by Seward, Chase and Blair, and on the morrow it became a part of history.

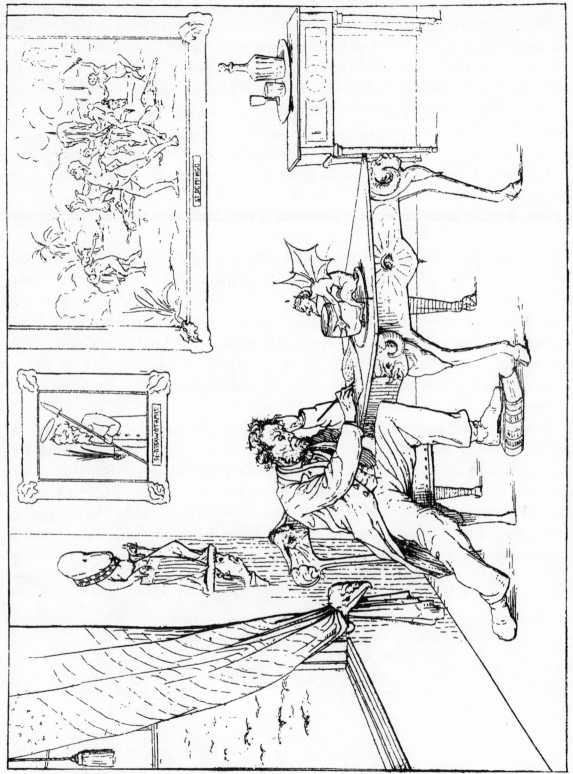

PLATE No. 96   Writing the Emancipation Proclamation, Engraving by Volck, Baltimore, October, 1862

The cartoon, Daring American Acrobat by Matt Morgan appeared in London Fun on November 15, 1862. Watched by an anxious audience which includes John Bull, the rulers of France, Italy, and Austria, and a cheering mob of the commonalty, Acrobat Lincoln is shown, head downward, making a perilous advance from one ring to another. He has already put behind him rings labeled Buncombe and Brag and Paper Money and from the ring Emancipation is about to go on to the ring Utter Ruin.

This caricature no doubt prompted admiring approval from some of the readers of Fun, but there were also in the England of 1862 men of breadth and vision who took another and more catholic view of American affairs.

One of these, as we know, was John Bright who, although a heavy loser by the war between the sections, successfully sought with tongue and pen to persuade his countrymen that right and justice were on the side of the North. "Slavery has measured itself with freedom," wrote Bright in his journal in April, 1865, when news reached him of Lee's surrender to Grant," and slavery has perished in the struggle. How often have I longed and prayed for this result, and how much I have suffered from anxiety whilst it has been slowly working out, I only know! This great triumph of the republic is the event of our age. The friends of freedom everywhere should thank God and take courage—they may believe the world is not forsaken by those who made it and rule it."

A few days later came the news of Lincoln's murder, and in his journal Bright paid tribute to the dead man's worth. "In him I have observed," he wrote, "a singular resolution honestly to do his duty, a great courage—shewn in the fact that in his speeches and writing, no word of passion, or of panic, or of ill-will has ever escaped him—a great gentleness of temper and nobleness of soul, proved by the absence of irritation and menace under circumstances of the most desperate provocation, and a pity and mercifulness to his enemies which seemed drawn as from the very fount of Christian charity and love. Good men everywhere will mourn for him, and history will place him high among the best and noblest of men."

Thus one great soul rendered deserved homage to another.

PLATE No. 97   Daring American Acrobat, Matt Morgan in London Fun, November 15, 1862

The cartoon by Stephens, Keep on the Track, appeared in Vanity Fair on November 22, 1862, and was prompted by the election that occurred in that month. Mr. Lincoln is made to do duty as a locomotive engineer, and to remark to his fireman (Secretary Seward) who is staggering under a load of fagots, each bearing the label Democratic Majority: "I've got the right fuel now and I guess I can keep her steady. Chuck in more, William."

Nevertheless, the outcome of the State and Federal elections of 1862 was a grave disappointment to the President and his friends. The popular judgment was clouded by defeats in the field and the antislavery policy of the administration, and the great States of New York, Pennsylvania, Ohio, Indiana, Illinois and Wisconsin, all of which two years before had cast their electoral votes for Mr. Lincoln, now declared against the party in power, and in each of them the Democrats made conspicuous gains in the new House of Representatives. But New England, Michigan, Iowa, Kansas, Minnesota, California, Oregon and the Border States now, or in the following year, elected Republican representatives, old or new, and that party retained a safe working majority in both branches of a Congress, which before it ran its course was to submit the Thirteenth Amendment to the States for an approval that was promptly given, thus making effective the Emancipation Proclamation of September 22, 1862.

Thereafter, with few recessions, the tide ran steadily in favor of the Union cause, and resulted in 1864 in Mr. Lincoln's reelection by an overwhelming majority. Meanwhile there was no faltering in his faith in final success. Witness his message delivered to the Congress elected in 1862 when it assembled for its final session in December, 1864: "While I remain in my present position I shall not attempt to retract or modify the Emancipation Proclamation. Nor shall I return to slavery any person who is free by the terms of that Proclamation or by any of the acts of Congress. If the people should by whatever mode or means, make it an Executive duty to re-enslave such persons, another and not I, must be their instrument to perform it."

Less than three months later the resolute spirit that breathed in this message had fitting reward in the passage of the Thirteenth Amendment by Congress. It is also to be noted that the new members of the popular branch of that Congress included five men who in future years were to play a large part in public affairs: James G. Blaine of Maine, James A. Garfield of Ohio, William B. Allison of Iowa, Samuel J. Randall of Pennsylvania and William R. Morrison of Illinois. Garfield and Morrison came fresh from duty in the field, one as major general and the other as colonel of volunteers. Three of the newcomers voted in due course for the Thirteenth Amendment.

PLATE No. 98   Keep on the Track, Vanity Fair, November 22, 1862

This cartoon by Morgan, Abe's Last appeared in London Fun on December 27, 1862, and reflects the disasters an influential element in England then believed and no doubt hoped would soon overtake the Union cause.

During the Civil War the so-called Palmerston-Russell ministry was in power in England, with Lord Palmerston premier, Earl Russell secretary for foreign affairs and Gladstone chancellor of the exchequer. There can be no question that Palmerston was a Confederate sympathizer while neither Russell nor Gladstone was friendly to the Northern cause. Thus it is one of the ironies of history that differences as to methods of procedure which arose between the trio in the early October of 1862, alone prevented a heavy if not fatal blow to that cause. In the preceding months the North had met with a series of dismaying reverses, and so it is not surprising that in mid-September Palmerston wrote Russell, then at Gotha in attendance on Queen Victoria, suggesting that the time had come "to consider whether, in such a state of things, England and France might not address the contending parties and recommend an arrangement on the basis of separation."

Russell promptly approved of this suggestion, adding in his reply to Palmerston: "I agree further that, in case of failure," (of an offer of mediation) "we ought ourselves to recognize the Southern States as an independent state." In the end it was arranged between them that on October 23 there should be a meeting of the British Cabinet to formally approve the offer of mediation. Meanwhile, an elaborate Cabinet circular went to its members to advise them of the weighty step in contemplation. Then, while Charles Francis Adams, our minister in London, mustered courage to face a blow he could not avert, the unexpected intervened to assure favoring winds and a smooth sea to Navigator Lincoln.

On October 7, sixteen days before the scheduled Cabinet meeting, Gladstone, chancellor of the exchequer who had been consulted about and given his hearty approval of the proposed programme, but now speaking out of order, delivered a speech at Newcastle in which he declared that Davis had "made a nation" and that dissolution of the Union and the independence of the Confederacy were as certain "as any event yet future and contingent could be." There long had been deep-seated and mutual distrust between Palmerston and Gladstone, the elder regarding the younger man as a future rival for the premiership. He now resented the Newcastle speech as an attempted forcing of his hand at a critical hour. Accordingly, he lost no time in commanding one of his lieutenants to publicly disclaim Gladstone's speech, and then postponed, as it proved, for good and all, the proposed cabinet meeting.

PLATE No. 99   Abe's Last, Matt Morgan in London Fun, December 27, 1862

The cartoon, Columbia Confronts the President, appeared in Harper's Weekly on January 3, 1863. Columbia faces the President and demands an accounting for the thousands slain the preceding month in the battle of Fredericksburg. "This reminds me of a little joke," says Mr. Lincoln. "Go tell your joke at Springfield," is the angry rejoinder. All of which recalls a story once told the writer by Andrew Gregg Curtin, governor of Pennsylvania in Civil War days. It was after the slaughter at Fredericksburg, and Governor Curtin had gone to the scene of conflict to look after his State's dead and wounded in person. While thus engaged he received a telegram from Mr. Lincoln, bidding him come to Washington. He responded at once and reaching the White House late in the evening found that Mr. Lincoln had retired. Seated by the President's bedside, he told what he had seen. "It was not a battle," said he, "it was a slaughter. Many of the wounded have received no attention, and thousands of the dead are still unburied. From the bottom of my heart, Mr. President, I wish we could find some way of ending this war."

Mr. Lincoln listened patiently, but with manifest anxiety, to the Governor's statement. When it was finished, he said:

"Curtin, it's a big job we've got on hand. It reminds me of what once happened to the son of a neighbor of mine out in Illinois. In the old man's orchard was an apple tree of which he was especially choice and one day in the fall his two boys, John and Jim, went out to gather the apples from this tree. John climbed the tree to shake the fruit off, while Jim remained below to gather it as it fell. There was a boar grubbing in the orchard, and seeing what was going on, it waddled up to the tree and began to eat the falling apples faster than Jim could gather them from the ground. This roiled Jim, and catching the boar by the tail he pulled vigorously, whereat the latter, with an angry squeal, began to snap at his legs. Afraid to let go, Jim held on for dear life, until finally, growing weary, he called to his brother to help him. John, from the top of the tree, asked what he wanted. 'I want you' said Jim, between the rushes of the boar, "to come down here and help me to let go of this darned hog's tail.' And Curtin," added the President, "that's just what I want of you and the rest. I want you to pitch in and help me let go of the hog's tail I have got hold of."

Before beginning this story Mr. Lincoln had been deeply depressed. When it was finished he laughed as heartily as did his auditor, and seemed instantly to recover his wonted spirits. "Pardon me, Mr. President," said the Governor, prompted by this change of mood, "but is not this story-telling habit of yours a sort of safety valve for you?"

"You have hit it, Curtin," was the quick reply. "If I could not tell these stories I think I should die."

PLATE No. 100 Columbia Confronts the President, Harper's Weekly, January 3, 1863

This cartoon which appeared in Harper's Weekly, January 10, 1863, and which showed Mr. Lincoln holding General Halleck and Secretary Stanton over the side of the ship of state, had appended to it the significant legend: "Universal Advice to Abraham—Drop 'Em." That Halleck, to whom Mr. Lincoln looked for sound advice and capable leadership when in July, 1862, he appointed him general in chief with headquarters in Washington, where he served until peace returned, speedily proved a great disappointment to the President is one of the familiar facts of Civil War history. How he soon came to be regarded by those who as a result of close contact had a right to judge him is clearly revealed in the diary of Edward Bates, Mr. Lincoln's shrewd and hard-headed attorney general. "I found him a frank, straightforward man," Bates wrote of Halleck when they first met in November, 1861, but the secretary soon came to regard with keen distrust the general who invariably avoided responsibility for weighty decisions, and on August 11, 1862, ending a comment on Halleck's conflicting testimony in a disputed matter, Bates tersely observed "a liar ought to have a good memory." After four score years Stanton's rightful place in the history of an eventful era is still a matter of sharp difference of opinion between those who study it with care and without prejudice. Suffice it to say that he had great qualities, but loyalty to his superiors was not always one of them.

PLATE No. 101   Universal Advice to Abraham, Drop 'Em, Harper's Weekly, January 10, 1863

The cartoon Bad News from Fredericksburg appeared in Harper's Weekly on January 17, 1863. It may be regarded as another footnote to, perhaps, the gloomiest chapter in the story of Mr. Lincoln's long and costly search for a general who could command success. A servant announces to a disappointed Lincoln the Union defeat at Fredericksburg to which Halleck and Stanton also listen with manifest chagrin. It was on November 7, 1862, that the President relieved McClellan of command of the Army of the Potomac and ordered him to turn it over to Burnside, this because McClellan after his success at Antietam had permitted Lee to cross the Blue Ridge and place himself between Richmond and the Army of the Potomac.

A West Point graduate, Burnside was a fine figure of a man, whose straightforward manliness never failed to compel the respect alike of friend and enemy, but he doubted his own capacity to successfully command a large body of men and this doubt had early and tragic confirmation. At Fredericksburg on December 12 with an army of 113,000 men he attacked 72,000 Confederates under Lee. The latter, however, had carefully prepared for his coming, planting riflemen in a sunken road which faced the Union advance. The result was the needless slaughter of thousands of brave men. The Union losses totaled 12,653 men, more than double those of the Confederates. For forty-eight hours many of the wounded lay uncared for in the winter cold, while others burned to death in long, dry grass set afire by cannon. But Mr. Lincoln unsubdued in spirit, issued an address to the Army of the Potomac, back on the northern bank of the Rappahannock, in which he said, among other things: "the consummate skill and success with which you crossed and recrossed this river in the face of the enemy, show you possess all of the qualities of a great army, which will yet give victory to the cause of the country and to popular government."

Eleven days later came New Year's Day of 1863, and Mr. Lincoln, still unsubdued in spirit, attached his name to the Emancipation Proclamation, remarking to Secretary Seward, who had brought him the engrossed copy for signature: "I never, in my life, felt more certain that I was doing right, than I do in signing this paper." And to another he remarked: "We are like whalers who have been on a long chase. We have at last got the harpoon into the monster, but we must now look how we steer, or with one flop of his tail he will send us all into eternity." And so Burnside, in addition to his own self-distrust having lost the confidence of his officers and men, Mr. Lincoln, after long pondering of the matter, on January 25, 1863, ordered General Hooker to the command of the Army of the Potomac.

Burnside went to the Army of the Ohio, later under Grant again serving with the Army of the Potomac. When peace returned he was elected governor of Rhode Island and at the time of his death in 1881 was serving as a federal senator from that state.

PLATE No. 102   Bad News from Fredericksburg, Harper's Weekly, January 17, 1863

PLATE NO. 103

The cartoon, An Ice Party, or Letting Things Slide on the Rappahannock was drawn by William Newman whose career is dealt with in another place. Put out early in 1863, it also represents in an effective way Northern reaction to the Fredericksburg disaster. A party of skaters headed by General Burnside, which includes Halleck and Stanton, with Mr. Lincoln bringing up the rear, is threatened with a plunge into the icy waters of the Rappahannock. "Don't be in such a hurry," Burnside cautions Halleck, who makes reply: "Taint me that's pushing; it's Stanton," while the secretary of war pleads: "It's Abe's fault and Uncle Sam." McClellan and Fremont gloomily watch the skaters from the river bank, and Uncle Sam cheers them on with a: "Go ahead, boys; keep it up."

PLATE No. 103   An Ice Party, or Letting Things Slide on the Rappahannock, Cartoon by Newman, 1863, Owned by the
American Antiquarian Society

PLATE NO. 104

The cartoon, Uncle Abe Welcomes Ben Butler appeared in Harper's Weekly on January 17, 1863, accompanied by this bit of dialogue:

Uncle Abe—"Hello! Ben, is that you? Glad to see you!"

Butler—"Yes, Uncle Abe. Got through with that New Orleans Job. Cleaned them out and scrubbed them up. *Any more scrubbing to give out?*"

Mr. Lincoln's relations with Butler, a self-seeker of the first order, were of a varied and often trying sort. Butler's brigade of 1200 men from Massachusetts was one of the first to reach Washington following the fall of Fort Sumter in April, 1861, and thereafter its irrepressible commander, with an unfailing flare for publicity, was never for long out of the newspapers of the period. He was made a major general of volunteers in May and later had a part in the capture of the Confederate forts at Hatteras Inlet. In 1862 he led the land forces which joined Admiral Farragut in the capture of New Orleans, and then for eight months as military governor ruled that city with a ruthless hand. Its people nicknamed him Beast Butler, and his high-handed and not always scrupulous methods were denounced throughout the South.

Late in 1862 Butler was removed from his post at New Orleans at the instance, he always claimed, of Secretary Seward, who, it may be noted, had no use for the man and his ways. During the remainder of the war his conduct as a general was invariably attended by controversy and failure. As commander of the Department of Eastern Virginia he allowed his army to be caught at Bermuda Hundred—"bottled up" in Grant's terse phrase—and held helpless by a lesser Confederate force, and late in 1864 abandoned an attempted capture of Fort Fisher only to see it taken up and accomplished by an abler and better soldier. Grant disliked and feared him. The President, it is safe to assume, neither feared nor trusted him.

Nevertheless, if Butler is to be believed, in the spring of 1864 he was offered and refused second place on the ticket which presented Mr. Lincoln for reelection. What would have been the course of events had Butler and not Johnson succeeded to the Presidency is one of the intriguing ifs of history.

PLATE No. 104 Uncle Abe Welcomes Ben Butler, Harper's Weekly, January 17, 1863

PLATE NO. 105

The cartoon etching Lincoln and Butler as Don Quixote and Sancho Panza was drawn by Volck early in 1863 and distributed from Baltimore. It amusingly reflects Southern reaction to the relations of Mr. Lincoln with Ben Butler, who all his days sought selfish ends and was a provoker of strife and contention for those who sought to labor with him. It is doubtful if Mr. Lincoln ever respected or trusted him, for, in sympathy for their fellows and the selfless desire for service, they were as far apart as the master and man made immortal by Cervantes. The cartoon under consideration, now owned by the Maryland Historical Society, is the last of the uncollected etchings by Volck of which there is record. After the Civil War, despite his unusual gifts, he appears to have done little if any work as an artist. Instead he was for many years a practicing dentist in Baltimore, where he died in 1912 at the age of eighty-four years.

PLATE No. 105 Lincoln and Butler as Don Quixote and Sancho Panza, Etching Cartoon by Volck, 1863, Maryland Historical Society now owned by

The cartoon, by Tenniel, Scene from the American "Tempest," appeared in Punch, January 24, 1863. News of the emancipation of the slaves by Mr. Lincoln had reached England earlier in the month, and Punch, for the nonce showing good will for the Union cause, depicts the President, clad in the uniform of a Union soldier, handing a copy of his proclamation to a grinning negro, who points to a glowering Confederate in his rear and says: "You beat him nough, massa! Berry little time, I'll beat him too."

Approval of Mr. Lincoln's action by English champions of freedom for all races and conditions of men took other and more impressive forms. The Non-conformists now earnestly espoused the Northern cause, and Spurgeon, then the most popular of their preachers, made the thousands congregated in his Tabernacle pray together: "God bless and strengthen the North; give victory to their arms. Bondage and the lash can claim no sympathy from us." Richard Cobden, who had seen some striking popular movements in his time, wrote of a great meeting in Exeter Hall: "I know nothing in my political experience as striking," while in March, 1863, John Bright, addressing the trade unions of London in St. James Hall, pointed out with lofty and compelling eloquence the inner and permanent meaning for the common people of England of the contest being waged in America. "I wish you to be true to yourselves," he told his hearers. "Dynasties may fall, aristocracies may perish, privilege will vanish into the dim past; but you, your children and your children's children, will remain, and from you the English people will be continued to succeeding generations.

"You wish for the freedom of your country," he continued. "You strive for it in many ways. Do not then give the hand of fellowship to the worst foes of freedom that the world has ever seen, and do not, I beseech you, bring down a curse upon your cause which no after-penitence can ever lift from it. You will not do this. I have faith in you. Impartial history will tell that, when your statesmen were hostile or coldly neutral, when many of your rich men were corrupt, when your press—which ought to have instructed and defended—was mainly written to betray, the fate of a continent and its vast population being in peril, you clung to freedom with an unfaltering trust that God in His infinite mercy will yet make it the heritage of all His children."

The passage of the years has confirmed the force and truth of the great Quaker's vision.

PLATE No. 106 Scene from the American "Tempest," London Punch, January 24, 1863

The cartoon, Manager Lincoln, appeared in Harper's Weekly on January 31, 1863. Mr. Lincoln, standing before the lowered curtain of a theatre, thus addresses an invisible audience: "Ladies and Gentlemen, I regret to say that the Tragedy, entitled The Army of the Potomac, has been withdrawn on account of Quarrels among the leading Performers, and I have substituted three new and striking Farces or Burlesques, one, entitled *The Repulse of Vicksburg*, by the well-known popular favorite E. M. STANTON, ESQ., and the others, *The Loss of the Harriet Lane* and *The Exploits of the Alabama*—a very sweet thing in Farces, I assure you—by the Veteran Composer, GIDEON WELLES." (Unbounded Applause by the COPPERHEADS)

This caricature which appeared four weeks after the costly but, for the Union cause, successful battle of Murfreesboro or Stone's River, recalled past disasters and foreshadowed future ones. In the last days of January, 1863, the Army of the Potomac, Hooker having succeeded Burnside as its commander, was making ready for a new disappointment at Chancellorsville and for the victory at Gettysburg which was to doom the Confederacy to final and irreparable defeat. Grant had met with repulses and baffling obstacles before Vicksburg, but was to push on through five months of dogged fighting to the capture of that city, which was also to make the Mississippi an open road for Union commerce and for its warships and gunboats, and, a crippling blow, cut the Confederacy into two parts, both thereafter most difficult to defend.

The Harriet Lane was sunk and her commander killed when, early in January, 1863, the Confederates under Magruder, recaptured Galveston and raised for a few days the Union blockade of that city. In this same month of January the Confederate raider Alabama was building in a British shipyard. Later she was allowed to sail through the negligence of British officials, and ably commanded by the Confederate, Raphael Semmes, but manned in the main by British seamen and gunners, between August, 1863, and June, 1864, cruising in the South Atlantic and Indian oceans, she captured sixty-two Northern vessels, and burned all but five of them at sea, causing direct losses in excess of $19,000,000.

But in June, 1864, the Union Kearsarge, under Captain John A. Winslow, which had long trailed the Alabama ran her to cover in the harbor of Cherbourg. A Sunday morning duel between the two vessels off Cherbourg, a duel witnessed by thousands of spectators on the French shore five miles away, ended after ninety minutes in the sinking of the Alabama, with forty of its crew, while the Kearsarge emerged practically unharmed, and with only one of its men to die of his wounds. Eight years later, as the result of an agreement to arbitrate, an international tribunal decreed—a ruling promptly observed—that Great Britain should pay the United States fifteen and a half million dollars for the losses caused by the Alabama.

PLATE No. 107   Manager Lincoln, Harper's Weekly, January 31, 1863

PLATE NO. 108

The cartoon, Lincoln's Dream, or There is a Good Time Coming, appeared in Frank Leslie's Illustrated Newspaper, on February 14, 1863, and is one of the most arresting of the early caricatures of William Newman, for some years a member of the Leslie group of artists, whose fondness for detail has in a later time often caused his work to be confused with that of Thomas Nast. Mr. Lincoln, asleep on a couch decorated with stars, dreams of the generals whom he has beheaded for their short-comings—McDowell, McClellan and Burnside—and of the members of his cabinet, Seward, Welles and Stanton, and of Halleck, his chief adviser in military affairs, who with bowed heads and blanched faces, now await the axe.

Each of the President's victims, past and prospective, demand a word. McClellan after Antietam never again commanded a Union army, but McDowell, at first Bull Run clearly the victim of the haste or tardiness of other men, proved in subordinate posts a capable if not always fortunate commander. Burnside, as recorded elsewhere, left the army in 1865 to fill important posts in business and public life. When he died in 1881 he had been for seven years a member of the Federal Senate from Rhode Island, and one of the writer's memories of a youthful first visit to Washington re-calls a glimpse of Burnside and his fellow senator Anthony strolling arm-in-arm and in leisurely fashion through the streets of the capital.

Secretaries Seward and Welles remained members of Mr. Lincoln's cabinet until his death, and then served his successor, Johnson, but if we are to believe Mrs. Lincoln, who held Seward in slight regard, the latter would have been replaced early in Mr. Lincoln's second term by another and a different man. Secretary Stanton also continued a member of Lincoln's cabinet until death put a period to its history, and after that for stormy months served Johnson in like capacity; but the measure of loyalty he gave to his great chief and the latter's plans for the restoration of the Union is still sharply debated by students of the Civil War period.

Perhaps none of his appointments to high station brought Mr. Lincoln so large a measure of vexation and disappointment as did his naming of Halleck as general in chief of the Union Army in August, 1862 with the understanding that he was to re-main in Washington as adviser to the President and secretary of war. Halleck was a West Point graduate turned lawyer who had written in an authoritative way on military art and science; but he shunned responsibility, and in no long time gave way to Grant. He, nevertheless, did not return to the law, in which, prior to the conflict between the sections, he had achieved substantial success, but ended his days in the army. He was commander of the Department of the South, with headquarters at Louisville, when he died in January, 1872.

PLATE No. 108 Lincoln's Dream, or There is a Good Time Coming, Frank Leslie's Illustrated Newspaper, February 14, 1863

The cartoon, by Morgan, Yankee Pancakes, appeared in London Fun on February 21, 1863. Secretary Chase is shown frying pancakes, each of which adds to the National Debt, while Mr. Lincoln, watching the process remarks: "Go it, Chase. Keep the pot a biling." All of which may have amused the readers of Fun, but the fact remains that the chief concern of the head of the federal treasury both before and after February, 1863, was not making new debts, but the adoption by Congress of a banking system and a stable currency which would assure the prompt payment of old ones.

Indeed it was on February 25, 1863, four days after the cartoon under consideration appeared in Fun, that Congress by a close vote in both houses, in response to the earnest and continuous urging of Secretary Chase, passed the first national bank act. But this legislation did not accomplish the ends the secretary had in mind. Accordingly after much labor and persuasion, a second and broader bill was passed by Congress on June 3, 1864, and under its provisions before the year's end nearly six hundred national banks came into being, vested with authority to issue bank notes in an amount equal to ninety per cent of the value of the government bonds owned by them.

Not, however, until March 3, 1865, long after Chase had ceased to be secretary, did the national bank system assume final form. Then Congress levied a tax of ten per cent on the notes issued by State banks and as a result of this levy there soon came into being 1600 banks subject to national supervision and having a note circulation of more than four hundred million dollars. Chief credit for the planning and adoption of a national bank system belongs to Chase. By assuring the acceptance of United States securities as a basis for notes he created a continuing demand for government bonds, and at the same time brought into being a currency at once uniform and safe. It is, therefore, only just to accord Salmon P. Chase, who kept a great cause a solvent one, a high place among the little group of able and devoted men who saved the Union.

PLATE No. 109   Yankee Pancakes, Matt Morgan, in London Fun, February 21, 1863

The cartoon, The Bad Bird and the Mudsill, appeared in Frank Leslie's Illustrated Newspaper on February 21, 1863. A tree beside a swamp holds a nest labeled Richmond from which Jefferson Davis, taking the form of a bird of ill omen, gazes with satisfaction at a helpless Lincoln stalled in the mud below him. "Ah, you may laugh," retorts Mr. Lincoln, "but if it weren't for this Mud I would soon fetch you out of that."

It is proper to recall that mud at times was a delaying and disastrous factor in the operations both of the Army of the Potomac and of the Union armies in the West. When Burnside, after his costly defeat at Fredericksburg, planned late in January, 1863, another attack on Lee, rain which quickly became sleet, turned the roads north of the Rappahannock into mud in which horses, mules and wagons sank and stuck. On January 25, Hooker succeeded Burnside as head of the Army of the Potomac, but for weeks rain and mud kept the new commander company, and not until May was Hooker ready for Chancellorsville, where, in addition to his defeat by Lee, he lost for good and all his reputation as a general who could compel success. Meanwhile before Vicksburg, Grant, dogged and determined, had found ways to master General Mud, and again at the close of 1863, when, before a river route was opened, ten thousand animals in a few weeks perished hauling rations through mud and rain to the pent-up garrison in Chattanooga, Grant again triumphed over untoward conditions, confirming the remark of one of his men: "Where that man goes things always seem to git." Early in the new year the Army of the Potomac found in him the general who was to lead it to dearly bought but final victory.

It may also be noted that the word mudsill, of which Leslie's artist made use in the present instance, was a favorite epithet with Southern speakers and journals in the years immediately preceding Fort Sumter. In a speech in the Senate in 1858 James H. Hammond, then an arrogant member of that body from South Carolina, declared that labor constituted the "mudsill of society," contending that "the manual laborers and operatives" of the North were "essentially slaves." He drew one distinction between the slaves of the South and the free laborers of the North. "Our slaves," he said, "are hired for life and are well compensated; yours are hired by the day, and not cared for."

One of those who replied to Hammond on the floor of the Senate was Henry Wilson, of Massachusetts, who had begun life as a village cobbler, and whose heated and moving defence of Northern labor quickly won for his speech a place in school readers. In the writer's boyhood it was still a favorite recitation of a Friday afternoon with the hopeful pupils of country schools.

Ah! you may laugh — but if it wern't for this Mud I'd soon fetch you out of that.

RICHMOND

PLATE No. 110   The Bad Bird and the Mudsill, Frank Leslie's Illustrated Newspaper, February 21, 1863

The cartoon, The Coming Men, appeared in Frank Leslie's Illustrated Newspaper on February 28, 1863. There was wit and some truth in this drawing which, with a disturbed Welles and Stanton in the background, shows the great and only Barnum presenting Tom Thumb and Commodore Nutt to Mr. Lincoln, the moral being enforced by this bit of dialogue:

Barnum—"Mr. President, since your military and naval heroes don't seem to get on, try mine."

Lincoln—"Well, I will do it to oblige you, Friend Phineas, but I think mine are the smallest."

Tom Thumb was the nickname of Charles S. Stratton, a Bridgeport midget, who put money into the purse of Barnum, when it stood in sore need of replenishment. Born in 1810, a year after Mr. Lincoln, Barnum has been aptly described as a Yankee brother of Colonel Mulberry Sellers. His varied career as a showman is set forth at great length and in beguiling fashion in the sucessive editions of his autobiography in the writing of which, there is good reason to believe, he had many assistants.

Barnum's real financial success began with Tom Thumb. Nobody had seen any possibilities of profit in the midget until Barnum took him in hand in November, 1842, and began an association which made both men famous in Europe as well as America. When the drawing under consideration appeared in Leslie's this association, which included many crossings of the Atlantic, still continued, and Tom Thumb headed a group of dwarfs who were then appearing at Barnum's Museum in New York. Indeed, the story of the rivalry of Tom Thumb and Commodore Nutt for the hand of the handsome midget, Lavinia Warren, and her eventual marriage to the former fills diverting pages in Barnum's autobiography.

Lavinia Warren's sister Minnie, who also belonged to Barnum's midget quartet, later married another dwarf known as Major Newell. They were still in their honeymoon days when, along with Mr. and Mrs. Tom Thumb, they came to the writer's home town in Pennsylvania and appearing at the only hall in the place, gave him one of the memorable experiences of his boyhood. Among cherished and touching reminders of that boyhood is a newspaper clipping announcing the death of Minnie Warren a year after her marriage. When she was about to become a mother the doctors told her that to save her life they would have to destroy her baby. The tiny image of womanhood pleaded with them not to touch her baby; if the child could not live, she wished to die with it. The notice of her death tells how this wish had tragic fulfilment.

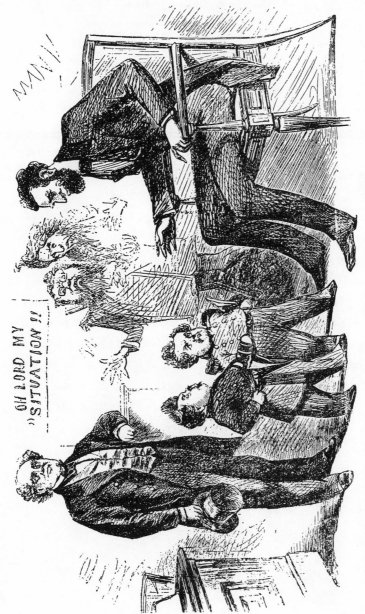

PLATE No. 111   The Coming Men, Frank Leslie's Illustrated Newspaper, February 28, 1863

PLATE NO. 112

The cartoon by Tenniel The Great "Cannon Game" appeared in London Punch on May 9, 1863—the eve, one recalls with a smile, of the decisive Union victories at Gettysburg and Vicksburg. The same issue of Punch contained an article entitled The Great American Billiard Match which, without design on the part of its author, but with a like blindness to the events of the morrow, affords an appropriate footnote to Tenniel's drawing. "Considerable excitement," we are told, "has been caused in sporting circles by this long protracted match . . . no one now dare prophesy when it will be finished. As for old Abe Lincoln, the champion player of the North, his backers, we believe, are as confident as ever that he is the best man, although at times his play has not appeared to prove it. There is no doubt that he has more strength at his command, but strength is of small use without knowing how to use it. Abe Lincoln may have skill, but he has not shown much of it, and certainly he more than once has shown himself outgeneraled.

"How the game will end we won't pretend to prophesy. There are plenty of good judges, who still appear inclined to bet in favor of the South and longish odds are offered that the game will be a drawn one. Abe's attempt to pot the niggers some put down as a foul stroke, but whether foul or not, it added little to his score. Upon the whole we think his play has not been much admired, although his backers have been vehement in superlatively praising it. There is more sympathy for the South, as being the weaker side—a fact which Jeff's supporters indignantly deny, and which certainly the North has not done much as yet toward proving. Without ourselves inclining one way or the other, we may express a neutral hope that the best player may win; and we certainly shall echo the desire of all who watch the game if we add that the sooner it is now played out the better."

PLATE No. 112   The Great "Cannon Game" London Punch, May 9, 1863

PLATE NO. 113

This cartoon by Matt Morgan, Honest Abe's Rudder, appeared in London Fun on May 9, 1863. It depicts Mr. Lincoln as a bulldog speeding away from danger, with divers tin cans labeled Ironside and Monitor tied to his tail, and remarking as he flies: "I'm being licked tarnation well! Only 'cos my rudder won't act." When Morgan drew this caricature news had just reached London of the sharp disappointment which preceded the Union victories of July, 1863—the thwarted naval attempt to capture Charleston on April 7 of that year. A fleet of iron-clads which had been carefully fitted out at heavy cost and of which great things were expected by the navy department and the Northern public, failed under Admiral Du Pont to reduce Fort Sumter and retake Charleston.

This reverse was due to Du Pont and a goodly number of the officers under him, who shared some part of their chief's timidity; but it was not wholly a surprise to Secretary Welles, a shrewd judge of men, who had already taken an imposing pretender's measure. "Received Admiral Du Pont's report with those of his officers," Welles recorded in his famous Diary on April 20. "The document is not such as I should have expected from him a short time ago, but matters of late prevent me from feeling any real disappointment. The tone and views of the sub-report have the ring or want of ring, of the admiral in command. I am by now no means confident that we are acting wisely in expending so much strength and effort on Charleston, a place of no strategic importance; but it is lamentable to witness the tone, language, absence of vitality and vigor, and want of zeal among so many of the best officers of the service. I cannot be mistaken as to the source and cause."

Ten days later Secretary Welles confided to his diary another acid estimate of Du Pont. "I fear," ran this second entry, "he can be no longer useful in his present command, and I am mortified and vexed that I did not earlier detect his vanity and weakness. They have lost us the opportunity to take Charleston, which a man of more daring energy would have improved. All Du Pont's letters show . . . that he went into the the fight with a predetermined conviction it would not be a success. . . . It is evident that he has no taste for rough, close fighting."

Du Pont without delay was shorn of the greater part of his fleet, and did not again hold responsible command at sea. Sumter, a mass of ruins, remained in Confederate hands until February, 1865, when the advance of Sherman's army compelled the evacuation of Charleston. By a tragic coincidence the Union flag was again raised over Sumter with impressive ceremonies on the last day of Mr. Lincoln's life—April 14, 1865.

PLATE No. 113 Honest Abe's Rudder, Matt Morgan in London Fun, May 9, 1863

The cartoon, Mr. Lincoln Dismisses John Bull, appeared in Harper's Weekly on May 16, 1863. The President is shown leaning on a fifteen-inch cannon and confronting John Bull in plaintive mood. "Hi want my cotton bought at fi' pence a pound," pleads the Briton. "Don't know anything about it, my dear sir," is the curt reply. "Your friends, the rebels, are burning all the cotton they find and I confiscate the rest. Good morning, John." And there is abundant proof that the state of public opinion in England in May, 1863, remained, as it had been since April, 1861, a mixed one. For a variety of reasons a majority of the aristocracy and upper middle class hoped for the failure of the Northern cause, while, with few exceptions, that portion of the British middle class engaged in commerce and manufacture earnestly desired an early end of the war so that they could secure sorely needed cotton and resume the sale of manufactured goods to America.

The Saturday Review of London declared the cotton famine the saddest thing that had befallen England for many a year. "There have been gloomy times enough before this," wrote one of the editors of that journal. "We have seen Ireland perishing from actual starvation, and England half ruined from commercial distress. But in the worst of our calamities there has seldom been so pitiable a sight as the manufacturing districts present at this moment." Nevertheless the mill workers of the North of England, who suffered most from the lack of cotton, were unfaltering supporters of the Union cause. They were told that their troubles would cease only when the war ended, but aware that "the struggle was one of freedom against slavery they resisted all attempts to excite them to a demonstration against its continuance. They saw their families in want even to the prospect of lacking bread, yet they desired the North to fight out the contest."

And at last the sun broke through the clouds. After Gettysburg and Vicksburg few Englishmen longer looked for or desired the success of the South. Instead, there was evident a growing measure of good-will rather than of hostility to the North, and a $15,000,000 loan, underwritten in Paris and based on cotton as security, which at first was well received in the end sold at a heavy discount or found no takers. Liberty, after troubled and uncertain days, was justified of her children.

PLATE No. 114 Mr. Lincoln Dismisses John Bull, Harper's Weekly, May 16, 1863

The cartoon, Brooms! Brooms! appeared in Vanity Fair, on May 23, 1863, when that lively journal's brief career was drawing to a close. It had for a sub-title: "Showing how each of the Press Gang thinks he has a new broom that will sweep up the rebellion quicker than the old one—General Hooker; but the President doesn't seem to see it." With Bryant, Bennett, Greeley, Raymond, and two other editors crowding an ante-room, an attendant announces to Mr. Lincoln: "New York Editors outside with new brooms to offer," but the President, hands in pockets and a collection of brooms at his right, makes curt reply: "Hang their new brooms—the old one is good enough yet."

Thus were heralded the early departure of General Hooker from command of the Army of the Potomac and the turning of another leaf in the story of Mr. Lincoln's long and thus far fruitless search for a general who could assure success for the Union cause. Late in January, 1863, Burnside at his own request was relieved of duty and General Joseph E. Hooker ordered to the command of the Army of the Potomac. A day later Mr. Lincoln supplemented the order to Hooker with a letter to the latter in which he gave shining proof of his patient yet resolute common sense and his rare understanding of wayward and impatient spirits.

For a time all went well. Hooker was an excellent organizer, and during February, March and April labored with splendid results to restore order and confidence to a beaten army. "I have never known men to change from a condition of the lowest depression to that of a healthy fighting state in so short a time," wrote General Couch, who was soon to become one of Hooker's severest critics. However, when late in April Hooker took the offensive Lee and Jackson out-generaled him at Chancellorsville, and when Lee in turn invaded Maryland and Pennsylvania, Hooker failed not only to check his advance but, having given his army a rest of some weeks, clearly unequal to the task ahead of him, made such captious demands on the authorities at Washington that when, in a fit of petulance, he asked by wire to be relieved of his position, Mr. Lincoln acted with decision and dispatch.

Thus at an early hour in the morning of June 28 an officer sent from Washington arrived at Fredericksburg and the headquarters of General George G. Meade, commander of the Fifth Corps of the Army of the Potomac then trailing Lee into Pennsylvania, and delivered to that officer an order relieving Hooker and appointing Meade in his place. "As a soldier," Meade wired Washington a few hours later, "I obey the order placing me in command of this army, and to the utmost of my ability will execute it." And within a week, aided by able lieutenants, he kept his promise by defeating Lee at Gettysburg.

PLATE No. 115 Brooms! Brooms! Vanity Fair, May 23, 1863

The cartoon, Mr. Lincoln Calling for Volunteers, appeared in what was to prove the last issue of Vanity Fair on July 4, 1863. The President is depicted holding aloft the flag while from every quarter volunteers are responding to his summons to service. Returning Fourths of July, it is proper to record, played an appropriate part in the life of Abraham Lincoln. Perhaps the first of which he had remembrance occurred in his seventh year when Thomas and Nancy Lincoln were making their home on Knob Creek, a few miles from the town of Hodgenville in what is now Larue County, Kentucky. Then for fourteen years, during which Mr. Lincoln grew from youth to manhood, each returning Fourth of July found him a resident of Spencer County, Indiana. There in the summer of 1826, a youth of seventeen, he learned that at last, in the white winter of age, the halting summons had come to John Adams and Thomas Jefferson, and that on the Fourth of July in that year two builders of the republic had passed from life.

The Fourth of July in 1831 found young Lincoln just returned from a second flatboat trip to New Orleans and arresting contacts with slavery and about to begin the six years' residence at New Salem which was for him to take the place both of academy and college. The Fourth of July in 1832 found him serving as a captain of volunteers in the Black Hawk war. On its return in 1837, a member of the bar, he had begun his residence of a quarter of a century in Springfield.

On the Fourth of July in 1860 Mr. Lincoln had been for several weeks the Republican nominee for President. "We know not what a day may bring forth," he wrote that day to his old friend A. G. Henry now residing in Oregon, "but today it looks as though the Chicago ticket will be elected." The Chicago ticket was elected, and on the Fourth of July in 1861 President Lincoln sent to Congress the first of the masterly messages that were to prove that the future of the Union was in the keeping of a man of strength and wisdom.

Mr. Lincoln, recently nominated for a second term, passed a portion of his last Fourth of July in 1864, which was also the day on which Congress was to adjourn, at the Capitol signing bills. One bill, which he did not sign clearly indicated what his course would have been on right means to restore the Union had he been permitted to serve out his second term. The measure in question cleared the way for the return of the Southern States to the Union, but made no provision for negro suffrage in any form, whereas it was known that Mr. Lincoln believed that the right to vote should be accorded to intelligent Negroes, especially to those who had served in the Union Army. "They would probably help in some trying time to come," he wrote Michael Hahn of Louisiana on March 13, 1864, "to keep the jewel of liberty within the family of freedom." Pregnant words full of meaning for the men of a later time!

PLATE No. 116   Mr. Lincoln Calling for Volunteers, Vanity Fair, July 4, 1863

[233]

PLATE NO. 117

The cartoon by Morgan, Tricks vs. Honours, appeared in London Fun on July 18, 1863. Mr. Lincoln is shown, with the cards he had planned to play dropping from nerveless hands, cringing before a Confederate soldier, whose belabeled jacket proclaims his part in the actions at Bull Run, Fredericksburg, Fort Hudson and Charleston, and who remarks with self-evident complacency: "Oh! don't give up, Abe; try another trick. I don't mind. I hold all the honours."

News then on the way from America to England was about to give the lie to an unfriendly conception of Mr. Lincoln's plight. We do not know when the ill-natured drawing under consideration left the artist's hands, but when it was published Meade had met and defeated Lee at Gettysburg; Pemberton had surrendered to Grant at Vicksburg, and the outcome of the contest between North and South was no longer in doubt. And so on the morning of the Fourth of July this word went out to the people of the North: "The President announces to the country that news from the Army of the Potomac, up to 1 p. m. of the 3rd, is such to cover the army with the highest honor, to promise a great success to the cause of the Union, and to claim the condolence of all for the many gallant fallen, and that for this he especially desires that on this day, He, whose will, not ours, should ever be done, be everywhere remembered and reverenced with profoundest gratitude."

At a later hour of a fateful Fourth of July word came that Vicksburg had surrendered to Grant, and on July 15 the President by proclamation set aside "a day for national thanksgiving, praise and prayer," but not before he had dispatched a characteristic letter to the silent soldier who by deeds not words was hewing his way to chief command of the Union armies. "I do not remember that you and I ever met personally," Mr. Lincoln wrote General Grant on July 13. "I write this now as a grateful acknowledgment of the almost inestimable service you have done the country. I wish to say a word further. When you first reached the vicinity of Vicksburg, I thought you should do what you finally did—march the troops across the neck, run the batteries with the transports, and thus go below; and I never had any faith, except a general hope that you knew better than I, that the Yazoo Pass expedition and the like could succeed. When you got below and took Port Gibson, Grand Gulf, and vicinity I thought you should go down the river and join General Banks, and when you turned northward, east of the Big Black, I feared it was a mistake. I now wish to make the personal acknowledgment that you were right and I was wrong."

When the sequel proved Mr. Lincoln in error either in thought or forecast, he rarely if ever failed to make prompt and frank admission of the fact.

PLATE No. 117 Tricks vs. Honours, Matt Morgan in London Fun, July 18, 1865

The drawing Worship of the North, put out at Baltimore in the summer of 1863, had a late place in the series of plates already referred to, engraved on copper by Adalbert John Volck, who through their underground circulation, became the most widely known Southern cartoonist of the Civil War period. It was not included in the portfolio of Confederate Etchings issued by Volck under misleading and clandestine conditions in 1864, and is now owned by the Whitney Museum of Art in New York. It is overcrowded with detail, a familiar and confusing practise with the artist who drew it, but its satire is all-inclusive and of a savage and unsparing sort. And it gives evidence of the state of mind that held sway both North and South in the summer of 1863, clearly the most trying year of the bitter struggle between the sections, when casualty lists mounted, and there were no manifest signs of the end.

As a result of the long debates of the slavery issue ending in armed and costly conflict the people of the South had come to regard those of the North as the victims of errant and evil forces, and Volck made stern use of this belief in drawing the caricature under consideration. In its center stands an altar which, with Puritanism as its foundation-stone, is built up of Negro Worship, Spirit Rapping, Free Love, Witch Burning, Socialism, Atheism and Rationalism. Atop this altar, bound and helpless lies the nation's youth about to be offered as a needless and reluctant sacrifice. Lincoln with the head of a clown sits at the right of the altar and at the left Henry Ward Beecher clutches the sacrificial knife, while near at hand Charles Sumner bears a torch and Horace Greeley guards a censer.

In the middle foreground kneels Benjamin F. Butler, the Union general most detested in the South, his knapsack stuffed with loot, while at the extreme right Harriet Beecher Stowe also kneels with a copy of Uncle Tom's Cabin as her support. To the rear of the altar the Chicago Platform is crowned by a Negro on the way to sainthood, and this is flanked by a statue of John Brown, labeled "Pray for us." Grouped to the right of Lincoln in varying mood are Seward, Stanton and other members of his cabinet, along with Generals Scott and Halleck. Last of all a group of greedy contractors march away to new fields of loot and profit with the banner More Blood at their head.

Surely a motley and unwholesome assembly, but be it remembered that the month in which Volck's drawing was given to the world was the month also of Vicksburg and Gettysburg, token and promise of the peace that was to follow war.

PLATE No. 118   Worship of the North, Engraving by Volck, July, 186,

The cartoon, "Rowdy" Notions of Emancipation appeared in London Punch on August 8, 1863, prompted by the Draft Riots which in the previous month dismayed and disgraced America's chief city.

At the left of the cartoon Mr. Lincoln stands with folded arms gazing gloomily into space, while in the foreground white ruffians assail unoffending Negroes and beat or stamp them into insensibility. All of which failed to place where it properly belonged the blame for a wanton and tragic breach of law and order. A federal draft law which went into effect on July 1, 1863, unwisely exempted from its operation all who should pay into the federal treasury the sum of $300. The discontent, thus produced was fomented in New York City by pothouse politicians, who declared the draft unconstitutional, and that it bore with unjust severity on the poor man.

Many vowed resistance and, borrowing courage from the fact that the city, to repel Lee's invasion of Pennsylvania, had been practically denuded of troops, made plans to attack the drafting officers. No trouble occurred on the first day of the draft, July 11, but on the second, Monday, July 13, an organized mob attacked and wrecked the provost marshal's office at the corner of Third Avenue and Forty-sixth Street. Then inspired by animosity towards the Negro race, the rioters raided a colored orphan asylum in Fifth Avenue above Forty-third Street and burned it to the ground.

A cry now went up to kill the police, and soon 500 rioters were marching down Broadway bent upon the destruction of police headquarters in Mulberry Street, but 200 policemen, ably led, barred their advance and a short and decisive fight cleared Broadway, except the rioters who with shattered pates strewed the pavement. Routed at one point, however, the mob rallied at another, and a few hours later, under cover of darkness, a determined attempt was made to sack and burn the office of the Tribune in Park Row. Again the police drove the rioters from the field with a heavy loss in killed and wounded; but it was now clear that the police force was too few in numbers to restore order, and all of the New York regiments were ordered to repair to the city.

During Tuesday and Wednesday, July 14 and 15, the mob continued to fire and loot property, and to maltreat and murder Negroes, but on the evening of the latter day the returning regiments began to arrive in the city. Bullets and bayonets now took the place of policemen's clubs, and on Friday, July 17, the mayor was able to announce the complete restoration of order. It became clear ere long that a lamentable affair had been mainly due to the timidity and hesitation of Horatio Seymour, the Democratic governor of New York, who sought to conciliate instead of sternly suppressing the rioters, and so permitted them to get out of bounds. When Seymour sought reelection as governor in 1864 he was beaten by a decisive majority.

Plate No. 119 "Rowdy" Notions of Emancipation, London Punch, August 8, 1863

The cartoon, The President's Order No. 262, appeared in Harper's Weekly on August 15, 1863. It was prompted by an emerging phase of the war which for a time provoked angry discussion both North and South. The Union arming of the blacks and their enrolment as soldiers, begun late in July, 1862, instantly aroused fear and hostility in the South, and, following Mr. Lincoln's two emancipation proclamations, the Confederate Congress passed a joint resolution, approved by Jefferson Davis on May 1, 1863, which prescribed that white officers of Negro Union soldiers —Negro regiments were by this time springing into full organization in many places—"shall, if captured, be put to death or be otherwise punished at the discretion of the court," by which was meant a military court attached to the army or corps making the capture.

Doubtless this law would have been promptly and summarily executed by the Confederate authorities had not the Washington administration adopted without delay an effective policy of retaliation. That policy took form in the following order issued by President Lincoln on July 30, 1863:

"It is the duty of every government to give protection to its citizens of whatever class, color or condition, and especially to those who are duly organized as soldiers in the public service. The law of nations and the usages and customs of war, as carried on by civilized powers, permit no distinction as to color in the treatment of prisoners of war as public enemies. To sell or enslave any captured person on account of his color, and for no offense against the laws of war, is a relapse into barbarism and a crime against the civilization of the age.

"The Government of the United States will give the same protection to all its soldiers, and if the enemy shall sell or enslave any one because of his color the offense shall be punished by retaliation upon the enemy's prisoners in our possession.

"It is therefore ordered that for every soldier of the United States killed in violation of the laws of war a rebel soldier shall be executed; and for every one enslaved by the enemy or sold into slavery, a rebel soldier shall be placed at hard labor on the public works and continued at such labor until the other shall be released and receive the treatment due to a prisoner of war."

This order was made up of "words with the bark on," and the Confederate authorities, despite the barbarous course they had officially proclaimed, did not fail to give careful heed to them. A few captured blacks were imprisoned, as hostages for whom an equal number of Confederate soldiers were ordered into confinement, by General Halleck, but in the end the death penalty was not inflicted on any of them.

PLATE NO. 120   The President's Order No. 262, Harper's Weekly, August 15, 1863

The cartoon, Brutus and Caesar drawn by Tenniel, appeared in London Punch on August 15, 1863. Mr. Lincoln as Brutus, reading a jest book in his tent at night, is confronted by a gigantic negro, the ghost of Caesar. "Wall, now! Do tell. Who's you?" exclaims the startled Brutus. "I am dy ebil genus, Massa Linking," is the reply. "Dis child am awful impressional."

Contrast with the contemptuous spirit reflected in Tenniel's drawing the account given by Frederick Douglass of his first meeting and talk with Mr. Lincoln about the time that the drawing appeared in Punch. It was in the summer of 1863 that Douglass, born a slave but long the most eminent representative of his race, called on the President to urge that if the black man was to do a soldier's duty then the government must assure him all the rights of a soldier. "I was never more quickly or more completely put at ease in the presence of a great man than in that of Abraham Lincoln," Douglass recorded in later years. "I at once felt myself in the presence of an honest man—one whom I could love, honor and trust without reserve or doubt.

"Mr. Lincoln listened with patience to all I had to say. He admitted the justice of my demand for the promotion of colored soldiers for good conduct in the field, but on the matter of retaliation he differed from me entirely. It was a terrible remedy, and one which it was difficult to apply. 'Once begun,' said he, 'I do not know where such a measure would stop.' If he could get hold of persons who were guilty of killing colored prisoners in cold blood he could easily retaliate, but the thought of hanging men for a crime perpetrated by others was revolting to his feelings. In all this I saw the tender heart of the man rather than the stern commander in chief of the American army and navy, and, while I could not agree with him, I could but respect his humane spirit."

So ended the first talk of Frederick Douglass with Abraham Lincoln. That the white man earnestly pondered what the colored man said to him became manifest when on July 30, 1863, the President issued the retaliatory order of which an account has been given in another place. Douglass had other meetings with Mr. Lincoln before the war's end, meetings which bred in the former slave growing and grateful regard for the President's absolute freedom from prejudice of class or condition. "He was the only man of distinction I ever met," wrote Douglass in old age, "who never reminded me by word or manner of my color."

PLATE No. 121 Brutus and Caesar, London Punch, August 15, 1863.

The cartoon, The Naughty Boy Gotham, Who Would Not Take the Draft, appeared in Frank Leslie's Illustrated Newspaper on August 29, 1863, set off by this plea from Mammy Lincoln: "There now, you bad boy, acting that way, when your little sister Penn takes hers like a baby." Naughty Boy Gotham from his high chair angrily spurns the contents of a bowl labeled Draft while in his rear a small girl, Philadelphia, accepts without protest the orders of its enforcers.

An ever growing need for fighting men was, almost from the first, one of Mr. Lincoln's most serious problems, and it became clear as time went on that volunteering and State action would not suffice to replenish the Union armies. Accordingly, early in February, 1863, a bill was introduced in the Senate which after long and angry debate, passed both branches of Congress, and on March 3, 1863, by approval of the President, became a law. It provided that, with certain exceptions set forth in detail, "all able-bodied male citizens and all persons of foreign birth who had declared their intentions to become citizens, between the ages of twenty and forty-five, should constitite the national forces," and the President was empowered to call them forth by draft.

Colonel James B. Fry, an officer of exceptional capacity for the task in hand, was made provost marshal general, being also charged with the entire work of recruiting volunteers. Thus was assured unity of action in the raising of troops. Enrolments began late in May, and were carried on with steadily increasing efficiency, and such complete success, that when in April, 1865, Mr. Lincoln was assassinated and recruiting ceased, there were a million soldiers in the field, while the national forces not called out totalled an additional two and a quarter million men. And in only one of our great centers of population, as pointed out in another place, was there serious opposition to the government's efforts to fill its depleted armies.

On January 1, 1863, Horatio Seymour, a Democrat, succeeded Edward D. Morgan, Republican, as governor of New York. Seymour regarded the conscription act as "a violation of the supreme constitutional law," and his failure to support it, a support earnestly invited by Mr. Lincoln, more than any other factor, led to the Draft Riots in New York City which in July caused the death or injury of more than a thousand unoffending men, women and children and a widespread destruction of property. Be it noted in conclusion that so long as Seymour remained governor he continued to wage war on the conscription act and the officers charged with its enforcement, but in November, 1864, the voters of New York retired him to private life. During the remainder of the war, Reuben E. Fenton, who succeeded him as governor, gave earnest and loyal support to the Lincoln administration.

PLATE No. 122   The Naughty Boy Gotham, Who Would Not Take the Draft,
Frank Leslie's Illustrated Newspaper, August 29, 1863

PLATE NO. 123

The cartoon The Sowers by Morgan appeared in London Fun on October 17, 1863. Mr. Lincoln in the role of a reckless maker of debts and taxes is represented as exclaiming: "Go it, Seward! Sow anything! We shall have a term of luck soon, and the next President will reap—Eh! Chase?" Thus cynical expression was given to the belief held by many in England that Mr. Lincoln was a desperate gambler who had only a divided people behind him. We know now that such was not the case.

Four days before Morgan's cartoon appeared in Fun John Brough, a stalwart War Democrat opposing the Copperhead Vallandigham, was elected governor of Ohio by a majority of over 101,000 votes. On the same day as the election in Ohio, Curtin of Pennsylvania, one of the most resolute and compelling of the war governors, was reelected by a substantial majority. Three weeks later, the voters in the November States registered in an unmistakable way their support of the Union cause. Massachusetts again chose Andrew as governor by 41,000 majority. The other Northern States, New Jersey excepted, voted with the Union Party which also carried Maryland, Kentucky and Delaware. "The success of the anti-slavery party and its steady increasing strength," wrote John L. Motley, a forecaster of vision and accuracy, "make it a mathematical certainty that, however the tide of battle may ebb and flow with varying results, the progress of the war is steadily in one direction. The peculiar institution will be washed away, and with it the only possible dissolvent of the Union."

"The war was never more popular than at this moment," wrote John Sherman to his soldier brother four weeks after the cartoon under consideration appeared in Fun; and at the same time James Russell Lowell was preparing for the North American Review a long review of the first three years of conflict entitled The President's Policy in which he measured with remarkable accuracy the forces behind Mr. Lincoln. "It was wise in Mr. Lincoln," Lowell wrote, "to leave the shaping of his policy to events. In this country, where the rough and ready understanding of the people is sure, at last, to be the controlling power, a profound common sense is the best genius for statemanship. Hitherto the wisdom of the President's measures has been justified by the fact that they have always resulted in more firmly uniting public opinion. If Mr. Lincoln continues to act with the firmness and prudence which have hitherto distinguished him, we think he has little to fear from the efforts of the opposition."

Mr. Lincoln read Lowell's long article and was grateful for its carefully measured praise. "I claim not to have controlled events," he wrote a little later to A. G. Hodges, "but confess, plainly, that events have controlled me." And this modest self-estimate has become the verdict of history.

PLATE No. 123   The Sowers, Matt Morgan in London Fun, October 17, 1863

PLATE NO. 124

The cartoon Extremes Meet appeared in London Punch on October 24, 1863. The good-will shown by Russia for the Union, when it stood without other friends among the nations, from the first was warmly resented by the ruling class of England, and British ill-will found characteristic expression in the present drawing. The Polish insurrection was then in progress, and the American President and the Russian Czar were depicted triumphantly clasping hands in the foreground of an arresting picture of rapine and desolation. The effect sought by the artist is made clear in the appended dialogue:

> Abe: Imperial son of Nicholas the Great,
> We air in the same fix I calculate,
> You with your Poles, with Southern rebels I,
> Who spurn my rule and my revenge defy.

> Alex: Vengeance is mine, old man; see where it falls,
> Behold your hearths laid waste, and ruined walls,
> Your gibbets, where the struggling patriot hangs,
> Whilst my brave myrmidons enjoy his pangs.

Russia displayed friendship for the Union, despite the fear entertained in high circles in St. Petersburg that its cause was a losing one. "Your situation is getting worse and worse," Prince Gortschakoff said to Bayard Taylor in late October, 1862; "the chances of preserving the Union are growing more and more desperate . . . Can you find no basis of arrangement before your strength is so exhausted that you must lose for many years to come your position in the world?" But Russia's lively concern for the welfare of the Union took form in deeds as well as words. A Russian fleet of war vessels arriving in New York City in September, 1863, was given an enthusiastic popular and official welcome, and when it visited Washington, the President being ill, marked attention was shown its admiral and officers by Secretary Seward, this "to reflect the cordiality and friendship which the nation cherishes toward Russia." It was widely believed that the fleet had been sent to American waters to help the United States in case of war with France or Great Britain. There was no tangible basis for this belief, but four years later, as will be noted in another place, it stilled opposition to the purchase by the United States of what is now the Territory of Alaska.

PLATE NO. 124   Extremes Meet, London Punch, October 24, 1863

The cartoon, "Holding a Candle to the xxxxxx" Much the Same Thing, appeared in London Punch on November 7, 1863. Again offering proof of how the tacit alliance between Russia and the United States grated on the sensibilities of certain high-placed Britons, the artist sought to move the multitude to laughter by depicting the President as Mephistopheles saluting the Russian bear. Mr. Lincoln was the victim of many forms of abuse both at home and abroad, but the writer fails to recall any other instance in which he was portrayed in Satan's livery. It stands to Tenniel's credit that not he but another was responsible for this vicious drawing.

Mr. Lincoln had been two years in his grave when the friendship between the United States and Russia had unexpected and surprising issue. For upward of a century Russia had held by right of discovery the vast stretch of North America now known as Alaska. This territory had never been brought under direct rule of the imperial government, but for the better part of seventy years its affairs had been directed by a monoply known as the Russian-American Company. The charter of this concern, which had sublet some of its privileges to the Hudson Bay Company, expired in 1861, and renewal was delayed while the imperial government pondered whether, instead of taking such action, it should make its American possessions the basis of a colonial system or sell them at a fair price to some friendly power.

The third alternative was finally decided upon by the czar's government, and in March, 1867, Stoeckle, the Russian minister at Washington and Secretary Seward began negotiations for purchase by the United States. A price of $7,200,000 was shortly agreed upon between them; this was promptly accepted by the authorities at St. Petersburg, and in a single night session, on March 29 a treaty of purchase took final form. In the forenoon of March 30 the President sent this treaty to the Senate, where it was adopted practically without debate, only two senators voting against it. Formal transfer of the purchase, to which Seward gave the name Alaska, occurred on October 11, 1867.

And so 577,396 square miles of land became United States territory because Russia wished to sell, and because a majority of the members of the Senate believed that in 1863 she had been ready to go to war with France or Britain in our behalf. Republics are not always ungrateful.

PLATE No. 125   "Holding a Candle to the xxxxxx" (Much the Same Thing), London Punch, November 7, 1863

The cartoon by Matt Morgan, The Yankee Guy Fawkes, appeared in London Fun on November 7, 1863. A Punch artist had just given Mr. Lincoln the garb and intent of the devil; now the youthful Morgan, prompted by the return of a holiday always welcomed by English boys, and in less ruthless mood, portrays him as a rampant Guy Fawkes who, as he shouts: "I'll warn yer. Your old Constitution won't do U. S." consigns to the flames an effigy of Washington. The effigy has Charter of American Laws—Geo. Washington inscribed on its breast, while documents labeled Suspension, Emancipation and the Draft add fuel to the bonfire that is destroying it.

Mr. Lincoln in his efforts to restore the Union had to resort with misgiving to many harsh measures, but no doubt the one he adopted with the greatest reluctance, after patient weighing of ways and means, was a proclamation, suspending in certain cases the writ of habeas corpus, issued on September 24, 1862, two days after the edict of emancipation was given to the world. It made "discouraging enlistment," and "any disloyal practice" violations of law; ordered that those guilty of such offences, along with those who gave "aid and comfort to the rebels" should be subject to trial and punishment by courts martial or military commissions," and for persons arrested on these charges suspended the writ of habeas corpus.

Prompted by military necessity this act was by many regarded as a usurpation of power. Democrats of a militant sort promptly denounced it as the act of a despot, but their protests did not for long have any shaping effect on public opinion. That "infringements of the bill of rights," writes James Ford Rhodes, "were not actively resisted, is explicable only by the confidence the people had in Abraham Lincoln. That he had assumed unwarranted powers might be true; but that he had done this with regret, that he had in his own loyal and unselfish nature a check to the excessive use of absolute power, was then almost as clear to his friends and opponents as it is now to the student of his character and acts. Indeed, there was a real majority of the people, who impatient of the law's delay, gave the President in the exercise of these extraordinary powers their faithful and earnest though unexpressed support."

Be it noted in closing that the story of Guy Fawkes and of his frustrated plan to blow up the Houses of Parliament and King James the First on November 5, 1605 is a familiar one. In England for the better part of three centuries on November 5, Guy Fawkes' Day, effigies of the conspirator were burned in all parts of the land as part of an annual celebration of the deliverance of Parliament. Guy Fawkes' Day is now observed only by the juvenile population of England, but there are frequent references to its customs in English literature, notably in the third chapter of The Return of the Native by Hardy.

PLATE No. 126   The Yankee Guy Fawkes, London Fun, November 7, 1863

The cartoon by Tenniel, Neutrality, appeared in London Punch on November 14, 1863. Here again the selfish disregard of some Britons for the puissant issues underlying the war between the States is again in evidence. A seated John Bull is shown, calmly enjoying his pipe and morning paper, while President Lincoln and Jefferson Davis, clad as old women, stand one on either side of him, engaged in this angry dialogue:

Lincoln, as Mrs. North—"How about the Alabama, you wicked old man?"

Davis, as Mrs. South—"Where's my rams? Take back your precious consuls—there!"

British neutrality in November, 1863, so far as it affected the Union cause, was of a sort that in the end was to afford John Bull little reason for the complacent mood in which Tenniel pictures him. The Confederate cruiser Alabama, built, equipped and coaled at Liverpool, was permitted to sail from that post on July 29, 1862, despite vigorous protests and efforts on the part of our minister in London to prevent it, and before its destruction by the Kearsarge off the French coast in mid-June, 1864, looted and sank many million dollars worth of American shipping. Not a few Englishmen refused to condone the ravages of the Alabama, and their anger found impressive expression in April, 1863, at a great meeting held in Manchester "to protest against the building and fitting-out of piratical ships in support of the Southern Slaveholders' Confederacy."

The principal speaker at this meeting was Goldwin Smith, then a professor at Oxford, and never did that champion of justice deliver an address that in after years gave him a fuller measure of satisfaction. "The duties of nations toward each other," he declared, "are not bound by the technical rules of law. They are as wide as the rules of morality and honor; and if in our dealings with America we violate the rules of morality and honor, we must abide the consequences of wrong doing, though our lawyers may advise us that we are secure. No nation ever inflicted upon another a more flagrant or maddening wrong. No nation with English blood in its veins has ever borne such a wrong without resentment. Built and equipped in a British port, manned by British seamen, with the English flag flying, the Alabama went forth to cruise from an English port against the commerce of our allies. That is the substantial grievance of the American government, and no technicalities can make it other than a heinous wrong."

When ten years later the British government paid without dispute the fifteen and a half million award of the Alabama Claims Tribunal it afforded tacit yet ample confession that Goldwin Smith's protest in 1863 had been a needed and righteous one.

PLATE No. 127 Neutrality, London Punch, November 14, 1863

PLATE NO. 128

The cartoon Drawing Things to a Head appeared in Harper's Weekly on November 23, 1863. The editor of that journal who had come to regard the success of the Union cause as no longer in doubt, makes Mr. Lincoln, ensconced in a snug apothecary shop and watched from the opposite side of the street by Napoleon and John Bull, remark to Secretary Seward, who is represented as an errand boy with a basket of Russian salve on his arm: "Mild applications of Russian salve for our friends over the way, and heavy doses and plenty of it for our Southern friend." When this cartoon appeared the battles of Gettysburg and Vicksburg had been fought and won and Grant had bested Bragg at Chattanooga. News of the thrilling conflict last named reached the people of the North on the fourth Thursday of November, and gave them their first genuine Thanksgiving since the fall of Sumter. There was no longer threat of foreign interference, but on all sides proof of the waning fortunes of the Southern cause. Mr. Lincoln, despite the heavy load he was carrying, could face the future with confident heart.

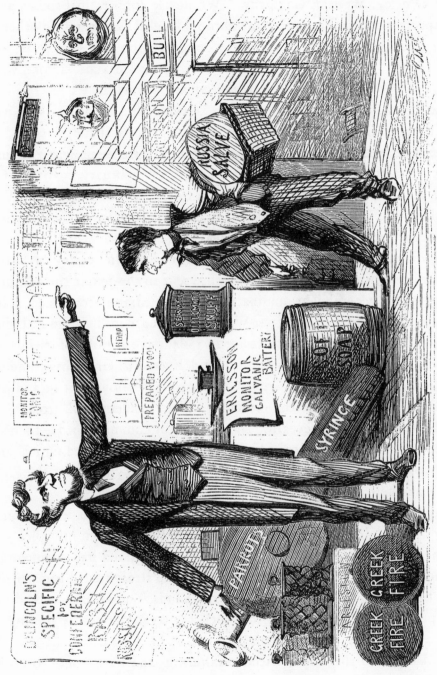

PLATE No. 128 Drawing Things to a Head, Harper's Weekly, November 28, 1863

The cartoon, Mr. Lincoln Finds a Broom to His Liking appeared in Frank Leslie's Illustrated Newspaper on March 7, 1864. A seated Lincoln, in a room adorned with the sign of Greeley, Weed & Company, "Wholesale Jobbers in Brooms and other Stocks" inspects with manifest approval a broom labeled Grant, while other brooms bearing the names of Pope, McClellan and Hooker, all the worse for wear, strew the floor behind him. "In a military point of view, thank Heaven!" wrote Motley, in the last days of December, 1863, "the 'coming man,' for whom we have so long been waiting, seems really to have come." To the President and his advisers, as well as to Motley, and other observers, Vicksburg and Chattanooga at long last had made it clear that Grant, with his record of battles fought and won, was the man who should command the Union armies. Accordingly on February 29, 1864, Congress revived the grade of lieutenant general, and gave the President authority "to place the General, whom he should so appoint, in command of the armies of the United States under his direction and during his pleasure."

This legislation promised welcome relief to Mr. Lincoln, weary of bearing the whole burden of military affairs, and he at once sent to the Senate the nomination of Grant as lieutenant general. The nomination was immediately confirmed, and Grant, then at Nashville, ordered to report at Washington. Late in life John P. Usher, who was Mr. Lincoln's secretary of the interior in 1864, gave a group of friends a revealing account of how on March 9 the President delivered to Grant his commission as lieutenant general "Mr. Lincoln," runs Usher's story, "thought it fit and proper to convene the cabinet to witness the ceremony. The President took from his table a scroll tin case, and opened it revealing the parchment commission. He then searched the table for what proved to be his address to General Grant," and which concluded with these words: 'The loyal people of the nation look to you, under the Providence of God, to lead their armies to victory.'

"Whereupon General Grant took from his vest pocket a paper containing his response to the President. He had read probably half of it when his voice gave out. Evidently he had not contemplated the effort of reading, and had commenced without inflating his lungs. But when his voice failed he straightened himself up in his fullest and best form, took the paper in both hands, one at each end, drew it up within proper reading distance and, commencing again at the beginning, read it through in a full strong voice. It seemed to me, as he did so, that he was thinking to himself; 'I can read this paper without faltering, and I am going to do it.' And he did."

Two weeks later Grant began the operations which were to end in Lee's surrender at Appomattox.

PLATE No. 129   Mr. Lincoln Finds a Broom to His Liking, Frank Leslie's Illustrated Newspaper, March 6, 1864

The cartoon, Just So! Fremont and Cochrane Call on Mr. Lincoln appeared in Harper's Weekly on June 18, 1864. It recalls a much debated, but, as the sequel proved, minor incident of Mr. Lincoln's second contest for the Presidency. John Charles Fremont, a picturesque figure honored far beyond his deserts, failed of election in 1856 when the first Republican nominee for President. He failed again in 1861, under conditions which proved his innate weakness of character, when entrusted by Mr. Lincoln with command of the Union forces in Missouri. Relieved of that command Fremont's career thereafter was in the main that of an angry and disappointed mischief-maker.

Thus early in 1864 he joined eagerly in the efforts of certain disgruntled Republican leaders to prevent the reelection of Mr. Lincoln and when on the last day of May a mass convention of some four hundred delegates—although an attendance of thousands had been anticipated by its projectors—was held for that purpose in Cleveland he promptly accepted its call to head a third party movement. Mr. Lincoln, however, refused to regard with misgiving the Cleveland gathering.

Events quickly proved that there was sound excuse for Mr. Lincoln's good humored contempt for the plotting of his enemies. On June 7 a National Union Convention met at Baltimore and accorded him a practically unanimous renomination, the votes of all the delegates except those of Missouri being recorded in his favor. The weeks that followed, however, brought losses to the Army of the Potomac under Grant and intense gloom both to the fighting forces and to the country at large. Thus, when the Democratic National Convention met at Chicago on August 29 it nominated McClellan for President on a platform that declared the war a failure . And during those gloomy days Thurlow Weed, a shrewd appraiser of popular opinion, wrote Secretary Seward that "the people are wild for peace," and that Mr. Lincoln's "reelection is an impossibility."

But there followed a sudden and complete change of sentiment in favor of the Union cause and its leader. On August 5, Farragut, lashed to the rigging of his flagship, fought and won the great battle of Mobile Bay; a few weeks later the Western army under Sherman captured Atlanta, and on September 3, the President asked the people when they gathered in their churches the following Sunday, to make "devout acknowledgment to the Supreme Being" for the Union victories. And "on the Sunday appointed by the President, the people, with one accord, thanked God and took courage."

Thereafter doubt was no longer entertained by the discerning as to the result of the election in November.

PLATE No. 130   Just So! Fremont and Cochrane Call on Mr. Lincoln, Harper's Weekly, June 18, 1864

[261]

PLATE NO. 131

The cartoon, The Hardest Shell Yet: Jeff Davis' breakfast spoilt by a shot from Baltimore, appeared in Frank Leslie's Illustrated Newspaper on July 2, 1864. There is no clue to the identity of the artist by whom it was drawn, but there is little doubt of the state of mind in which Mr. Davis received the news of Mr. Lincoln's renomination, and there is abundant evidence of the grim condition of affairs which then faced the Confederate leader. "The rebels have now in their ranks their last man," wrote Grant to Washburn in the letter cited in another place. "The little boys and old men are guarding prisoners, guarding railroad bridges, and forming a good part of their garrisons for entrenched positions. A man lost by them cannot be replaced. They have robbed the cradle and the grave equally to get their present force. Besides what they lose in frequent skirmishes and battles, they are now losing, from desertion and other causes, at least one regiment per day. . . . Their only hope now is a divided North. . . . I have no doubt but the enemy are exceedingly anxious to hold out until after the Presidential election. They have many hopes from its effects. They hope a counter-revolution; they hope the election of the Peace candidate. In fact, like Micawber, they hope for something to 'turn up.'"

General Grant saw clearly into the future. The something hoped for by Mr. Davis and his associates did not turn up. Mr. Lincoln was not only renominated, but he was also reelected, proving that at long last the people of the North were united in the resolve to win. Thomas destroyed Hood's army at Nashville; Sherman marched from Atlanta to Savannah and thence northward to and through the Carolinas, while with hammer blows the Union forces reduced and beat into helplessness the Army of Northern Virginia, so that on April 9, 1865, Lee's surrender to Grant at Appomattox brought the end of the war and the restoration of the Union.

PLATE NO. 131   The Hardest Shell Yet, Frank Leslie's Illustrated Weekly, July 2, 1864

PLATE NO. 132

The cartoon The Rail Splitter at Work Repairing the Union, drawn by Baker and put out by Currier and Ives in July, 1865, supplies a suggestive footnote to the work of the Union National Convention which in the preceding month had chosen Abraham Lincoln and Andrew Johnson as its candidates for President and Vice President. Johnson, reverting to his old trade of tailor, his modest means of livelihood when he began an unusual career in State and national politics, is shown uneasily seated on a huge globe, bearing on its face a disrupted map of the United States, which Mr. Lincoln, also reverting to early activities, is trying to move with one of the rails he split in his youth. "Take it quietly Uncle Abe, and I will draw it closer than ever," says Johnson, a pair of shears dangling in front of him, and Mr. Lincoln makes reply: "A few more stitches, Andy, and the good old Union will be mended."

All of which recalls what, as the sequel proved, was the weightiest act of Mr. Lincoln's last year of life—his decision, made known to a few trusted friends on the eve of the Baltimore convention of June, 1864, that Andrew Johnson and not Hannibal Hamblin should be its nominee for Vice President. Chauncey M. Depew, then New York's secretary of state, and a rising man in political affairs, learned of the President's wishes from Secretary Seward when on the eve of the convention he and William H. Robertson, a now half-forgotten but then influential Republican leader, dined with that gentleman; and in old age Mr. Depew delighted to tell of his own and his friend's part in what followed at Baltimore.

Mr. Seward, Depew relates, "eulogized Andrew Johnson of Tennessee, and gave a glowing description of the courage and patriotism with which Johnson, at the risk of his life, had advocated the cause of the Union and kept his State partially loyal. 'You can quote me to the delegates,' he said to us, 'and they will believe I express the opinion of the President. While he wishes to take no part in the nomination for Vice President, yet he favors Mr. Johnson.' When we arrived at the convention this interview with Mr. Seward made us a center of interest, and at once changed the current of opinion which before that had been for Daniel S. Dickinson. It was finally left to the New York delegation. The meeting of the delegates from New York was a stormy one. Mr. Dickinson had many warm friends, and the State pride to have a Vice-President was in his favor. Upon the final vote Johnson had one majority. The decision of New York was accepted by the convention, and he was nominated for Vice President."

Recalling Johnson's stormy days as President one wonders what would have been the course of history had Daniel S. Dickinson in his stead succeeded Abraham Lincoln on April 15, 1865.

PLATE No. 132   The Rail Splitter at Work Repairing the Union, Currier and Ives, July, 1864

The cartoon, Mike, Remove the Salmon, drawn by Bellew, appeared in Harper's Weekly on July 16, 1864. Drawing and title suggest the state of mind in which late in the preceding month Mr. Lincoln had accepted the resignation of Salmon P. Chase as Secretary of the Treasury. It is the verdict of history that Chase had many elements of greatness, but that an over-weening ambition to be President distorted his vision and brought him at times dangerously near to disloyalty to a wise and forbearing chief.

During the opening weeks of 1864 Mr. Chase was an active and hopeful, if perhaps unseemly seeker for the Republican nomination for President to succeed Mr. Lincoln, but his prospects faded when his own State of Ohio endorsed the candidacy of Mr. Lincoln, and somewhat ungraciously he withdrew from the field. Thereafter those who accorded due weight to his capacity for public service, but looked askance at ambitions which seemed to them out of place, hoped he would continue a member of the cabinet until a great task was fully accomplished. However, early in June, 1864, differences arose between Mr. Chase and the senators from New York as to the filling of certain Treasury posts in that State, vacant or about to become vacant. The Secretary contended that his preferences should govern in the matter, and when Mr. Lincoln failed to agree without dissent to this point of view for a fifth time tendered his resignation. Much to his surprise, Mr. Lincoln who had grown weary of their recurring differences, promptly accepted this resignation and named William P. Fessenden as his successor. Thus, in a manner that at first confused him Mr. Chase's official life came to an end.

But not Mr. Lincoln's high regard for the rare moral and intellectual qualities of his late secretary of the treasury. "Chase," he told a friend, "is about one and a half times bigger than any other man that I ever knew." And he had been only a few weeks in private life when Mr. Lincoln informed the Senate Committee on Finance that he should appoint him Chief Justice if there were a vacancy. Such a vacancy occurred when aged Chief Justice Taney died in October, 1864, and in due course Mr. Lincoln, in the face of protests from leading Republicans the country over, carried out the purpose he had announced in July. On December 6 he sent to the Senate the nomination of Chase for the chief justiceship, and the nomination was confirmed by that body without reference to committee.

For eight and a half years Chase filled with dignity and ability the exalted post Marshall and Taney had held before him, but, as Mr. Lincoln had anticipated, he continued to covet and strive for the Presidency, and, twice refused a sought-for nomination by the Democratic party, died in May, 1873, a disappointed and embittered man.

PLATE NO. 133 "Mike, Remove the Salmon," Harper's Weekly, July 16, 1864

PLATE NO. 134

This poster cartoon to which was given the title The True Issue, or "That's What's the Matter," was distributed by Currier and Ives in August, 1864, shortly after the Democratic National Convention at Chicago, putting aside Horatio Seymour, had made General George B. McClellan its nominee for President. Lincoln and Davis are depicted trying to rend in twain a map of the United States, while McClellan intervenes to prevent threatened destruction.

It was on this plea that the late commander of the Army of the Potomac based his hope of victory at the polls, and at the outset so strong was its appeal to short-sighted advocates of peace that for a time, as noted elsewhere, Mr. Lincoln's defeat appeared to be a foregone conclusion. "This morning, as for some days past," he wrote on August 23, on the eve of the Democratic Convention which was to nominate McClellan and declare war a failure, and while waiting a session of his Cabinet, "it seems exceedingly probable that this Administration will not be reelected. Then it will be my duty to so cooperate with the President-elect as to save the Union between the election and the inauguration; as he will have secured his election on such grounds that he cannot possibly save it afterward."

Mr. Lincoln's secretaries record that "he then folded and pasted the sheet in such manner that its contents could not be read, and as the Cabinet came together he handed this paper to each member successively requesting them to write their names across the back of it. Under date of November 11, 1864, John Hay recorded the rest of the story in his diary. "At the meeting of the Cabinet today," wrote Hay, "the President took out a paper from his desk and said: 'Gentlemen, do you remember last summer I asked you all to sign your names to the back of a paper of which I did not show you the inside? This is it.' He then read this memorandum (and), said: 'You will remember that this was written six days before the Chicago convention. I resolved in the case of the election of General McClellan, being certain that he would be the candidate, that I would see him and talk matters over with him. I would say, "General, the election has demonstrated that you are stronger, have more influence with the American people than I. Now let us together, you with your influence, and I with the executive power of the Government, try to save the country. You raise as many troops as you possibly can for this final trial, and I will devote my energies to assist and finish the war.'

" 'And the General,' said Seward, 'would have answered you, "Yes, Yes," and the next day, when you saw him again and pressed these views upon him he would have said, "Yes, yes," and so on forever, and would have done nothing at all.'

" 'At least', said Lincoln, 'I should have done my duty and have stood clear before my own conscience.' "

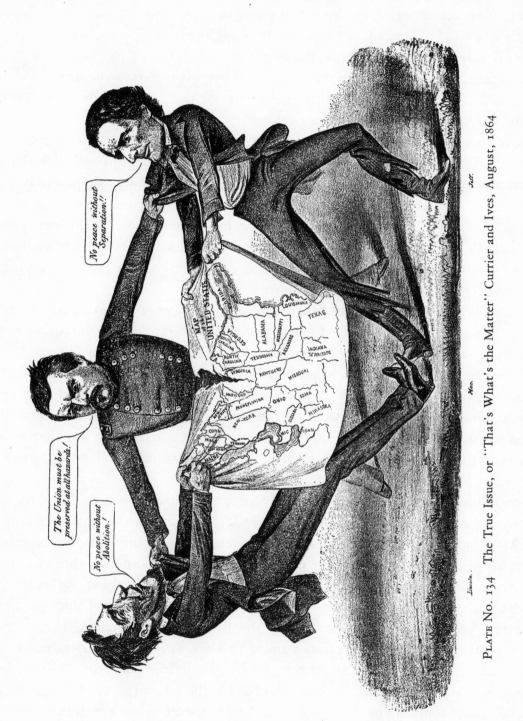

PLATE No. 134   The True Issue, or "That's What's the Matter" Currier and Ives, August, 1864

The cartoon, Niagara Doves, drawn by Morgan, appeared in London Fun on August 13, 1864, accompanied by this bit of dialogue:

Uncle Abe:—"Say Greeley, what 'ave you brought back?"

Dove Greeley:—"Narey nothink, nunkey!"

The artist depicts Mr. Lincoln with a look of disgust receiving the doves which are the only visible fruit of the ill-starred efforts of the editor of the New York Tribune to restore peace between the sections.

One of the nondescript individuals who found it an easy matter to establish intimate relations with Mr. Greeley was an adventurer who called himself "William Cornell Jewett of Colorado" and whose capacity for mischief was limited only by opportunities to exercise it. He claimed that he enjoyed the confidence of eminent statesmen both North and South, and early in July, 1864, he wrote Greeley from Niagara Falls that he was an accredited intermediary from the Confederate authorities to make propositions for peace. The next day Jewett sent a telegram saying: "Will you come here? Parties have full power."

The credulous Greeley accepted practically without reserve these flamboyant assurances. He sent Jewett's letter and telegram with a perfervid message of his own to Mr. Lincoln, and urged the President to take prompt action upon them.

"If you can find any person anywhere," Mr. Lincoln, who had no faith in Jewett, wrote in reply, "professing to have any proposition of Jefferson Davis in writing, for peace, embracing the restoration of the Union, and abandonment of slavery, whatever else it embraces, say to him he may come to me with you, and that if he really brings such a proposition he shall at the least have safe conduct . . . to the point where you shall have met him."

There followed a comedy of pretence and misrepresentation in which the editor of the Tribune was made to play a sorry part. On July 16, after further correspondence with Mr. Lincoln, who supplied him with a safe conduct to and from Washington for the alleged representatives of the Confederacy, Greeley journeyed somewhat reluctantly to Niagara Falls, there to discover that Jewett was without authority of any sort nor had the accredited Confederate agents in Canada—Clay, Thompson and Holcombe—power to speak for or commit the Richmond government. In the end the disgruntled editor returned empty-handed to New York, perversely refusing to admit that, trusting to shady characters, he had committed an error. Instead, he charged that Mr. Lincoln had been responsible for the farcical issue of his journey to Canada; nor could he be persuaded to advocate the President's reelection until, according to one of his biographers, being always an eager seeker for office, he was promised the post of postmaster general after March 4, 1865.

PLATE NO. 135   Niagara Doves, London Fun, August 13, 1864

The poster cartoon, A Little Game of Bagatelle, between Old Abe and Little Mac was put out by Currier and Ives in September, 1864. It furnishes proof that men could find causes for laughter in a political contest charged with issues so weighty that their acceptance or rejection was certain to shape through the long future the destiny of a nation. Mr. Lincoln with a cue labeled Baltimore is depicted winning a game the progress of which is watched with interest by half a dozen of the men then active and prominent in public affairs.

Clement Laird Vallandigham, seated at the end of the board, perhaps the one wholly self-satisfied member of a remarkable group, makes this biting comment on McClellan's part in the issue of the game: "There is nothing the matter with the CUE or the PLATFORM; you had the first red and didn't make anything; now he'll win the game."

A man of imposing presence, sonorous speech and unfailing self-righteousness, Vallandigham had ability and courage, but also a gift for taking the wrong side of a great question, and so lives in history as the one man in the North, who, when the Union was for the moment rent in twain, sought to give the South aid of a peculiarly provoking kind. By turns editor and lawyer, equally belligerent in the use of tongue and pen, he was for five years following 1858 an Ohio member of the popular branch of Congress, but, an extreme pro-slavery man, he opposed Mr. Lincoln's policy as President, and in 1862 lost his seat in that body. Thereafter he was the stormy petrel of a stormy period. Treasonable utterances caused his arrest by the Union military authorities in 1863, and Mr. Lincoln, who knew how to disarm an enemy, shrewdly ordered him banished to the Confederacy.

Vallandigham, however, had only a perfunctory welcome in the South, and in no long time made his way first to Bermuda and thence to Canada where he remained until the end of the war. Nevertheless, the Washington authorities, alert to his capacity for mischief in the house of his friends, in August, 1864, permitted him to attend the Democratic National Convention at Chicago, where as chairman of the platform committee he drafted and forced the passage of a resolution declaring the war a failure, and by so doing assured the defeat at the polls of the convention's nominee for President. At the same election, having been chosen during his exile the Democratic candidate for governor of Ohio, he likewise was beaten by an unprecedented majority. Reverses did not dismay him, and in 1868 he again met defeat as a candidate for senator from Ohio. He died three years later an embittered and disappointed man.

PLATE No. 136   A Little Game of Bagatelle, between Old Abe and Little Mac, Currier and Ives, September, 1864

PLATE NO. 137

The poster cartoon, Running the "Machine" like Plate 136 was put out by Currier and Ives in September, 1864, when the contest which resulted in the reelection of Mr. Lincoln was nearing its most heated stage. It borrows its title from a letter, which its author no doubt lived to regret, written on the morrow of Bull Run by Edwin M. Stanton to James Buchanan, whom in the closing days of the latter's administration, he had served for a brief period as attorney general. "The imbecility of this Administration," Stanton then in private life wrote his former chief, "culminated in that catastrophe (Bull Run), and irretrievable misfortune and national disgrace never to be forgotten are to be added to the ruin of all peaceful pursuits and national bankruptcy, as the result of Mr. Lincoln's 'running the machine' for five months."

The cartoon for which Stanton unconsciously supplied a title is poorly drawn, but has vigor and directness. A total of $432,000,000 in greenbacks were issued between 1861 and 1865, and the artist depicts Secretary Fessenden with anxious face turning the crank of Chase's Patent Greenback Mill, while two war contractors greedily view the fruits of his labors, and Stanton, now a devoted lieutenant of Mr. Lincoln, receives with joy the news of some minor Union victory. The President at Stanton's left laughs at one of his own stories and at the other side of the table long-bearded Gideon Welles, former Connecticut editor, offers proof of his alleged ineptitude as secretary of the navy.

Secretary Fessenden, however, is the outstanding figure in the artist's drawing and recalls the interesting manner in which he succeeded Chase as head of the Treasury. When Chase resigned in a pet in the summer of 1864 it was feared in some quarters that it would be difficult for the President to adequately fill his place, but Mr. Lincoln promptly and with characteristic adroitness solved the problem thus presented to him. William Pitt Fessenden of Maine, a man of great ability, wholly devoted to the Union cause, was then chairman of the Senate committee on finance, and Mr. Lincoln instantly concluded that he was the right man to succeed Chase. Wedding action to decision the President at once sent his nomination to the Senate, and when Fessenden called to recommend Hugh McCulloch for the place he was told that his own nomination had been sent to the Senate. "You must withdraw it. I cannot accept," he told the President. "If you decline," said Mr. Lincoln, "you must do it in open day, for I shall not recall the nomination." At the end of a long talk Fessenden, alert to the call of duty, reluctantly accepted; the Senate without dissent confirmed his nomination, and he filled a difficult post with patient wisdom until March, 1865, when he felt that he could with propriety resign it to Hugh McCulloch and return to his old seat in the Senate there to end his days.

PLATE No. 137   Running the "Machine," Currier and Ives, September, 1864

The poster cartoon The Grave of the Union, or Major Jack Downing's Dream, "Drawn by Zeke" was issued by a New York publisher in September, 1864. Jack Downing was the comic Yankee character created a generation earlier by Seba Smith, and his dream as visualized by "Zeke" clearly reflects the crimes with which the Lincoln Administration was charged by its numerous and noisy critics. Treason open or covert is always an ugly thing with which to deal, and in its suppression the President and his advisers were early compelled, much against their will, to resort to measures which, on the face of things, appeared to violate traditions of civil rights long held in reverence in all parts of the Anglo-Saxon world.

Thus on the last day of July, 1861, the first war Congress, which did much else to assure it an honorable place in history, passed a sweeping Conspiracies Act, and less than a year later placed on the statute books a rigid law for the suppression of treason. Attorney General Bates and the Federal courts, however, were slow in enforcing these acts, and in September, 1862, Mr. Lincoln, resorting to more direct measures, issued a proclamation "directing trial by court martial or military commissions of all persons who impeded the draft, discouraged enlistments or committed other disloyal acts." Under this proclamation a great number, variously estimated at from 20,000 to 38,000 persons, were arrested, denied the right of habeas corpus and held in jail until brought to trial.

Horatio Seymour and other Democratic leaders, among them Clement L. Vallandigham, whose story is set forth in another place, denounced this summary policy as a fatal blow to liberty and the Constitution, but in retort Mr. Lincoln asked this cogent and telling question: "Must I shoot a simple-minded soldier boy who deserts, while I must not touch a hair of the wily agitator who induces him to desert?" And it is the pondered judgment of history that the course adopted by the President and his advisers by rigorously stamping out treason in high places helped in a substantial and effective way to restore the Union.

In September, 1864, however, "Zeke" was moved to picture Mr. Lincoln and a group made up of Greeley, Sumner, Chase, Welles and Seward burying the Constitution, Free Speech, the Habeas Corpus and the Union, while Henry Ward Beecher lifts his voice in prayer, and Secretary Stanton gazes with approval on the four War Democrats—Cochrane, Butler, Meagher and Dickinson—who are drawing the car in which he is seated, at the same time remarking: "My jackasses had a load, but they pulled it through bravely." It may also be noted that this is the only Civil War cartoon time has spared us in which the pastor of Plymouth Church is shown in approving company with Mr. Lincoln.

PLATE No. 138   The Grave of the Union, or Major Jack Downing's Dream, Cartoon "Drawn by Zeke," September, 1864

PLATE NO. 139

The cartoon, Compromise With the South by Thomas Nast appeared in Harper's Weekly on September 3, 1864. It holds a place apart in the history of caricature in America for it brought to an artist then only twenty-four years of age national recognition as a master cartoonist, and it helped in a trenchant and persuasive way to make sure the reelection of Mr. Lincoln to the Presidency. As pointed out in another place in the late summer of 1864 the Republican or Union Party seemed destined to defeat at the polls in November, but when in the last days of August the Democratic National Convention assembled at Chicago it nominated McClellan for President on a platform that demanded an armistice and declared the war a failure. This implied confession of defeat, despite McClellan's protestations that if elected he would prosecute the war with vigor and resolution, caused an early and sharp change of sentiment in the North.

Millions of copies of the arresting cartoon here reproduced, "dedicated to the Chicago Convention" were circulated as campaign documents, and prompted in generous measure the searching of hearts that went on among the plain but liberty-loving men of the North, growing in depth and intensity as one week of debate and discussion followed another in the September and October of 1864. There was in very truth during this fateful period a new birth of the national spirit. At last they recognized in the man in the White House, who declared: "I do not lead; I only follow," a fit leader in uncertain times, and soon the result of the election was no longer in doubt. On October 13, with that event less than a month away, Mr. Lincoln during one of his daily visits to the war telegraph office penciled on a telegraph blank his estimate —experience had taught him never to be over-hopeful in his predictions—that in the Electoral College he would get 117 votes against 114 for McClellan. Out of 231 votes he could see himself winning by a majority of three. But when the returns came in on the night of November 8 it was found that he had received practically unanimous support in the North or 212 out of a total of 231 electoral votes.

Plate No. 139 Compromise with the South, Harper's Weekly, September 3, 1864

PLATE NO. 140

The cartoon This Reminds Me of a Little Joke appeared in Harper's Weekly on September 17, 1864, at a stage in the pending contest for the Presidency when it was becoming clear to shrewd observers that the prospects of the Democratic candidate were of a dubious sort. The artist depicts the President holding his opponent in his upturned left hand, and regarding him with good-humored indifference, a situation in keeping with the facts, for Mr. Lincoln's estimate of the creator of the Army of the Potomac, slowly and reluctantly shaped under the stress of repeated disappointment of his hopes, after four score years, has become the verdict of history.

There is little doubt that McClellan was a lover of the Union and deeply concerned for its restoration, but he was also a man of inordinate and consuming ambition, ever prone to lend an attentive ear to the counsel of evil advisers. Perhaps what Donn Piatt wrote of him in 1887, fresh from a reading of that singular book McClellan's Own Story, was close to the truth. "McClellan," he tell us, "can be summed up in a few words. He had the egotism of a weak character, that he and his friends mistook for the confidence of genius. This made him arrogant on parade and timid in the presence of a grave responsibility. He habitually magnified obstacles into impossibilities and deferred great deeds to a future that had no possibility."

In Mr. Lincoln's homely idiom "McClellan had the slows," and so he failed when he faced an abler and more alert general in the field, and he failed yet more miserably when he sought to wrest the Presidency from a greater man.

PLATE No. 140   This Reminds Me of a Little Joke, Harper's Weekly, September 17, 1864

The cartoon, Mrs. North and Her Attorney appeared in London Punch on September 24, 1864. It shows President Lincoln crouched at his desk and nervously gnawing a goose quill, while a veiled woman sitting at his side says: "You see, Mr. Lincoln, we have failed utterly in our course of action. I want peace, and so, if you cannot effect an amicable arrangement I must put the case in other hands."

A large section of British opinion had not yet taken into account the force and direction of the tide then running in Mr. Lincoln's favor in the Northern States and thus Punch, one of its mouthpieces, voiced the belief, still held by many in England, that his defeat at the approaching election was a foregone conclusion. None are so blind as those who refuse to see. A short seven weeks later Mr. Lincoln triumphed at the polls, and before another half year had run its course Lee surrendered to Grant at Appomattox.

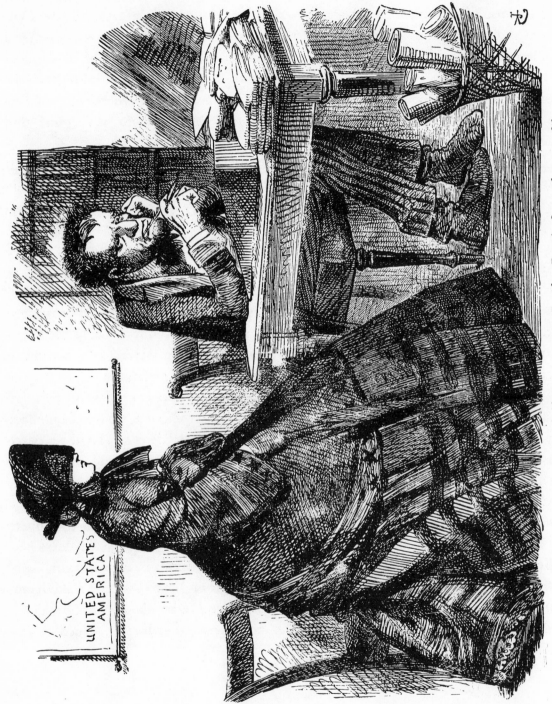

PLATE No. 141   Mrs. North and Her Attorney, London Punch, September 24, 1864

PLATE NO. 142

The poster cartoon, McClellan Tries to Ride Two Horses was put out by the campaign managers of the National Union Party late in September 1864. It was probably the first use of caricature by those responsible for the outcome of elections. McClellan is shown astride two horses, one a patient steed labeled Peace, and the other a restless charger wearing a War blanket. At his left and rear Mr. Lincoln, depicted as a clown, observes: "You tried to ride them two horses on the Peninsula for two years, Mac, but it wouldn't work." And McClellan replies in confidence: "Curse them balky horses—I can't manage the act no how. One threw me in Virginia, and the other is bound the other way."

It has been recorded elsewhere how the Democratic National Convention at Chicago had declared the war a failure and demanded a cessation of hostilities as prelude to a convention of the States assembled to secure peace by the restoration of the Federal Union. It also has been recorded how McClellan promptly put out a letter repudiating the pivotal resolution of the Democratic platform, but this protest proved unavailing and the man in the street shortly reached the decision which on August 23 Mr. Lincoln, as we know, had recorded in a secret memorandum, which the members of his Cabinet signed in reverse without being at the time informed of its contents, that in case he should not be reelected it would be his duty to help the President-elect save the Union between the election and the inauguration "as he will have secured his election on such grounds that he cannot save it afterward."

The average man, without regard for party affiliations, was not slow to perceive that there were solid reasons for Mr. Lincoln's grim prediction, and as September merged into October, signs multiplied that McClellan faced defeat. "To have 'peace on any terms,' " Grant wrote Washburne, "the South would demand the restoration of their slaves already freed; they would demand indemnity for losses sustained, and they would demand a treaty which would make the North slave hunters for the South." Meantime the platform pleas for McClellan's election put forth by Robert C. Winthrop, Horatio Seymour and speakers of like caliber and persuasiveness had telling answers in the bulletins of Union successes. "Sherman and Farragut," declared Secretary Seward in a brief speech at Washington, "have knocked the bottom out of the Chicago nominations," and less than a week later the first of Sheridan's brilliant victories in the Shenandoah Valley made new votes for Mr. Lincoln. The rest is history.

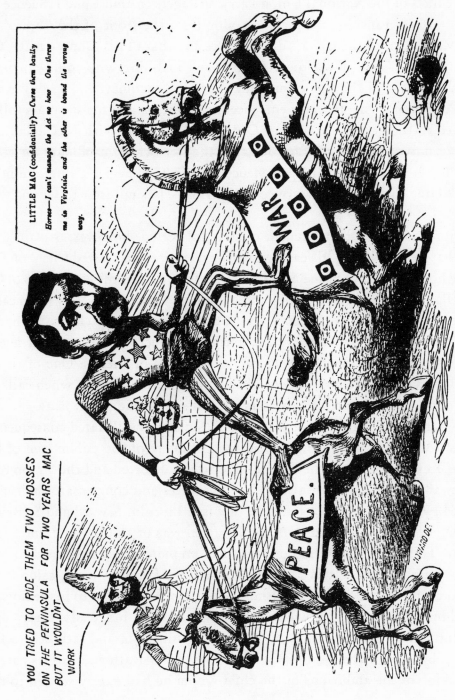

PLATE No. 142   McClellan Tries to Ride Two Horses, National Union Party Cartoon, September, 1864

The poster cartoon, Policeman Lincoln Orders McClellan Off the Capitol Grounds, was distributed in late September or early October, 1864. It represents another of the pictorial efforts of the National Union Party managers to amuse and influence doubtful voters. Officer Lincoln is depicted driving from the front of the Capitol Organ Grinder McClellan, to the latter's discomfiture and that of his running mate, George Hunt Pendleton, a man of aristocratic birth and inclining who could not have enjoyed his portrayal in the role of monkey. Born in Cincinnati and a lawyer by profession, Pendleton made an early entrance into politics, and for six years following 1857 served in the popular branch of Congress. His defeat with McClellan in 1864 was followed five years later by his defeat as the Democratic candidate for governor of Ohio, but he had the gift of persistence, and in 1879 began a single term in the Federal Senate. His last public service was performed as minister to Germany under Cleveland.

Pendleton's interest for the student of a fateful period, however, is mainly due to the fact that he was during his early years the intimate and trusted friend of Thomas M. Key, who, with a large measure of truth, has been termed the evil genius of George B. McClellan. A man of great ability and a lawyer by profession, Key at an early age was called to the bench of the Superior Court of Cincinnati, whence he had come from his native Kentucky, and, by his upright conduct and exceptional legal acumen, won the respect and confidence of a wide circle of friends. One of these was George B. McClellan, then a resident of Cincinnati, who in 1861, when called from civil life to the camp, invited Key to serve on his staff as judge advocate.

Thus began an association that was to have sinister and ill-fated consequences for McClellan. A Democrat, sharing the outlook of many of the public men of his native State, Key hoped to see the Confederate armies defeated and the Union restored to its prewar basis. He desired also to free the slaves and compensate their masters, but moved by his love for the South, he despised Lincoln, Seward and Stanton, and his contempt for the Washington Administration was of an utter and unrelenting if secret sort. This strange blending of views and prejudices Key passed on to McClellan, "who was a Democrat because he was a West Pointer," and, aside from the driving force of his own innate egotism, most of his errors prior to his removal from command by Mr. Lincoln, he owed to the counsels of his judge advocate.

Key contracted a mortal illness on the field of Antietam and returned to Cincinnati to die, but his influence on McClellan survived his death and had its part in the final wrecking of the ambitions of the chief whom he had vainly striven to make a great man.

PLATE No. 143   Policeman Lincoln Orders McClellan Off the Capitol Grounds, National Union Party
Cartoon, September, 1864

The drawing A Roland for an Oliver appeared in Frank Leslie's Illustrated Newspaper on October 3, 1864, when the Northern press was again printing rumors of covert negotiations for peace between the sections. George Nicholas Sanders, an odd and amusing busybody who before and during the war, played a noisy but barren part in events, is represented as saying to Mr. Lincoln: "Won't you accept an Olive branch for me? the emblem of Peace, you know." To which the President, who earlier in the year had been given good reason to suspect Sanders and his ways, makes scornful reply: "What! an Olive branch with Blackberries growing upon it! Never!"

Sanders was a native of Kentucky but also by innate and irrepressible inclining a citizen of the world. A man of rare personal charm, he knew how to make friends, but he was also an adept in breeding enemies, and it became his favorite boast, a boast fairly earned, that no one ever controlled him. Late in 1851 he secured direction of the Democratic Review, a moribund New York monthly and in its columns lashed out savagely in all directions at the enemies of Douglas.

The latter sought in vain to restrain Sanders; in no long time his attacks had such deadly effect on the prospects of Douglas that Andrew Johnson with grim truth termed the Illinois senator a "dead cock in the pit," and in June, 1852, the Democratic National Convention on the forty-fifth ballot chose as its nominee Franklin Pierce who triumphed at the polls over his old commander, General Winfield Scott.

The new President, who made his old friend, Nathaniel Hawthorne, consul at Liverpool, gave Sanders a recess appointment to the London consulship, and the impatient Kentuckian hurried off to his new post without waiting for its confirmation by the Senate. Inevitably and as a matter of course his London home became a meeting-place for Mazzini and other political exiles who found the British capital a safe and congenial place in which to plot the overthrow of the governments that had expelled them. Sanders devised effective if unconventional ways to aid them, and news of his activities reaching Washington the upholders of things as they are in the Senate refused to confirm his appointment.

Sanders who died in New York in 1873 passed most of his latter years in England and France. An agitator until the end of his days, during the seige of Paris he helped to man the barricades, as he had done in 1848, and by so doing quickly won a place in the councils and hearts of the French radicals who made a hero of the militant American with an irrepressible urge to shape events. A full-length biography of Sanders, slurring no phase of a flamboyant, many-sided career, would provide a most diverting as well as informing volume for students of the Civil War and the stormy period that preceded it.

PLATE No. 144   A Roland for an Oliver, Frank Leslie's Illustrated Newspaper, October 3, 1864

PLATE NO. 145

The double poster cartoon Your Plan and Mine was issued by Currier and Ives in October, 1864, a few weeks before Mr. Lincoln's reelection was to make doubly sure the freedom for the black men of the South promised two years before in the Emancipation Proclamation. Pointing its own moral it recalls in an arresting if clumsy way the doubt then growing among thoughtful men in the North as to how McClellan in case of his election would deal with the slavery question. In the left panel Jefferson Davis, bowie knife in hand but much the worse for wear, claims a kneeling negro soldier to whom McClellan holds out the olive branch. "Well, Master Fire Eater," says the Democratic candidate for President, "as you have found the war, which you have waged against the Government for the last four years, an unsuccessful experiment and are nearly used up, the Party I represent beg you to accept the 'Olive branch,' take back your Nigger, and promising that you shall do as you please in the future, with both White and Black men, earnestly entreat your return to the Union." And to this timorous gesture Davis makes characteristic reply: "I see the Olive branch and take the Nigger, and am glad to hear that you are willing to be governed once more by your Southern masters." While the kneeling black man pleads: "Why general! I am a Union soldier! I have shed my blood in defence of liberty and law, and will you give me back again to Slavery?"

The second panel shows Mr. Lincoln thrusting a bayonet at a beaten and suppliant Davis with this ultimatum: "Your unconditional submission to the Government and laws is all that I demand, and the great magnanimous NATION that I represent have no desire for revenge upon you, but they will never allow you to again enslave those who have been made free by your rebellion."

"Hold Mr. President!" Davis replies. "I surrender unconditionally and own up that the rebellion is a failure. I beg of you to let me come back into the Union and not to punish me too severely for my madness and folly."

While at the right and rear of an unrelenting Lincoln, a laughing black soldier, no longer uneasy as to the future interjects: "Ha, Ha, **Massa** Secesh, guess you won't fool time with this child any more!"

McClellan never had opportunity to prove if as President he would enforce or attempt to undo the Emancipation Proclamation for the evening of November 8, 1864, found him a badly beaten man, and on January 31, 1865, Congress adopted the measure Mr. Lincoln had most at heart, the Thirteenth Amendment to the Constitution, which, in due time ratified by three-fourths of the States, forever abolished slavery in the United States.

PLATE No. 145   Your Plan and Mine, Poster Cartoon issued by Currier and Ives, October, 1864

PLATE NO. 146

The pen drawing, the work of an unknown artist, The Commander-in-Chief Conciliates the Soldiers' Vote on the Battlefield was published in New York in October, 1864. Plainly the work of an amateur, and misleading and malicious in its origin, nevertheless, it was, perhaps the most effective of the anti-Lincoln cartoons produced during a campaign in which malice and falsehood had full sway. Mr. Lincoln had visited the battlefield of Antietam on the morrow of that conflict, and gross misrepresentations of his conduct during the visit furnished a theme for the cartoon under consideration.

Thus on September 9, 1864, the New York World, whose editor, Manton Marble, was one of Mr. Lincoln's most persistent and unrelenting critics, printed an account of an incident which it alleged had occurred on the battlefield of Antietam a few days after the fight. "While the President," ran the World article, "was driving over the field in an ambulance, accompanied by Marshal Lamon, General McClellan, and another officer, heavy details of men were engaged in the task of burying the dead. The ambulance had reached the neighborhood of the old stone bridge where the dead were piled highest, when Mr. Lincoln, suddenly slapping Marshal Lamon on the knee, exclaimed: 'Come, Lamon, give us that song about Picayune Butler. McClellan has never heard it.' 'Not now, if you please,' said General McClellan, with a shudder, 'I would prefer to hear it some other place and time.' "

A Philadelphia friend of Lamon sent the latter a copy of the World article, asking "in behalf of others, as well as myself, whether any such occurrence took place," and requesting an immediate reply. There followed an arresting but long unknown example of how Mr. Lincoln could meet a trying situation. Lamon showed the President a draft of his proposed reply to his Philadelphia correspondent. Mr. Lincoln carefully read Lamon's letter and shook his head. "I would not publish this reply," he said, "it is too belligerent in tone for so grave a matter, and you are at times too fond of a fight. Let me try my hand at it." Whereupon the President, slowly and with care, wrote out the statement he would have Lamon send to his correspondent, a statement which in admirable fashion gave the lie to the World's charges.

Upon second thought, Mr. Lincoln advised Lamon to wait a few days before mailing this statement to his friend—then other pressing matters drove it from the minds of both men, and so the admirable reply Mr. Lincoln had prepared was not made public until more than thirty years after his death, surely a record of facts deserving a place in the present chronicle.

PLATE No. 146   The Commander-in-Chief Conciliates the Soldiers' Vote on the Battlefield, Drawing by Unknown Artist, October, 1864

PLATE NO. 147

The poster cartoon, The Old Bull Dog on the Right Track, was issued by Currier and Ives in October, 1864. It was one of the first instances in which Grant furnished a theme for the caricaturists who thereafter for more than a dozen years were to find the silent soldier an appealing subject. Here he is shown in the guise of a bulldog seated on the Weldon railroad, and gazing at the crouching pack, Lee, Davis and Beauregard among them, assembled in and around a kennel in the distance labeled Richmond. "You ain't got this kennel yet, old fellow!" they tell Grant, but "I am bound to take it," is his confident prediction. At the left Candidate McClellan points to his successor and remarks to Mr. Lincoln: "Uncle Abraham, don't you think you had better call the old dog off now? I am afraid he will hurt those other dogs if he catches hold of them."

And the President, arms akimbo, makes reply: "Why, little Mac that's the same pack of curs who chased you aboard of the gunboat two years ago. They are pretty much used up by now, and I think it's best to give the old bulldog full swing to go in and finish them."

All of which recalls Wilkeson's comparison of Grant and McClellan in his Recollections of a Private. "The enlisted men," he tells us, "spent much time in comparing Grant with McClellan. The latter had many warm friends among the soldiers. He only of all the men who had commanded the Army of the Potomac was personally liked and admired by his troops. Soldiers' eyes would brighten when they talked of him. Their hard, lean, browned faces would soften and light up with affection when they spoke of him—and still it was affection only; they did not as a rule concede to him military talent. And the general opinion among them was, given Grant command of the army in 1862, and the rebellion would have been crushed that year. Asked how McClellan would have done with the army of 1864 under his command, they shrugged their shoulders and said dryly: 'Well he would have ended the war in the Wilderness—by establishing the Confederacy.' "

PLATE No. 147   The Old Bull Dog on the Right Track, Currier and Ives, October, 1864

The poster cartoon, Abraham's Dream: "Coming Events Cast Their Shadows Before" was issued by Currier and Ives in October, 1864. Lincoln's dream, disturbing uneasy slumbers, shows at the right the Goddess of Liberty driving from the White House a crestfallen President who wears a Scotch cap which an imaginative reporter made a part of his garb in his secret night journey from Harrisburg to Washington in February, 1861, and who now remarks as he speeds on his way: "This don't remind me of any joke." And at the right McClellan is shown, bag in hand, ascending the steps of and ready to occupy the White House.

If some of his friends are to be believed Mr. Lincoln now and again gave weight to and told of unusual dreams, and in late August and early September, 1864, there was fair excuse for the vision depicted in the cartoon under consideration, but while October was running its course McClellan's prospects underwent a sea change, and the observing without regard for party were not slow to predict their luckless ending. "I have seen your despatch," Mr. Lincoln wired Grant on the morning of August 17, when the Northern press was filled with criticisms of that general's campaign in Virginia, "expressing your determination not to break your hold where you are. Neither am I willing. Hold on with a bulldog grip, and chew and choke as much as possible."

This grim resolve to accomplish a desired purpose had eloquent emphasis in a speech delivered by Carl Schurz in Philadelphia on September 16. "You have heard of the people of Germany," Schurz told an applauding audience, "pouring their gold lavishly into the treasury of the United States. You have heard of a loan of a thousand millions having been offered and being now in progress of negotiation. Would these people who are standing by us so generously in our embarrassments, would they have done so if they did not trust in our ability and determination to carry through the war?"

Such a question could have only one answer, and that answer was given by the voters of the North on November 8.

PLATE No. 148   Abraham's Dream: "Coming Events Cast Their Shadows Before," Currier and Ives, October, 1864

The cartoon, The American Brothers; or How Will They Get Out of It appeared in London Punch on November 5, 1864. It pictures Mr. Lincoln and Mr. Davis bound to adjacent benches by ropes, significantly labeled "Debts." Thus Punch again voiced the impression then prevalent in certain circles in England that Mr. Lincoln's defeat at the approaching election was a foregone conclusion. Happily this impression was a mistaken one. Tenniel's cartoon was still wet from the press when Mr. Lincoln was reelected by the largest majority in the electoral college up to that time ever given to a candidate.

PLATE No. 149   The American Brothers; or, How Will They Get Out of it, London Punch, November 5, 1864

PLATE NO. 150

The poster cartoon, The Giant Majority Carrying Abe Lincoln Safely Through Troubled Waters to the White House, drawn by Frank Bellew and now in the collection of Harry MacNeill Bland of New York, was distributed by a New York publisher, shortly after the election of 1864. On the whole it was one of the most appealing cartoons which during his lifetime had Mr. Lincoln for a subject. He had in truth come "through troubled waters" to a second term as President, and the spirit, resolute but generous, with which he faced an unfinished task, found timely expression in the brief speech he made to a group of serenaders on the evening of November 10. "Now that the election is over," he asked his hearers, "may not all having a common interest reunite in a common effort to reunite our common country? For my own party I have striven and shall strive to avoid placing any obstacle in the way. So long as I have been here I have not willingly planted a thorn in any man's bosom. While . . . duly grateful, as I trust to Almighty God, for having directed my countrymen to a right conclusion as I think, for their own good, it adds nothing to my satisfaction that any other man may be disappointed or pained by the results. May I ask those who have not differed from me to join with me in this same spirit toward those who have?"

PLATE No. 150   The Giant Majority Carrying Abe Lincoln Safely Through Troubled Waters to the White House, Poster Cartoon by Frank Bellew, November, 1864

PLATE NO. 151

The cartoon, The Black Draft, drawn by Tenniel appeared in London Punch on November 19, 1864. Here Mr. Lincoln and Mr. Davis again keep company, the one at the pistol's point and the other with a rawhide forcing two frightened negroes to drink from bowls labeled "Conscription." But this satire loses part of its force when the fact is recalled that every man of color who served in the Union Army did so as a volunteer. The men of the Fifty-fourth Massachusetts—the first colored regiment of the North to enter the war—who fell with their white colonel, Robert Gould Shaw, in the gallant but hopeless assault on Fort Wagner in July, 1863, were volunteers.

So were the 180,000 other men of color who, following their example, enlisted under the Union flag before the war's end. The employment of colored soldiers early became a matter of hopeful concern to Mr. Lincoln. "I am told," he wrote on March 23, 1863, to Andrew Johnson, then military governor of Tennessee, "you have at least thought of raising a negro military force. In my opinion the country now needs no specific thing so much as some man of your position and ability to go to this work. When I speak of your position, I mean that of an eminent citizen of a slave State and himself a slaveholder. The colored population is the great available and yet unavailed force for restoring the Union. The bare sight of 50,000 armed and drilled black soldiers upon the banks of the Mississippi would end the rebellion at once."

And in August, 1863, after the fall of Vicksburg, the President addressed General Grant in like manner regarding the enlistment of colored troops. "I believe," he wrote, "it is a resource which, if vigorously applied now, will soon close this contest. It works doubly—weakening the enemy and strengthening us. We were not fully ripe for it until the river was open. Now I think at least 100,000 can and ought to be organized along its shores, relieving all the white troops to serve elsewhere." And Grant promptly replied: "By arming the negro we have added a powerful ally. They will make good soldiers, and taking them from the enemy weakens him in the same proportion they strengthen us."

Mr. Lincoln and General Grant proved true prophets. Until the war ended colored volunteers fought gallantly on many sections of the battle front, and, after the lapse of four score years, the widows of a goodly number of them still hold places on the pension rolls at Washington.

PLATE No. 151   The Black Draft, London Punch, November 19, 1864

The drawing Long Abraham a Little Longer, drawn by Frank Bellew in one of his happiest moments, appeared in Harper's Weekly on November 17, 1864. It gave fitting, whimsical expression to the glad relief with which the loyal people of the North welcomed the reelection of Mr. Lincoln. Now there could be no further debate of the doubtful policy of "swapping horses while crossing a stream" or of Mr. Lincoln's right to complete the weightiest task that up to that time had ever challenged the wisdom and patience of an American President.

Mr. Lincoln himself welcomed the news of his reelection with a full measure of satisfaction, charged with quiet humor, which found expression in an unconventional way. Charles A. Dana who was then Secretary Stanton's chief assistant, in his Recollections of the Civil War affords a welcome glimpse of him receiving the election returns. "I went over to the War Department about half past eight o'clock in the evening," writes Mr. Dana, "and found the President and Mr. Stanton together in the Secretary's office. General Eckert, who then had charge of the telegraph department of the War Office, was coming in constantly with telegrams containing election returns. Mr. Stanton would read them, and the President would look at and comment upon them. Presently there came a lull in the returns and Mr. Lincoln called me to a place by his side.

" 'Dana,' said he, 'have you ever read any of the writings of Petroleum V. Nasby?'

" 'No sir,' I said, 'I have only looked at some of them, and they seem to be quite funny.'

" 'Well,' said he, 'let me read you a specimen', and, pulling out a thin yellow-covered pamphlet from his breast pocket, he began to read aloud. Mr. Stanton viewed these proceedings with great impatience, but Mr. Lincoln paid no attention to that. He would read a page or a story, pause to consider a new election telegram, and go ahead with a new passage. Then the reading was interrupted (and) Mr. Stanton beckoned me into the next room. I shall never forget the fire of his indignation at what seemed to him to be mere nonsense. That when the control of an empire was to be determined by a few figures brought in by the telegraph, the man most deeply concerned, not merely for himself but for his country, could turn aside to laugh at such frivolous jests was, to his mind, repugnant, even damnable. He could not understand apparently, that it was by the relief which these jests afforded to the strain of mind under which Lincoln had so long been living, and to the natural gloom of a melancholy and desponding temperament that the safety and sanity of his intelligence were maintained and preserved."

PLATE No. 152   Long Abraham a Little Longer, Harper's Weekly, November 26, 1864

PLATE NO. 153

The cartoon, Jeff Davis's November Nightmare, appeared in Frank Leslie's Illustrated Newspaper on December 3, 1864. The president of the Confederacy is depicted as aroused from sleep to find Mr. Lincoln seated by his side. "Is that you still there Long Abe?" he asks, and his visitor makes reply: "Yes! And I am going to be FOUR YEARS LONGER." But as a matter of fact Jefferson Davis in the closing weeks of 1864 faced a darkening future with undaunted spirit. When in January, 1865, Mr. Lincoln sanctioned a visit of the elder Francis P. Blair, an old friend of the head of the Confederacy, to Richmond on a mission of peace, Davis listened quietly to his visitor's declaration that slavery was doomed, and agreed to send commissioners to meet representatives of the Union at Hampton Roads, but directed them to accept nothing less than peace between "the two countries!"

And when the Confederate commissioners reported to him their failure to reach an agreement with Mr. Lincoln, his speech to an excited crowd was shaped in a spirit of angry defiance. "With the Confederacy I will live or die!" he told his listeners. "I thank God that I represent a people too proud to eat the leek or bow the neck to mortal man!" Thereafter events moved swiftly to their predestined conclusion—the flight of Mr. Davis on April 3, still hoping against hope, from a capital about to yield to the Union forces.

PLATE No. 153   Jeff Davis's November Nightmare, Frank Leslie's Illustrated Newspaper, December 3, 1864

PLATE NO. 154

The savage cartoon The Federal Phoenix by Tenniel appeared in London Punch on December 3, 1864, and gives unwelcome proof of the angry mood in which the English Conservative leaders and a majority of their followers received the news of Mr. Lincoln's reelection. It must also have been that one of his Lincoln caricatures to which their author in after days looked back with deepest regret. Its title explains its character. It shows one of the birds to which the ancients gave the name of Phoenix, on whose neck the artist has placed the head of Mr. Lincoln, rising from a pyre the fuel for which is furnished by commerce, credit, the Constitution, a free press, habeas corpus and state rights. How it impressed the public for whom it was intended can only be conjectured, but to one who was a babe in arms when the man thus held up to condemnation passed from life, it seems as brutal in motive as it was misleading in fact.

PLATE No. 154   The Federal Phoenix, London Punch, December 3, 1864

The cartoon "You Have Swollen the Earth With the Blood of My Children" appeared in London Fun on December 3, 1864. No doubt intended as that journal's comment on the presidential election of the preceding month it was not drawn by Matt Morgan, but by F. Wilfred Lawson, an artist who then enjoyed a moderate measure of popularity with the British public. It was from the first the policy of Fun, as noted elsewhere, to disparage Mr. Lincoln and the Northern cause and Lawson's drawing and the text which accompanied it were no exceptions to this rule. Columbia confronting the lately reelected President thus upbraids him: "Lincoln, you have brought me to this, yet I have not flinched to perform my part of the contract. I still cling to you that you may fulfill yours. You have swollen the earth with the blood of my children. Show me what I am to gain by this, or look for my dire vengeance in the future."

Vain words as events were soon to prove, but so long as Mr. Lincoln lived Fun, blind to the meaning of events on this side of the sea, continued to portray him as the leader of a lost cause.

PLATE No. 155   "You Have Swollen the Earth with the Blood of My Children," London Fun,
December 3, 1864

PLATE NO. 156

The twin drawings to which was given the title Topics of the Hour appeared in Frank Leslie's Illustrated Newspaper on December 24, 1864, and amusingly reflected the mood in which the people of the North made ready to observe what was to prove their last Civil War Christmas. In one of them a seated Mr. Lincoln approvingly pats the shoulder of one of the colored soldiers who were then doing their part to assure the success of the Union cause; and in the other he is shown lustily belaboring the smeared and beaten leader of the Confederacy. Perhaps it is not out of place to recall that Mr. Lincoln was one of the strongest men of his time, and in his youth always prepared and ready to give proof of his prowess.

It was a favorite story of General James Grant Wilson of how, during a social hour in 1858, when the debates between Lincoln and Douglas were running their course, an old friend who had guided Wilson to the shabby law office of Lincoln & Herndon in Springfield, told their host that he had lately learned some interesting facts about Washington from George Washington Parke Custis, the General's adopted son who lived with him at Mount Vernon for many years. One of these was that Washington in his youth was a famous wrestler, never having been thrown. "It is a curious thing, my young friend," said Mr. Lincoln to Wilson, "but that is also my record. I could outlift any man in Southern Illinois when I was young, and I never was thrown. If George was loafing around here now I should be glad to have a tussle with him and I rather believe that one of the plain people of Illinois would be able to manage that aristocrat of old Virginia."

Half a dozen years later "one of the plain people of Illinois" proved his ability to manage another Southern aristocrat, Jefferson Davis of Mississippi.

PLATE No. 156   Topics of the Hour, Frank Leslie's Illustrated Newspaper, December 24, 1864

PLATE NO. 157

The cartoon The Threatening Notice appeared in London Punch on February 18, 1865, when Tenniel caricatured the living Lincoln for the last time. It represents the President remonstrating with the American eagle in the dress of Uncle Sam over the Senate's proposed abrogation of Canadian treaties. "Now, Uncle Sam," Mr. Lincoln is reported as saying, "you are in a darned hurry to serve this notice on John Bull. Now, it is my duty, as your attorney, to tell you that you may drive him over to that cuss, Davis." But John Bull was not to be driven "over to that cuss, Davis." Two months later the war was ended, Mr. Lincoln dead, and Mr. Davis in flight from what proved early capture by Union troopers.

PLATE NO. 157   The Threatening Notice, London Punch, February 18, 1865

The cartoon Lincoln Triumphs in Act to Amend the Constitution appeared early in February, in 1865, in the Budget of Fun, one of the numerous publications at that time conducted by Frank Leslie. It was drawn by William Newman, an artist of British birth and breeding, and, it may be added, fondness for detail, who began to contribute to London Punch when that journal was founded in 1841, and who continued to work for it for twenty years, although never on its staff. Spielmann records in his history of Punch that "owing to Newman's lack of breeding and common manners he was never invited to the (weekly) dinner nor did any of his colleagues care to associate with him," this despite the fact that his drawings were long a welcome feature of Punch.

Spielmann tells us that in the end Newman, "disappointed at the little advance he had made in the world, emigrated to America where more lucrative employment awaited him." This was in 1861, and arrived in America he found congenial employment on the publications of Frank Leslie, who, also an Englishman, may have been responsible for his coming to America. Be this as it may Newman's unusual cartoons for a decade claimed a prominent place in the Leslie periodicals, particularly the Budget of Fun, which flourished for a brief period only, and of which no complete file is now believed to be in existence.

Congress on January 31, 1865 submitted to the States for ratification an amendment to the Constitution which made the abolishment of slavery a part of the organic law of the republic. A movement with this end in view, an end regarded as necessary by many of the Republican leaders both in and out of Congress, began on December 14, 1863, when Ashley of Ohio and Wilson of Iowa each introduced such an amendment into the House. Similar propositions were brought before the Senate by Sumner and Henderson of Missouri, and were duly referred to its judiciary committee, whose chairman, Lyman Trumbull reported as the joint resolution to be considered by the two branches of Congress what is now the Thirteenth Amendment of the Constitution. This resolution on April 8 was passed by the Senate by a vote of 38 to 6, but when the House voted on it on June 15, with 23 not voting, the yeas were 93 and the nays 65. Thus it failed of the two-thirds requisite for its passage.

There the matter rested until January 6, 1865, when Ashley again called the resolution up for consideration. It was debated at intervals during the remainder of the month, and on January 31 came to a vote. Then of 94 Republicans, 64 Democrats and 25 Union men from the Border States who composed the House, 119 voted for it and 56 against it. And so the Thirteenth Amendment went on its way to sure and swift ratification by the needed number of States.

PLATE No. 158 Lincoln Triumphs in Act to Amend the Constitution, Budget of Fun, February, 1865, Redrawn by Ernest W. Ryerson

The drawing Uncle Abe's Valentine Sent to Columbia appeared in Frank Leslie's Illustrated Newspaper on February 25, 1865, and offers another treatment by William Newman of the event then most discussed by all classes of men—the submission by Congress for ratification by the States of what is now the Thirteenth Amendment. Mr. Lincoln, remarking with a smile, "This is like a dream I once had in Illinois," is shown studying a valentine which, freed from the chains that lately hampered it, now gives unfettered expression to the national purpose.

It is interesting to recall how the States one after another gave assent to the amendment submitted to them by Congress. Kentucky and Delaware did not ratify it, but nineteen Northern States did so without undue delay, and when the Southern legislatures met in the fall of 1865 President Johnson required of them that they take similar action. This was promptly done in the Carolinas, Georgia and Alabama. These four with the four States reconstructed by Mr. Lincoln—Virginia, Tennessee, Arkansas and Louisiana—added to those of the North which had taken affirmative action made the necessary three-fourths, and on December 18, 1865, Secretary Seward issued a proclamation certifying that the Thirteenth Amendment had become "valid as part of the Constitution of the United States."

It may be added that four additional Northern States ratified the amendment in December, 1865, and January, 1866. Florida and Texas took like action, the one in December, 1865 and the other in February, 1870—making a total of 33 out of 36 States in the Union when Secretary Seward issued his proclamation. Thus was made clear the great gulf which separated the United States of the last month of 1865 from the perplexed Union of the opening weeks of 1861 when Congress, vainly seeking to appease the Southern States, had voted that, "No amendment shall be made to the Constitution which will authorize or give to Congress the power to abolish or to interfere within any State with the domestic institutions thereof including that of persons held to labor or service by the laws of said State."

PLATE No. 159   Uncle Abe's Valentine Sent to Columbia, Frank Leslie's Illustrated Newspaper,
February 25, 1865

The poster cartoon The Peace Commission was put out by Currier and Ives in March, 1865, the last of the many caricatures of Mr. Lincoln designed by the artists of that famous house. It shows the President with outstretched arms extending a welcome to the three Confederate commissioners—Alexander H. Stephens, John A. Campbell, and Robert M. T. Hunter—whom in mid-January of 1865 Jefferson Davis, perhaps prompted thereto by a recent visit from the elder Francis P. Blair, had selected to negotiate a possible peace with the Union authorities. Stephens and his associates appeared at General Grant's headquarters at City Point on the evening of January 29.

Advised of this fact, Mr. Lincoln sent Secretary Seward to Fortress Monroe with written instructions to tell the Confederate envoys that there were three conditions on which peace might be effected: The national authority must be restored throughout all the States; the South must accept the abolition of slavery, and there could be no cessation of hostilities short of an end to the war. Minor matters, however, would be considered in a spirit of give-and-take. But before Seward had met and talked with the Confederate envoys, Mr. Lincoln, influenced by a long telegram from General Grant, decided to have a part in the negotiations, and so informed the Union commander.

Accordingly on February 2 the President on a naval vessel steamed down the Potomac to Hampton Roads alongside Fortress Monroe. The rest of the story is told in a report which on February 10 he made to Congress "On the morning of the third," Mr. Lincoln recorded, "Messrs. Stephens, Hunter and Campbell, came aboard of our steamer, and had an interview with the Secretary of State and myself of several hours' duration. . . . The conference ended without result."

And so the war went on to its inevitable conclusion. Nevertheless the Fortress Monroe conference offered appealing proof of the later declaration that "Mr. Lincoln was always doing something for somebody." Twenty years earlier he and Stephens had served together as Whig members of Congress. Now they met as friends, and during an interlude in the discussions which had brought them together Mr. Stephens told Mr. Lincoln of his nephew John A. Stephens, a Confederate lieutenant then an ailing prisoner of war at Johnson's Island, Ohio.

Mr. Lincoln promised to effect the young man's release, and from Washington on the following day telegraphed the commander at Johnson's Island to parole him and have him report in person to the President. Six days later he wrote to Mr. Stephens: "According to our agreement your nephew, Lieutenant Stephens goes to you bearing this note. Please, in return, select and send to me that officer of the same rank imprisoned at Richmond, whose physical condition most urgently requires his release."

PLATE No. 160 The Peace Commission, Currier and Ives, March, 1865

PLATE NO. 161

The drawing From Our Special Correspondent appeared in Harper's Weekly on April 15, 1865. Here with unconscious pathos, as the sequel proved, a Harper artist for the last time made the living Lincoln a subject for his pencil. It was on the morning of April 3, 1865, that troops of General Weitzel occupied Richmond, abandoned within the hour by the Confederates and partly in flames which were quickly brought under control as was the rioting of commissary looters. Late in the afternoon of the same day Mr. Lincoln came by boat from General Grant's headquarters at City Point where he was a guest, and made his first visit to Richmond.

The crowd which received him was made up entirely of Negroes, but its welcome was a fervent and reverent one, some of its members kneeling and bowing at the President's feet. "Don't kneel to me," said Mr. Lincoln. "Kneel to God only and thank him for your freedom." Then, guarded by twelve armed sailors and leading his little son Tad by the hand, he visited all parts of downtown Richmond, including Libby Prison where so many Union officers and men had undergone confinement, hunger and wasting illness. Later with General Weitzel and a cavalry escort, he rode over Richmond in a carriage. In the evening he returned to City Point and on Sunday, April 9, was back in Washington to receive from General Grant the news of the surrender of Lee's army.

The Harper artist depicts Mr. Lincoln, with a drumhead for a table, writing from City Point: "All seems well with us," but when on April 15, the issue of the journal in which his drawing appeared reached its readers, Booth's bullet had done its work, and Abraham Lincoln lay dead in the East Room of the White House.

PLATE No. 161   From Our Special Correspondent, Harper's Weekly, April 15, 1865

PLATE NO. 162

The cartoon Britannia Lays a Wreath on Lincoln's Bier appeared in Punch on May 6, 1865, and with Tom Taylor's fine tribute in verse quoted elsewhere made atonement for the grudging treatment that journal had accorded Mr. Lincoln through four troubled years, not, however, with the whole-hearted assent of some of the men responsible for the policy of Punch. Layard in his biography of Shirley Brooks affords us an informing glance behind the Punch curtain, in the late April of 1865. He makes it clear that its editorial staff was divided as to Tom Taylor's verses, Shirley Brooks vainly leading the opposition to their publication. In support of this contention, Layard prints the following entry from Brooks' diary:

"Dined Punch. All there. Let out my views against some verses on Lincoln in which T. T. (Tom Taylor) had not only made P. eat humble pie, but swallow dish and all."

In the end Punch ate what Brooks termed humble pie, and, looking back across the years, a later generation on both sides of the sea must regard its act as an honorable and manly one.

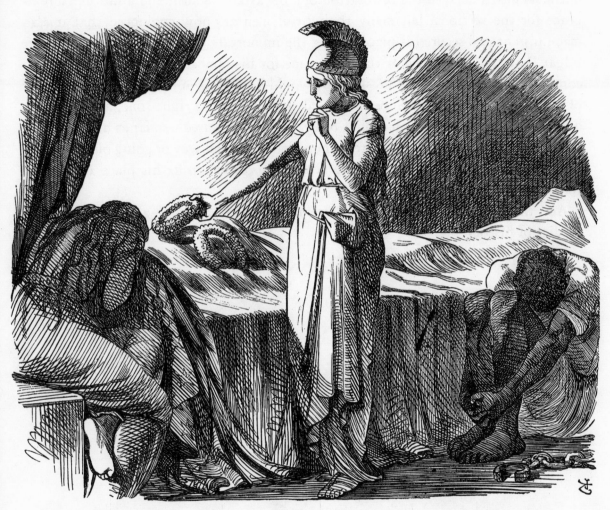

PLATE No. 162   Britannia Lays a Wreath on Lincoln's Bier, London Punch, May 6, 1865

PLATE NO. 163

The cartoon Attained appeared in London Fun on May 6, 1865, and, as Punch did on the same day, pays belated tribute to Mr. Lincoln's worth and work, things to which hitherto it had been preversely and persistently blind. Drawn by Lawson it shows him reaching for the urn of Victory at the fateful instant chosen by the assassin for his undoing. It has become clear through the years that the President's untimely death delayed the restoration of a devastated South, and a full measure of peace for the sections; but many thoughtful men are now convinced that it also made instant and secure his place among the immortals. "Mr. Lincoln," writes Dr. Edgar Dewitt Jones, "died at the right time for his fame. I believe had he lived to complete his second term as President it would have broken him politically and his place in the sun would have been delayed. He died at the right time, and while he died in a dreadful way which cannot be explained or excused—so far as his own fame was concerned, if he had deliberately chosen the time and way of going out, no other time or way of his going could have been more certain to fix his place among the stars."

And this measured weighing of facts may be safely accepted as the unchanging verdict of history.

PLATE No. 163   Attained, London Fun, May 6, 1865